RETURN *of the* DRAGON

CONTEMPORARY ASIA IN THE WORLD

CONTEMPORARY ASIA IN THE WORLD

David C. Kang and Victor D. Cha, Editors

This series aims to address a gap in the public-policy and scholarly discussion of Asia. It seeks to promote books and studies that are on the cutting edge of their respective disciplines or in the promotion of multidisciplinary or interdisciplinary research but that are also accessible to a wider readership. The editors seek to showcase the best scholarly and public-policy arguments on Asia from any field, including politics, history, economics, and cultural studies.

Beyond the Final Score: The Politics of Sport in Asia, Victor D. Cha, 2008

The Power of the Internet in China: Citizen Activism Online, Guobin Yang, 2009

China and India: Prospects for Peace, Jonathan Holslag, 2010

India, Pakistan, and the Bomb: Debating Nuclear Stability in South Asia, Šumit Ganguly and S. Paul Kapur, 2010

Living with the Dragon: How the American Public Views the Rise of China, Benjamin I. Page and Tao Xie, 2010

East Asia Before the West: Five Centuries of Trade and Tribute, David C. Kang, 2010

Harmony and War: Confucian Culture and Chinese Power Politics, Yuan-Kang Wang, 2011

Strong Society, Smart State: The Rise of Public Opinion in China's Japan Policy, James Reilly, 2012

Asia's Space Race: National Motivations, Regional Rivalries, and International Risks, James Clay Moltz, 2012

Never Forget National Humiliation: Historical Memory in Chinese Politics and Foreign Relations, Zheng Wang, 2012

Green Innovation in China: China's Wind Power Industry and the Global Transition to a Low-Carbon Economy, Joanna I. Lewis, 2013

The Great Kantō Earthquake and the Chimera of National Reconstruction in Japan, J. Charles Schencking, 2013

RETURN *of the* DRAGON

Rising China and Regional Security

Denny Roy

COLUMBIA UNIVERSITY PRESS New York

Columbia University Press
Publishers Since 1893
New York Chichester, West Sussex
cup.columbia.edu

Library of Congress Cataloging-in-Publication Data

Roy, Denny, 1960–
Return of the dragon : rising China and regional security / Denny Roy.
pages cm.— (Contemporary Asia in the world)
Includes bibliographical references and index.
ISBN 978-0-231-15900-5 (cloth : alk. paper) — ISBN 978-0-231-52815-3 (e-book)
1. China—Foreign relations—21st century. 2. World politics—21st century. 3. China—International status. 4. National security—China. I. Title.

DS779.47.R68 2013
355′.033051—dc23

2012042059

∞
Columbia University Press books are printed on permanent and durable acid-free paper.
This book is printed on paper with recycled content.
Printed in the United States of America

c 10 9 8 7 6 5 4 3 2 1

COVER ILLUSTRATION: Sail Byrnes
COVER DESIGN: Faceout Studio

CONTENTS

RETURN *of the* DRAGON

Chapter One

INTRODUCTION

Everyone who follows and thinks about international affairs is aware that the rise of China is changing our world.

The economic aspect of China's rise is well known—perhaps too well known, to the point of exaggeration. Most Americans who responded to a 2011 Gallup poll thought China already had the world's largest economy, even though at that time the U.S. economy was more than double the size of China's and America's per capita gross domestic product was more than ten times the figure for China.[1] The basic consequences are straightforward. The world is buying more from China and selling more to China. China's economic development is providing lower-priced products for the world's consumers, but it is also driving many foreign companies out of business and increasing the competition for some global resources.

The international security aspect of China's rise—its effect on the ability of countries and peoples to protect themselves from intimidation or the use of force against them by other governments—is at least as important as the economic aspect. The emergence of China as a great power is the preeminent global security issue of the twenty-first century. But what does this mean? Identifying and specifying the security consequences of a stronger China is relatively challenging.

Some observers, including members of the U.S. Congress, see China as a reincarnation of Nazi Germany—but with a larger resource and population base. Alarmist authors say China is driving for "global dominance" and predict "a shooting war within the next ten years" between China and the United States. Other commentators, however, assure us that conflict between China and the other major powers is unlikely because continued

Chinese prosperity, and by extension the legitimacy of China's ruling party, depends on avoiding military conflict.[2]

Certainly, neither of these two simplistic and extreme views is reliable. We should not expect Chinese troops to march into the capitals of Asian states, nor is Beijing lusting for a war against the United States so China can become the new superpower. At the same time, however, we can count on high tensions and a risk of military conflict during the next couple of decades, as the growth of Chinese power increases international friction and sharpens strategic disputes.

China is sometimes called the next "superpower." A superpower is not simply the world's strongest country. It is a historically rare breed of state that can bring decisive political or military power to bear in any region on earth. This may be in China's distant future, but for now the PRC is clearly emerging as a great power: a country that ranks among the world's top few states in its political influence, economic strength, and military capabilities.

This book assesses the effect of China as a great power on important security and strategic issues. The main focus is on the major Asia-Pacific countries most affected by a stronger China. I will argue that the increased tensions naturally resulting from the rapid rise of an indignant new great power will meet powerful moderating forces, but ultimately China's expectation of a sphere of influence will create or worsen dangers for China's neighbors. On balance, the rise of an extraordinarily strong China will decrease security for the region.

The rise of China will generate strategic tensions. This is partly because of the nature of international politics. Since the international community cannot guarantee the safety of states, the dangers of military attack and invasion are ever present facts of life for national governments. States cannot fully trust each other and must therefore see one another as potential adversaries. To increase their security, states try to make themselves powerful relative to other states. This is the surest way to deter would-be adversaries from attacking. States that succeed in making themselves strong, however, draw greater suspicion because they can cause greater harm to other states in the event of war. Strong states are able to bully other states or to contemplate starting a war. Tension is especially likely between a new great power and an established great power that seeks influence over the same region—in this case, China and the United States.

Another reason the rise of a new great power leads to increased tension is that newly strong countries raise their aspirations. A great power's foreign policy agenda will become more expansive as the country becomes more powerful than its neighbors. More ambitious goals become feasible. All states wish they could dominate their environment. Only a few are strong enough to try. The question for China and other powerful states is whether striving for domination is worth the cost and risk that result from other states resisting.

Even if China does not intend to dominate its neighbors, the increase of Chinese capabilities is enough to cause alarm and defensive counteraction among the PRC's neighbors. A state's attempt to make itself more secure can create what international relations scholars call the "security dilemma."[3] Countries can never know the true intentions of other governments. Even if a government appears to have benign intentions now, those intentions might change later. The distinction between defensive and offensive military forces is practically meaningless. When a state becomes relatively strong, the neighboring states must prepare for the worst by increasing their own capabilities. The likely result is worsening mutual suspicions. This dynamic is prominent in East Asia. The Chinese insist their military buildup is solely for defensive purposes. Other Asia-Pacific countries such as the United States and Japan question the intentions underlying China's military growth and strengthen their own capabilities in response. Beijing views the response as part of an unjustified strategy to suppress China's legitimate development. There is a danger that two sides will become locked into a spiral of rising tensions.

A second source of tensions attending the rise of China is the PRC's unique worldview. The international political environment works similarly on various great powers, resulting in similarities in their behavior. China will be subject to these same tendencies. Each great power, however, also has unique characteristics that may cause peculiarities in its foreign policy. A country's interpretation of its own historical experience is one of the most potent of these characteristics. History influences perceptions of opportunities and threats in the external environment, which in turn colors national foreign policy making. China's past glory and more recent "shame" has given the Chinese strong expectations about China's proper place in the world. China is not only a rising great power, it is a *returning* great power, arguably the first in history. The PRC's domestic economic and political circumstances and its keen desire for international prestige also affect Chinese foreign relations. The Chinese perceive their neighbors and international affairs in some ways differently than do other countries in the region. The differences between Chinese and non-Chinese viewpoints creates disagreements between Beijing and other Asia-Pacific governments over whether certain policies by either China or its neighbors are justified.

Most states in the Asia-Pacific region have anxieties about the growth of China's power and influence. The level of anxiety varies depending on the state's circumstances, such as its size, proximity to China, and relationship with the United States. A more powerful PRC will be more capable of harming or attempting to dominate other states. Some states in the region will perceive coercion or encroachment by China. They will face difficult choices about whether to stand up for their interests against Chinese disapproval. As the PRC's relative power increases, so will the internal pressure for China to try to change international relations in the Asia-Pacific region to more closely match China's interests. If China insists on faster or deeper changes than residual American power can tolerate, a U.S.-China conflict could undermine regional prosperity and drag other states into an unwanted and polarizing conflict. Regional governments that are satisfied with the American-sponsored status quo may not see themselves better off under a redesigned Chinese order.

China has an identifiable "grand strategy" at a general level, but more specific Chinese security goals in different areas frequently come into conflict and create quandaries for the leadership. A long-term and overarching problem is striking a balance between assertiveness and assurance. On one hand, Beijing hopes to avoid frightening its neighbors and causing them to cooperate defensively against China. Beijing therefore assures the world that a strong China will be peaceful and cooperative. Chinese officials, scholars, and media insist that China is a "principled" country, different from the typical bullying and self-interested great power, and seeks only mutually beneficial economic development and international justice. On the other hand, the PRC government is under strong, persistent pressure from some elite groups and from the Chinese mass public to fulfill expectations that the leadership will stand up for China's interests and national Chinese dignity. These expectations will grow along with China's perceived relative power. Many Chinese believe that, having suffered a long and historically anomalous period of weakness and humiliation, China should now grasp the fruits of its international resurgence.

The dangers of conflict in a world with China as a great power are potentially offset by robust bulwarks that support peace. The status quo is formidable, backed by enduring American strength. China is prospering under the current international system and is largely satisfied with many aspects of it. The alleged American "containment" campaign has not prevented the PRC from thriving. China has strong disincentives from seeking regional domination (defined as forcing other states to subjugate their major policy decisions to Chinese approval). Chinese behavior perceived as threatening would bring about multinational military cooperation against China. Beijing is keenly aware of this danger and anxious to avoid it. Even as the strongest Asia-Pacific power, China could not dominate a region in which most national governments formed an anti-China coalition. Thus, Beijing's need to maintain the image of a good neighbor could check a Chinese inclination to pursue an aggressive foreign policy, precluding serious conflicts over many disputed issues. Peacefully integrating a strong China into a region long dominated by the United States will require patience on the part of the Chinese and often unwelcome adjustments on the part of other Asia-Pacific states, but it is not impossible. The United States has already shown it will not actively block the rise of China if China follows the accepted rules of international relations. There are few actual issues for China and America to fight over.

Unfortunately, there remains a substantial risk of conflict. China in principle supports peace and justice in international affairs. The Chinese believe their country is an exceptionally benign great power. The Chinese, however, hold strong and peculiarly Chinese viewpoints on many security issues. While "principled" in Chinese eyes, these views herald PRC behavior in some instances that will appear to others in the Asia-Pacific region as the kind of self-interested bullying that is historically typical of powerful countries. The danger of conflict arises from those areas in which China believes it is acting in defense of its legitimate rights to security and prosperity, while other states perceive China is acting aggressively and illegitimately. The risk of resort to military action is increased when clashing policies involve what both sides regard as vital national interests. In some cases, strategically short-sighted domestic political pressure may force the Beijing leadership to act against its own wishes and pursue risky foreign policies. A few intractable points of friction between the interests of some of the Asia-Pacific governments and China's vision for the new regional order are already apparent. If not contained, such frictions could lead to war. Prominent among these danger areas are the Taiwan Strait and the seas of China's east and southeast coasts.

China's deep political, social, and economic weaknesses potentially constrain the assertion of its power abroad by making Chinese leaders cautious about overreaching. PRC aggressiveness might disrupt the flow of goods and investment upon which China heavily depends, divert resources away from the civilian economy, or lead to a loss of Chinese face before the international community. The Party leadership must consider whether the strain of trying to impose Chinese self-interest upon a resisting world would raise preexisting domestic discontent to levels the Party could no longer control. But weakness can also have the opposite effect. Under some circumstances, such as when foreigners jab the Chinese in a sensitive place, the awareness of domestic weakness may lead PRC leaders to lash out as a way of protecting perceived vulnerabilities.

This overview highlights several important themes, including security dilemmas, the battle between the forces restraining conflict and the factors contributing to conflict, and the rise of China's ambitions to match the increase in its relative capabilities. These themes pervade the discussions of the specific security issues and bilateral relationships involving China that the following chapters cover.

How My Book Fits Into the Field of Study

(This section is for scholars and students of international relations theory; other readers might want to skip ahead to chapter 2.)

My theoretical framework could be called neorealism with a couple of modifications. My approach is close to neoclassical realism, which posits that the international distribution of power determines a strong, general direction for a particular state's security policy but that domestic political considerations intervene to exert influence over policy making.[4] I accept most of the basic neorealist assumptions. Anarchy compels survival-seeking states to try obsessively to acquire relative power as a way of protecting themselves. States necessarily see others as potential foes. Because the intentions of other states are changeable and unknowable, security dilemmas are a common feature of international politics. Contiguous great powers are natural adversaries except when they are united in opposition to a common enemy. States tend to balance against the most threatening concentrations of power unless balancing is not a viable option.

Now for the modifications. Neorealism holds that maintaining the security of the state against external military threats is the top priority of governments. Keeping invaders out is necessary but not always sufficient for national leaders to keep their jobs. In my view, regime security takes precedence over state security in those rare instances where the two objectives conflict.

Neorealism is a material rather than an ideational theory in that it sees national leaders acting on the basis of purportedly concrete conditions such as the economic and military capabilities of states. Ideas, however, play an important role in international politics, primarily in two ways. First, in their pursuit of security, national policy makers knowingly or unknowingly base their decisions and strategies on perceptions of the international system, their own country's ideal and actual place within it, and the intentions and capabilities of other countries. These perceptions are shaped by many idiosyncratic factors. A community's particular interpretation of history is one of the most important of these factors. Second, national policy makers (even in authoritarian regimes) are under pressure to meet the expectations of a mass public. One important ramification is that the objective of delivering prosperity to the people rivals the goal of maintaining state security in the minds of national leaders who want to stay in power. The imperative of raising the country's living standards often forces the government to take uncomfortable steps that deepen cooperation with (and vulnerability to) other states. Another ramification is that public pressure can sometimes force leaders to take actions the leaders believe are shortsighted or unwise. In China's case, the mass public is deeply steeped in the belief that the world owes China respect and room to return to its former glory.

Thus, my approach enhances (or corrupts, depending on one's point of view) neorealism with principles from constructivism and liberalism. It would be preferable to keep my analysis within the confines of a single elegant theory if this were possible. I will not, however, insist on parsimony at the expense of accuracy. International relations in Asia involve a complex set of factors that demand an eclectic approach.

The dichotomy between offensive and defensive realism forces realist analysts to choose a side. My view is that both phenomena are visible in international politics in varying circumstances. Some regimes, such as Nazi Germany, are unusually aggressive for reasons unique to their case. The same country might be offensive in one period and defensive in another (wartime Japan versus postwar Japan). Most pertinently, I find rising China to be highly assertive in keeping with the expectations of offensive realism in the PRC's immediate neighborhood but more supportive of the status quo in a defensively realist fashion when it comes to global strategic issues outside the region.

Typically, analysts who employ a theory that predicts aggressive behavior by a strong China do not fully discuss the costs China would pay and the opportunities China would lose by following such a course. Similarly, optimistic theorists who argue that aggression doesn't pay tend not to consider the strength of the factors that impel the Chinese leadership to pursue conflict-generating policies. PRC policy makers need not be theoretically partisan; they weigh the respective costs and benefits of working within the established arrangements versus overthrowing them.[5] To measure the impact of a stronger China on international security, my book undertakes a net assessment of both the pacifying and the contention-causing forces that influence Chinese decision makers.

Several recent books cover the foreign policy of rising China.[6] I should explain the unique contribution that my book makes to this crowded field. Some of the books by my American colleagues focus on a chapter of history that has recently ended, but my book is forward looking. Robert Sutter's work *U.S.-Chinese Relations* explains how the often tumultuous U.S.-PRC relationship has settled into a status quo in which crises are less likely because of deep bilateral economic interdependence, the Beijing leadership's focus on solving problems inside China, and the resilience of U.S. strategic preeminence in Asia. The fundamentals of that status quo, however, are changing, which makes Sutter's book a history of a passing era rather than a guide to even the near future. Avery Goldstein's *Rising to the Challenge* is a well-researched analysis of the emergence in the late 1990s of a PRC grand strategy designed to facilitate China's continuing economic buildup and military strengthening without causing an international strategic backlash. This strategy included downplaying the strategic rivalry with the United States, cultivating relationships that would make other countries reluctant to challenge China's interests, and assuring the international community that China is peaceful and responsible. This book limits itself to a time period when China was a growing but still midsized power that needed to be cautious about challenging the United States and U.S. allies. Goldstein's book cannot necessarily tell us much about Chinese grand strategy in the present and future, when Beijing is more confident, more bulked up, and more strongly pressed by triumphalism at home.

Other prominent recent books concentrate on particular aspects of the rise of China in great depth, in contrast to the broader scope of my book. Robert S. Ross and Zhu Feng's book *China's Ascent* accepts that a rising power develops a more ambitious foreign policy and that the scenario of one great power catching up with another increases tensions. The authors argue, nonetheless, that military conflict is not an inevitable result of structural power shifts but will hinge on decisions and policies made by China and the United States and, more generally, on the way other countries react to the rise of China. Although this book contains two chapters that provide Korean and Japanese views, it mainly focuses on the power-transition problem in the U.S.-China relationship from several different angles. It does not attempt to depict the broad sweep of China's effect on regional security that my book aims for. The Ross and Zhu book is also more optimistic than mine. They conclude that the disincentives to conflict are strong enough to withstand the increased tensions without leading to a major war. My greater focus on the region leads to my more pessimistic conclusion that the rise of China is already infringing on the security of other countries. Like my book, Aaron L. Friedberg's *A Contest for Supremacy* takes into account multiple layers of influence on the PRC's current security policies, including the changing configuration of power among states, China's historical self-image, and the CCP's ideological outlook on foreign affairs. Friedberg's book, however, has a different purpose from mine. While my book is designed to assess a rising China's effect on regional security, Friedberg's presentation is organized around the goal of supporting a particular recommendation for U.S. policy toward China.

Advocating a certain American policy toward China is also one of the two main purposes of Susan Shirk's *China: Fragile Superpower*. The second purpose is to explain one of the important influences on Chinese foreign policy: the insecurity of the CCP regime. Shirk argues that China's leaders are too preoccupied by domestic politics to pursue an assertive foreign policy master plan, so Washington should strive to avoid provoking outbursts of Chinese nationalism that will force the regime to act aggressively abroad to placate angry mobs in the streets at home. I agree that domestic pressure could push an insecure CCP into an external conflict. My book discusses this danger, although less thoroughly than does Shirk's book. But I also argue that even absent such a domestic eruption, a rising China is threatening to its neighbors because of other factors: the PRC's increase in relative capabilities, the Chinese perception of the international political environment, and China's historical self-image.

David Kang's book *China Rising* takes a fundamentally different approach from mine, yielding different findings. Kang argues that traditional international relations theories, which mostly focus on differences in power as the cause of state behavior, wrongly predict that neighboring states will fear the rise of China and will band together in a defensive posture. Instead, says Kang, explaining Asia's international relations requires an understanding of the historical identities of Asian states. Historically, these states saw China not only as the natural leader of the region but also as mainly a force for stability. As a consequence, the Northeast and Southeast Asian governments of today do not fear a rising PRC, are accommodating rather than allying against China, and prefer a strong China to a weak China because the latter may create a power vacuum that another country tries to fill. The strength of Kang's approach, which is his respect for the region's unique history as the key to explaining contemporary Asian international relations, is also its weakness. Kang takes this approach so far that he undervalues or excludes the ways in which Asian countries are behaving as the traditional "Eurocentric" theories would predict. Much of China's behavior, for example, resembles that of a typical non-Asian great power. Consequently, some of Kang's conclusions are overstated or erroneous. Although Asian states want to trade with China and try to avoid antagonizing it, most have significant strategic fears of a stronger China, are taking low-key steps to protect themselves through defense cooperation with other countries, and increasingly appreciate a robust U.S. military presence in the region.

China's Search for Security by Andrew Nathan and Andrew Scobell is a thoughtful analysis deeply informed by both theory and history. Like me, these authors take an approach that combines neorealism with a respect for China's national experience and the role that perception plays in international politics. They reach the conclusions that China is inherently defensive and that long-term security challenges within the PRC and on its borders keep China from threatening the West. In contrast, I argue that the PRC's notion of self-defense cuts into the security of other states in the region. Furthermore, despite needing a heavy investment in security forces to protect the regime and preserve the empire, an economically vibrant China still has the resources and attention to carry out an assertive foreign policy. And again, an obsession with regime security can lead to foreign policy extroversion as well as introversion.

Chapter Two

A CHINESE VIEW OF THE WORLD

Chinese take great pride in their nationality. Originating between four thousand and five thousand years ago, China's is one of the world's oldest and greatest civilizations. It is distinguished for many accomplishments in engineering, art, premodern science, government, and philosophy. For centuries, China was superior to Europe in technology, standard of living, and organizational efficiency. At around the time of the birth of Jesus Christ, the life of the ancient Britons was still relatively primitive. They were divided into tribal groups that frequently warred against each other. They lived mostly in squalor. By comparison, the Chinese of this period had built a sophisticated canal and irrigation system; were using gunpowder, paper currency, mills operated by water power, wheelbarrows, and blast furnaces for the production of cast-iron tools and weapons; and had implemented a merit-based examination system for selecting civil service officers. China covered a large territory and encompassed a large population even in ancient times. The Han people, who constitute 92 percent of China's population, are the world's largest ethnic group. The Han are actually a collection of many culturally and linguistically distinct peoples, but the extraordinary longevity of the Chinese state provided sufficient time for these peoples to be absorbed and redefined as Han.

This assimilation of distinct peoples was not without resistance. Perhaps the greatest preoccupation of premodern Chinese rulers was unifying and preserving the Chinese empire. In practice, this involved conquering communities that did not wish to be included in the empire and then putting down periodic insurrections. There were several wars fought between rival kingdoms. A military campaign to reunify China politically occurred as recently as Chiang Kai-shek's Northern Expedition of 1926–1928. Chinese history is also punctuated by frequent uprisings against the rule of the central government. The largest of these, the Taiping Rebellion of 1850 to 1864, led to the deaths of an estimated twenty million people. Significantly, it also had a foreign connection, as the leader of the rebellion was influenced by Christian missionaries.

China was the preeminent political, cultural, and economic power in premodern Northeast and Southeast Asia for centuries. Some neighboring states adopted Chinese customs and thinking. China administered a sophisticated tributary system in which surrounding states displayed deference to China, by giving gifts and verbally acknowledging the superiority of the Chinese emperor, in exchange for opportunities to trade with China and occasional assistance from Beijing.

In principle, the Chinese tribute system had parallels with Confucian philosophy: all members of society were organized into a hierarchical relationship, harmony was highly prized, and that harmony was most likely to be realized if every individual acted properly based on his or her place in the hierarchy—loyal and obedient toward superiors and benevolent toward inferiors. In practice, many of China's neighbors found the Chinese arrogant and domineering. Historically, Beijing did not view other states as equals of China. The Chinese considered their head of state, the "Son of Heaven," to be the emperor of the known world; the leaders of other states were merely "kings." Those peoples that were not part of the tributary system were classed as barbarians.

Confidence in their superiority bred complacency among the Chinese elite. In one of the distant barbarian realms, a scientific and industrial revolution occurred that would reorder global politics. Great powers arose in Europe, with technology and productivity that overtook those of China. In 1792, a British delegation led by Lord George MacCartney called on the Chinese Qianlong emperor and requested an expansion of Britain's trade relationship with China. The emperor refused, saying China had no need for the "strange" and "ingenious" products of a barbarian country. For the Chinese, a disaster was in the offing.

Energized by capitalism, Europe had a strong and unrequited demand for Chinese goods such as tea, porcelain, and silk fabric. Beijing, however, assented only to very limited and tightly constrained trade with the European countries. The ruling Qing dynasty—China's last before the republican revolution in 1911—disliked international trade, believing it mostly created problems such as piracy and social unrest. Legal Sino-European trade was allowed only in a handful of designated ports, the busiest of which was Guangzhou (Canton, near Hong Kong). Furthermore, the Chinese would accept payment for their products only in silver, the hard currency of the day.

Britain had difficulty finding a product they could supply that the Chinese wanted to buy. The British government also wanted to reverse the outflow of silver, which Britain had to buy from other European governments. The solution was government-sponsored narcotics trafficking. Backed by the authority of the British government, the British East India Company held a monopoly over the production and export of Indian opium. The importation and use of opium had been banned in China since 1729. The British, however, found in China an eager market and local officials who could be bought off. The East India Company established an opium-smuggling network and required payment from the Chinese in silver.

By the early 1800s, the social ills of widespread opium addiction and the drain of silver from the Chinese economy became serious issues for the Qing government. In 1839, Beijing appointed the zealous Confucian official Lin Zexu to halt the opium trade in Guangzhou. Lin forced the British traders to hand over their stocks of opium, which Lin destroyed. These British traders complained to their home government that the Chinese government had taken their property and infringed upon their right to trade. The British sent a punitive military expedition. Superior Western military technology forced the Chinese government to capitulate in 1842, mainly because British vessels were able to sail up the Yangtze River and obstruct the flow of commerce that generated the revenue on which the Chinese government relied. International affairs rarely offer such a clear-cut case of good versus evil. A Chinese official of unusual integrity had attempted to enforce his country's longstanding ban on a harmful drug. For this, the smugglers' government launched a military attack on China. Worse, the postwar settlement yielded the first of what became known as the "unequal treaties" between China and stronger foreign powers. The Treaty of Nanking opened additional Chinese ports to British traders, ceded Hong Kong to Britain, and required the Chinese to pay Britain reparations of $21 million in silver, equal to about half China's annual revenue. The opium trade resumed.

Known as the Opium War or First Opium War (there was a second "Opium War" in 1856–1860), this conflict holds a prominent place in the

Chinese worldview. Chinese textbooks divide China's history into two main periods: before and after the Opium War. The Opium War also marks the beginning of what the Chinese call the "Century of Shame" or "Century of Humiliation" (alternative translations of *bainian guochi*). Many cases would follow in which foreigners seeking markets and cheap resources coerced China into granting concessions and privileges.

The declining Qing government, gradually slipping into rigor mortis, could not effectively repel foreign pressure. Chinese humiliation broadened when Japan, which the Chinese historically regarded as an inferior, defeated Chinese forces in an 1894–1895 war over influence in Korea. The Japanese government had responded to the Western challenge by rapidly assimilating Western technical expertise. Now the Japanese got not only Korea but also the Chinese island province of Taiwan. A 1911 revolution finally overthrew the moribund Qing and established a Republic of China, but China's travails were far from over. The Chinese people suffered through the fractionalization of the country into various warlord-controlled fiefdoms, Chiang's military campaign to bring the country nominally back under the control of a central government, the opening campaigns of the Chinese Civil War between Chiang's Kuomintang (Nationalist, KMT) forces and the Chinese Communist Party (CCP), the Japanese invasion of 1931–1945, and finally the denouement of the KMT-CCP struggle in 1945–1949. These conflicts killed tens of millions and caused comparably large amounts of human dislocation and economic damage.

National humiliation is probably the single most important theme in the history of modern China as taught by the PRC educational and propaganda system. By the CCP's reckoning, the Century of Shame ended in 1949, with the establishment of the People's Republic of China. (Some Chinese fix the date a few years later, with the Chinese "victory" in the Korean War.) The PRC displaced Chiang's Republic of China government, which fled to exile on the island of Taiwan. The CCP government has made sure its citizens are well aware of how much China suffered during this period. The Century of Shame is taught in the schools, commemorated in museums throughout the country, and reiterated through TV war movies, media articles, and speeches by officials. The message is that a feeble government left a formerly great China prostrate before rapacious foreign and domestic enemies but that the CCP government has made China strong and great again. In effect, the Century of Shame is used as a continuous campaign advertisement for CCP rule.

In sum, the Chinese draw three very strong and interrelated lessons from their past. First, China properly deserves recognition as the world's greatest country, a position it occupied through most of human history. China's greatness makes it the natural leader of its region. Second, dividing the country impedes its greatness. Lost territory must therefore be recovered and the unity of the country preserved. Third, China's vulnerability for a brief, anomalous period of its modern history led to massive molestation at the hands of predatory foreign powers. The world's great powers (other than China) are ruthless and exploitative.

These three lessons point toward a common conclusion: China must become strong. This goal has driven the Chinese throughout their modern history, with the other great powers used as a basis of comparison. The Qing dynasty reacted to the challenge of Western imperialism with the "Self-Strengthening Movement" (1861–1895), which attempted military modernization by borrowing from Western technology. The Chinese nationalist leader Sun Yat-sen sought to deliver China from Western imperialism by advocating the selective adoption of Western science, education, and political philosophy. He and Chiang prepared for the Northern Expedition by training military officers in an academy staffed by Soviet faculty. Chiang later experimented with the Italian/Nazi model of fascism as a vehicle for strengthening China. The stated goal of Mao Zedong's disastrous Great Leap Forward campaign of 1958 was to vault China into the ranks of the great powers through a crash program of increased steel production. The leading foreign countries were both rivals and models for a recovering China.

Fear of Separatism

Keeping the country together is considered a sacred duty of Chinese leaders. Threats to national unity take different forms. Some of China's many historical uprisings have involved cleavages along class lines—groups of socioeconomically disadvantaged people rebelling against a system they felt denied them the opportunity to prosper. Other rebellions have had a philosophical or ideological edge. A third category of unrest is ethnic separatism, which carries the danger of the permanent loss of Chinese territory. In keeping with the historically derived axiom that internal disorder is linked with foreign aggression (*neiluan waihuan*), the Chinese see minority ethnic nationalism as a vulnerability that China's enemies can exploit. During the Century of Shame, foreigners took advantage of Chinese weakness to take control of pieces of Chinese territory. The British got Hong Kong, and the Portuguese got the port of Macau (Aomen). Japan colonized Taiwan and later expanded into Manchuria. Tibet, which the Chinese considered part of their empire, was an independent kingdom while China floundered during the warlord era and the Japanese invasion. Part of the legacy of this history is that today's PRC government often blames "foreign forces" for internal problems, even when the connection is dubious. As an example, in May 2011, ethnic Mongolian students protested the environmental damage in the PRC province of Inner Mongolia caused by the rapid expansion of Han-owned mining industries. A Foreign Ministry spokeswoman said of the protest, "As to those foreign parties that are using the incident to stir up trouble, they have ulterior motives." When asked to identify the foreign forces and explain their motives, she responded, "You should ask those foreign parties that are stirring up trouble." The implication is that foreign governments want to weaken China from within.[1]

Thus, the issue of "separatism" stabs at two sensitive Chinese historical nerves: the imperative to keep the country together and the compulsion to redress the Century of Shame. With Hong Kong and Macau back under Chinese administration, Taiwan is the most prominent case of "lost" territory. The regions of Tibet and Xinjiang, however, remain restive and troublesome for Beijing even though foreign governments do not challenge the PRC's sovereignty claims. Both regions contain sizeable communities that are culturally and ethnically distinct from the Han Chinese. Many Tibetans and Uyghurs fear that their traditional lifestyles are threatened by PRC rule. Generations of Chinese leaders, however, have made clear that China intends to keep Tibet and Xinjiang as part of the PRC. Religion is a particularly volatile issue. Tibetans traditionally adhere to Lamaist Buddhism, Uyghurs to Islam. The CCP regime is fundamentally atheistic, influenced by the Marxist view of religion as a tool the ruling class uses to exploit the working classes in presocialist societies. The Chinese state sees religion as not only anachronistic but also a potential threat to the regime in that it represents a competing and inevitably foreign claim on the loyalty of the people.

Xinjiang, or "New Territory," is huge—making up one-sixth of China's total land territory—but sparsely populated. Uyghurs are the largest ethnic group with 8.4 million people and 45 percent of the population. The Han

Chinese population is about 7.5 million (41 percent). There is also a large Kazakh minority. Beijing has a policy of providing economic incentives for ethnic Han Chinese to relocate to Xinjiang. Han are already the majority in the provincial capital of Urumchi.

China is determined to keep Xinjiang for several reasons. The province provides the PRC with strategic depth between Central Asia and heavily populated eastern China. Xinjiang contains the Lop Nur lake bed, where the PLA tests its nuclear weapons. Finally, Xinjiang contains valuable resources, including oil and natural gas. Uyghur resentment against Han rule in Xinjiang is a persistent problem for the Chinese. In 2008, sixteen police officers died in an attack in the city of Kashgar that the Chinese government blamed on two Uyghur "terrorists." In Urumqi almost two hundred people, mostly Han Chinese, died in violence stemming from Han-Uyghur tensions in 2009. In 2010, seven died in a bombing targeting Chinese security personnel in Aksu. Beijing has been quick to allege the involvement of "foreign forces" in fomenting discontent among the Uyghurs. Human rights monitors frequently criticize Beijing for excessive crackdowns on the Uyghur community that do not distinguish peaceful activists from "terrorists." After 9/11, the PRC sought international recognition of "East Turkestan/Turkistan" activist groups as terrorist organizations, seeing an opportunity to transform a source of Western criticism into a tangible Chinese contribution to fighting the global "war on terror." This was controversial, as critics immediately accused China of trying to legitimize the persecution of Uyghurs. (The U.S. Department of State eventually included the East Turkistan Islamic Movement on one of its terrorist lists but not on the Foreign Terrorist Organizations List.)

Like Xinjiang, Tibet is a large but sparsely populated territory with natural resources and strategic importance. Chinese leaders consider it vital as a "national security screen" between China and India.[2] The Tibetan religion spawned a distinct sociopolitical system, with the Dalai Lama at its apex, that previously ruled Tibet. Historically, Chinese influence has been intermittent. In the most recent reassertion of Chinese control, the PLA marched into Tibet in 1951. After a failed uprising in 1959, the fourteenth Dalai Lama fled for exile in India. The second-highest religious figure in Tibetan Buddhism is the Panchen Lama. After the Panchen Lama died in 1989, in 1995 the Dalai Lama named as his successor and reincarnation a seven-year-old boy. In a ham-fisted power play, Beijing arrested the boy and named a CCP-approved Tibetan as the new Panchen Lama.

As with Xinjiang, the Chinese government offers incentives for Han Chinese to move to Tibet, which the Tibetan government in exile calls an attempt by Beijing to make Tibetans a minority in Tibet. The Chinese government argues that the Tibetan theocracy was unjust and backward and that Tibetans are more prosperous under PRC rule. Tibetan nationalists have accused the Chinese authorities of "cultural genocide" and of the massacre of Tibetan dissidents, monks, and nuns. Deadly riots broke out again in 2008, with the Chinese government and the Tibetan government in exile giving different figures on the size and ethnic composition of the casualties.

Beijing condemns the Dalai Lama as a separatist and demands that the rest of the world adopt this outlook. The Dalai Lama's dignity in defense of traditional Tibetan culture and religion, however, gained him great international prestige. He won the Nobel Prize in 1989. The United States awarded him a Congressional Gold Medal in 2007. Although Washington does not officially support Tibetan independence, in the 1960s the U.S. government trained Tibetan exiles in guerrilla warfare with the aim of preparing them to lead an insurgency in Chinese-occupied Tibet. Such episodes have fanned the deep-seated Chinese fear that ill-intentioned foreigners are encouraging separatism as a means of weakening China. For the United States and other governments, the prospect of a visit by the Dalai Lama creates a dilemma. An angry reaction from Beijing is inevitable, but to appear unwelcoming toward the Dalai Lama makes these governments look weak and unprincipled.

What Does China Want?

China's foreign policy goals and strategies can be charted in the form of a pyramid-shaped structure. At the top level are a small number of broad, unvarying, and highly important objectives. In the middle is a collection of general strategies. Taken as a whole, these can be considered China's "grand strategy." In the lower part of the pyramid are a large number of more specific subsidiary strategies, eventually generating China's agenda toward every foreign country and China's position on every international issue. Occasional changes in content are likely at the bottom of the pyramid but less likely the closer we move toward the top.

As the capstone, China has at least two main goals: prosperity and security. To one degree or another, all national governments share these same goals. Prosperity serves overlapping interests. There is no question that the Chinese government feels driven to continue to raise the overall living standards of the Chinese people. This is a duty and expectation of public officials. More to the point, individual leaders will not be considered competent and successful if they fail to meet this expectation. The legitimacy of the CCP and its right to a monopoly on political power will come under question if it cannot maintain economic growth at a pace that stays ahead of public discontent. PRC officials therefore emphasize that their overriding concern is with bringing prosperity to their people. This is believable, but it also has the advantage of obscuring the strategic dimension of China's economic development. Building a strong and prosperous economy now, even with the most benign of intentions, hardly precludes China from using that economic strength in more objectionable ways in the future. If Chinese leaders secretly harbored the forcible domination of the world as their no. 1 goal, they would similarly begin by building up their wealth, productive capacity, access to vital resources, and technological prowess.

Whatever Beijing intends, the starting point is economic development. It is the response to the most urgent demands on the Chinese leadership as well as the foundation for all of China's possible future aspirations.

When they think about national power and security, the citizens of Western countries usually think mainly about military forces. Chinese officials, on the other hand, often use the terms "comprehensive national power" (*zonghe guoli*) and "comprehensive security" (*zonghe anquan*). These terms express a basic Chinese belief that the strength and safety of the country depend on a very broad set of factors: not only on the strength of China's military but also on the civilian population, the economy, and the effectiveness of China's diplomacy. From this standpoint, security goes beyond the protection of people, assets, and territory from foreign military threats. It also includes safeguarding economic development, preserving social harmony, and precluding challenges to the PRC political system and the authority of the Chinese Communist Party (i.e., regime security). Accordingly, economic, political, and social disturbances can be as dangerous as military threats. Even challenges to China's dignity and status from within the international community can be considered serious dangers to China's security.

All national governments care about their reputation and make some effort to present their policies in a favorable light. Some states seem particularly insistent on gaining international respect. Many observers have placed China in this category based on two strong patterns in Chinese behavior: seeking international prestige and recognition as a great power and displaying great sensitivity and even overreaction toward perceived affronts to national pride. If so, we might consider adding "status" to the short list of China's most fundamental objectives.

The next two levels of the pyramid contain the elements of China's grand strategy. In the context of international politics, a grand strategy is a simple and broad statement of how a national government will employ its resources in pursuit of security. A grand strategy either explicitly or implicitly identifies high-priority interests and the most compelling perceived threats to those interests. The closest thing to an official and public PRC statement of its own grand strategy is "peaceful development" (*heping fazhan*), although this is better understood as the carefully crafted spearhead of an international public relations campaign. A better explication of China's grand strategy would begin with a broadly sketched but practical list of the means by which China tries to attain security, prosperity, and status. A reasonable list would include the following elements: achieve and maintain national unity, build up China into one of the major world powers and the preeminent regional power, maintain an external environment conducive to economic growth, increase China's international prestige, and minimize foreign resistance to the rise of China.

From the behavior and statements of PRC officials, we can identify the following as general strategies that China follows at least some of the time in its foreign relations:

- Get access to markets, suppliers and resources
- Make peace with neighbors
- Prevent Taiwan's independence and work toward unification
- Get other countries to oppose what Beijing calls "separatism"
- Build strong enough military forces to deter foreign aggression and uphold key Chinese offshore interests
- Advance the "peaceful China" notion and discredit the "China threat" notion
- Deter foreigners from opposing or cooperating against Chinese objectives
- Undercut U.S. attempts to limit China's regional leadership
- Promote international stability
- Cultivate relationships with regional states in which their governments make no major policy decisions that are against China's wishes
- Build a network of partnerships and friendly ties through diplomacy, multilateralism, and economic ties
- Maintain Chinese claims to disputed territory

The grand strategy is a plan for achieving the basic goals of security, prosperity, and status, but it is also itself a set of aims on which more specific Chinese policies are based. This is why the overview here includes both goals and strategies: the difference between the two can be blurry. The specific policies that fill out the wide base of the Chinese foreign policy pyramid are too numerous to list here, but a few examples will suffice:

China's policy toward the United States: maintain the constructive relationship that feeds China's economic development; avoid open confrontation except in the event of a direct U.S. challenge to a vital Chinese interest; parry anti-China U.S. policies while dissuading Washington of any need to try to block the rise of China.

China's policy toward Japan: work toward a Japan that is neutral, underarmed, assists in China's economic development, and does not compete with China for a regional leadership role. Limited U.S.-Japan military cooperation is acceptable for now, but increased Japanese military activity outside the alliance is not. Attempt to employ the "history card" judiciously, but not to such an extent that this emboldens Japanese conservative nationalists or seriously damages Sino-Japanese economic cooperation.

China's policy toward the Korean Peninsula: draw Seoul into closer economic partnership and political accommodation with China, preparatory to easing South Korea out of its alliance with the United States. As for North Korea: prevent a collapse of the regime, pressure Pyongyang to undertake economic reforms along the Chinese model, and urge the North Koreans to pursue peaceful relations with the other regional governments while prodding the United States, Japan, and South Korea to alleviate North Korea's sense of insecurity.

China's policy toward South Asia: attempt to stabilize relations with India and to discourage Indian participation in defense cooperation with other states against China but without weakening China's influence with other South Asian countries (especially Pakistan), the Chinese claim to disputed but strategically important territory near China's border with India, or China's control over Tibet.

When we examine even a partial set of China's foreign policy goals and strategies, we can easily see that the package is riddled with contradictions.

Even at the top level of the pyramid, we can foresee tensions between the most general objectives. The pursuit of security typically involves military strengthening and defense partnerships that can alarm other states and thereby restrict opportunities for trade (prosperity) and make China appear to some observers like an international troublemaker (status). One of these general goals can by itself generate self-contradictory policies. If the drive for status leads to Chinese overreaction to a perceived insult, the self-defeating outcome is that foreigners will look down on Beijing because of the overreaction. If the desire for security leads to a Chinese military buildup, the consequence might be increased suspicions and reactive arms buildups by China's neighbors that leave the Chinese less secure than before. The contradictions are clearer when we lay out China's various observed and stated policies. Making peace with regional neighbors conflicts with maintaining China's claims to disputed territories. Promoting international stability conflicts with sheltering North Korea from pressure to stop provocative and violent acts against South Korea. Threatening war over Taiwan independence conflicts with promoting the idea of a "peaceful" rise of China.

One might assert that China does not have a coherent grand strategy, given that it is composed of parts that imply contradictory subsidiary policies. We can see, then, that China has an enormous and continuous challenge in attempting to balance these various competing interests. The prevalence and depth of these contradictions work against stability and predictability in Chinese foreign policy.

As we try to anticipate how China will sort out these contradictions, it is useful to know who or what is the intended beneficiary of PRC policy making. In the case of security policy, we usually assume the driver is "national security." This, however, is a sloppy term. To be more precise, we can distinguish several possible referents of security.[3] The first is the "nation." In the field of political studies, nation means a group of people who share a common identity. The basis of their shared identity may be ethnic, religious, or philosophical. The security of the Chinese "nation" would mean the preservation of whatever the Chinese people see as the basis of their Chineseness. The second possible referent is the "state," which includes the country's political system, government institutions, and territorial boundaries. A third possible referent of security policy is the regime, which is the particular group of leaders or the political party controlling the top government positions. Finally, policy making might be aimed at providing for the safety and well-being of China's citizens, either collectively or individually. Some overlap among these different referents is possible. Chinese might see Taiwan's independence, for example, as a threat to all four referents of security: to the nation, if Chinese identify themselves closely with a traditional empire that includes Taiwan; to the state, if the PRC has territorial sovereignty over Taiwan; to the regime, which would lose legitimacy if it "lost" Taiwan; and to individual Chinese, through the loss of part of the "Chinese" public to a rival government. These distinctions among referents matter because a policy designed to protect one referent would not be ideal for protecting the others. What makes one referent more secure might make another less secure. A simple example is the case of a Chinese citizen who criticizes the central government: the security of the individual clashes with the security of the regime. I will argue that the regime sitting atop the policy-making apparatus gives its own interests top priority, potentially at the expense of other sets of interests.

The significance of this assumption is often missed. Neither China's nor any other country's national leaders will say publicly that they value their own skins over their sacred charge to protect the country's people, assets, territory, and good name. Political leaders do not reach the pinnacles of power without mastering the basic political skill of pursuing one's self-interest while appearing to promote the greater good. Most of the time, what is good for the country is also what is good for the regime. Occasionally, however, circumstances arise that pit the interests of the country and the interests of the regime against each other. If regime security is the driving interest of PRC policy making, China's national leaders will choose a policy that is good for them and marginally bad for the country over a policy that good for the country but bad for them. The top leaders in Beijing are constrained from taking a course of action that the Chinese people would recognize as clearly and seriously damaging to the country; grave malfeasance would lead to inexorable demands for the ouster of the regime. Even an authoritarian regime requires some level of legitimacy to stay in power.

In certain cases, however, the decision makers are liable to choose a policy that prioritizes their own personal interests over the broader interests of their countrymen. In May and June 1989, the regime faced a massive protest centered on thousands of students occupying Tiananmen Square in Beijing. A violent suppression of the protestors was certain to harm China's international prestige and opportunities for economic cooperation. But the top Chinese leaders with control over the military took this step anyway, seeing the protests as a serious challenge to CCP rule. The Chinese officials who favored the harsh crackdown rationalized that China's continued progress was predicated on CCP rule. This thinking equates regime security with the prosperity and security of the Chinese people—in effect establishing the principle that whatever is good for the regime is by definition good for the Chinese people. Other illustrative cases come from recent China-Japan relations. While the Chinese government has usually preferred to maintain good relations with Japan to further economic cooperation and undercut the growth of anti-China Japanese nationalism, on several occasions unanticipated events triggered upsurges of outrage toward Japan among the Chinese public, forcing Beijing to join in making gestures and statements condemning Japan, lest Chinese observers turn their wrath toward their own leaders for being too weak in defense of China's honor.

An Exceptional Great Power?

Demonstrating what could be called Chinese exceptionalism, the Chinese believe their country has been and will be a unique great power. There are at least three ways this uniqueness is made manifest. First, China is averse to traditional alliances. The Cold War–era principle that China follows an "independent" foreign policy remains part of the present-day foreign policy mantra. Originally, it meant that China does not ally with one of the superpowers. This idea taps into a deeper Chinese historical dissatisfaction with alliances. In the premodern world, China did not officially enter into alliances (although in practice Beijing sometimes had de facto alliances with neighboring governments) because China was at the top of the regional hierarchy and in principle could not enter into a relationship with another state that implied equality. In the modern age, Chinese tried to play one great power off against another. Siding with the victorious Allies in World War I, however, did not result in China regaining Shandong Province from the defeated Germans; instead, the Allies gave Shandong to Japan. The postwar alliance with Russia collapsed in acrimony. The Chinese dislike being either the major partner or the minor partner in an alliance. They also reject the notion that alliances contribute to peace, pointing to the U.S. wars in Korea and Vietnam. China today has only one formal alliance partner: North Korea. In recent years, Chinese leaders have made clear that although the Sino–North Korean Mutual Aid and Cooperation Friendship Treaty remains on the books, Beijing will not automatically send military forces to help the North Koreans if they get into a war. The Chinese insist that their relationships with Russia and with the Shanghai Cooperation Organization are not alliances because they are not aimed at another country.

Nevertheless, the practice of partnering with the enemies of China's enemies comes naturally to the Chinese. During the drive to unify China in the 1920s and the Japanese invasion of 1931–1945, China employed a "united front" strategy of putting aside ideological differences to join forces with potential adversaries against a more compelling common enemy. The CCP under Mao continued this practice during the Cold War. As a strategy of international politics, China's united front strategy closely resembles a balance-of-threat approach: identifying the most threatening state (not necessarily the most *powerful* state in the system) and forming a coalition against it. A history of friendly relations among the coalition members is helpful but not essential, as these countries' shared interest in opposing the threatening state takes precedence. In the 1950s, Beijing perceived its most threatening potential adversary to be the United States and aligned with the Soviet Union. In the 1970s, the Chinese saw the Soviets as most threatening and moved toward rapprochement and greater cooperation with the United States. In the post-Mao and post–Cold War era, China has returned to cooperating with Russia in significant ways to oppose the sole remaining superpower, although the balancing is relatively muted because China's sense of a direct and existential security threat is reduced and because China relies heavily on economic cooperation with the United States. In sum, China has a track record of pragmatic balancing behavior even while preferring not to use the term "alliance."

A second reason Chinese believe China is a unique great power is that the Chinese people know how it feels to be downtrodden. Chinese argue that their experience as victims of great-power imperialism has given China sympathy for weak and poor countries and credibility as their defender. Other than Russia and France enduring Nazi invasions during World War II, none of today's other great powers suffered anything resembling foreign imperialist molestation during the modern era. As Chinese would be quick to point out, their suffering lasted for a century and included both a long period of economic exploitation by avaricious foreign powers and a cruel military invasion by Japan that the CCP says killed twenty million Chinese—far surpassing the Jewish Holocaust. Throughout the Cold War, the Chinese government styled itself as the champion of the Third World. Much of modern China's unhappy experience with international politics is distilled into the Five Principles of Peaceful Coexistence, which originally arose from a joint statement by China and India in 1954. The newly established PRC and newly decolonized India both objected to what they saw as a historical pattern of domineering behavior by the great powers. The two governments announced that five principles should not only guide Sino-Indian relations but should also serve as the basis of all international relations: "mutual respect for sovereignty and territorial integrity, mutual nonaggression, noninterference in each other's internal affairs, equality and mutual benefit, and peaceful coexistence." This list of five principles subsequently became a standard part of the official PRC description of China's foreign policy. The five principles were the basis of the PRC's post–Cold War "New Security Concept," a condemnation of U.S. alliances in Asia as "Cold War thinking," and a commitment to reducing tensions through multilateral dialogue. During a 2005 speech to the United Nations, PRC President Hu Jintao introduced the Chinese objective of building a "harmonious world" (*hexie shijie*), an extension of his domestic "harmonious society" (*hexie shehui*) campaign. The substance of Hu's harmonious world is that states should seek security through trust building and multilateral cooperation rather than through "Cold War" alliances (like America's), the global economic system should be fair, individual countries should be free to choose their own domestic political and social systems (i.e., the West should stop pressuring human rights abusers), and international relations should be democratized (the United States should not dominate). If "harmonious world" rehashes well-known Chinese views about international affairs, its significance is that it is a step toward greater Chinese involvement in shaping the rules of international affairs. The idea suggests an international leadership role for China, which sees itself as a depository of wisdom on "harmony" because this is a key theme of Confucian thought. Ideally for China, this is a completely nonthreatening form of leadership.

A third reason why Chinese consider their country unique among the great powers is their belief in the (questionable) notion that China is inherently defensive and does not make war unless attacked. Chinese maintain that their historical track record proves China is peaceful. Even when strong, the argument goes, China eschewed aggression and fought only to defend itself. The explanation is reputedly found in Chinese culture. Traditional Chinese thought distinguishes between *wangdao* ("the kingly way"), which is benevolent leadership that relies on persuasion and moral example, and *badao* ("the tyrant way"), which is rule by force. Chinese extol *wangdao* and commonly believe that premodern China exemplified it. China, they say, had the power and technology to dominate its neighbors but instead opted to wield influence by sharing its culture and knowledge with countries that would appreciate it.[4] This is an idealized view; the historical reality was more complicated. (More on this later.) Chinese say their strong Confucian tradition also contributes to a peaceful foreign policy. Confucius (Kong Fuzi, or "Master Kong") taught that those in power should employ it ethically rather than selfishly. He also emphasized the importance of seeking and maintaining social harmony. Chinese leaders remain deeply influenced by Confucian values, the claim goes, so they are inclined to reach accommodation with other countries and disinclined to try to dominate smaller neighbors. Again, the historical record of premodern China does not show an absence of warfare or of attempts to push around weaker regional states, although the Chinese government was "Confucian" in that it consistently treated other countries as inferiors.[5]

Nevertheless, Chinese officials frequently assert with a straight face that "seeking hegemony [dominance] goes against China's cultural tradition," so for this reason alone the world should stop worrying about growing Chinese power.[6] The problem with this argument is that in an arena of intense competition for something scarce but highly valued, such as wealth or security, culture usually counts for little. This is why we see common features among high-achieving politicians across different cultural traditions. We also see similarities in behavior among an equally culturally diverse group of great powers throughout history.

The extent to which China's past serves as a guide to the future behavior of China as a modern great power is questionable. First, as we have seen, there are different interpretations of Chinese history. According to the official Chinese government view, "History shows that China has never invaded and occupied other countries' territory nor terrorized other countries, and it did not do so even when it was one of the most powerful countries in the world."[7] This, however, is not the whole story. It is true that premodern China influenced its neighbors using what in today's parlance would be called "soft power." The Ming dynasty, for example, sent Chinese teachers and books overseas, lent the assistance of Chinese technical experts to foreign governments, and hosted foreign students. In an idealized view of Chinese history, these are magnanimous efforts to share superior Chinese culture with neighboring states. Alternatively, however, we could see this exercise of soft power as part of a broader strategy of expanding and consolidating Chinese political domination, especially when we recognize that the Chinese mixed in the occasional use of force against challenger or recalcitrant states.[8] Some analysts have argued persuasively that despite their Confucian ideals, premodern Chinese rulers were not averse either to making alliances with smaller regional states or to using force against them, and that in these respects China differed little from the European powers.[9] The ancient Chinese fought in thousands of conflicts. When confronted with this fact, defenders of the idea of a peace-loving ancient China argue that each of these conflicts were defensive, necessary to unify the country, or instigated when China was under "foreign" ethnic Mongol or Manchu rule (Inner Mongolia and Manchuria are now part of the PRC). But the idea of China as a historically benevolent neighbor is a hard sell for the Vietnamese, who suffered several Chinese invasions, including one by the ethnically Han Ming dynasty in the fifteenth century. It is somewhat dubious that in the PRC's interpretation of history the Mongol and Manchu dynasties count as "Chinese" because the conquerors adopted Chinese culture and philosophy, yet their aggressive foreign policies do not count against China's reputedly peaceful track record. It is also dubious that Chinese conquest of what was then a neighboring country (such as the Qing dynasty's extermination of the Central Asian state of the Zunghars in 1756–1759) should subsequently be reclassified as domestic housekeeping because the modern world accepts as legitimate the expanded boundaries of today's PRC.

Even the significance of the fifteenth-century Chinese admiral Zheng He's voyages is a matter of debate. According to Chinese history, the Muslim Chinese eunuch led seven voyages—well before Columbus's journey to the Americas, the Chinese point out—to Southeast Asia, the Indian Ocean, the Middle East, and as far as the coast of Africa. Four of Zheng He's ships were over four hundred feet long (Columbus's flagship *Santa Maria* was only seventy feet long). His fleets were also numerically huge, comprising up to 250 ships and thirty thousand personnel (mostly soldiers) plus thousands of tons of goods for trade. The Chinese government celebrates the Zheng He voyages as evidence that China will be a peaceful and benevolent great power. According to Xu Zuyuan, the PRC vice minister of communications, "these were friendly diplomatic activities. . . . Zheng He did not occupy a single piece of land, establish any fortress, or seize any wealth from other countries. In commercial and trade activities, he adopted the practice of giving more than he received, and thus he was welcomed and lauded by the people of the various countries along his route." Premier Wen Jiabao cites Zheng He's voyage to make the point that "Hegemonism is at odds with our cultural tradition, and it runs counter to the wishes of the Chinese people." Some non-PRC scholars, however, challenge the view that the purposes of Zheng He's voyages were friendly and generous. James R. Holmes and Toshi Yoshihara assert that Zheng He's mission was to restore Chinese suzerainty over the region, which "had everything to do with power politics." Geoffrey Wade argues that Zheng He's voyages were "military missions with strategic aims": to demonstrate Chinese military superiority to both friends and foes, to gain control of foreign ports and trade routes, and to influence regional politics in the favor of pro-China factions. Zheng He's forces set up military bases and engaged in substantial combat in places such as Sri Lanka, Thailand, and what is now Indonesia.[10]

A second reason why China's past is not a reliable guide to China's future is that the circumstances of the modern world are substantially different from those of the premodern world. It does not necessarily follow that China will behave the same way in the future as it did in the past. Among the obvious differences are modern phenomena such as globalization, the heavy reliance of national economies on hydrocarbon energy resources, enhancements in the ability to project military power, and mass public pressure on national decision makers. Premodern Chinese elites apparently worried relatively little about foreign threats to national security, confident in the strength of Chinese civilization to absorb external challenges and "Sinicize" conquerors. Ancient China experienced nothing like the Century of Shame, which profoundly altered thinking about China's security and about the dangers posed by other great powers. Twenty-first-century China is entering historically uncharted territory with an unprecedented outlook.

Cooperation Versus Confrontation

Worldwide recognition of China as an emerging great power, a direct consequence of the PRC's post-Mao economic takeoff, coincided with a much-improved security climate for China. The situation had certainly improved since the first half of the twentieth century, when China was fighting for its life, and the latter half of the twentieth century, when China endured periods of high tension—and occasional combat—with both superpowers. Paramount leader Deng Xiaoping proclaimed in 1985 that the world had entered an era of "peace and development." China, he said, could focus on building its economy rather than preparing for war, should seek improved relations with the outside world, and could afford to make compromises on strategic disputes in order to increase China's access to the global economy. At the beginning of the twenty-first century, Chinese leaders reaffirmed this approach by proclaiming "an important period of strategic opportunity" (*zhongyao zhanlue jiyuqi*) that they anticipated would last through the year 2020. Their assessment, similar to Deng's, is that while China needs to remain attentive to the behavior of the other major powers during this period, the expectation of a major war is low, and thus China can concentrate on strengthening the nation through economic development. China could therefore afford to be patient in pursuing redress for its grievances with foreign governments.

Indeed, patience appeared to be the prudent course because based on Chinese strategic assessments, China would need a lot of time. Most Chinese international affairs analysts see the world as having moved from "bipolarity" to "unipolarity" during the last half-century. Under the bipolarity of the Cold War period, there were two superpowers as "poles" or power centers, with many other countries flocking to one side or the other. The breakup of the Soviet Union and the Eastern Bloc in 1989–1990 left the United States as the lone superpower. Unipolarity has meant neither world domination by the United States nor world alignment with the United States. Rather, it means an international system in which one country is so much more powerful than any of the others as to be in a class by itself. China favors a "multipolar" world in which China is one of several roughly equal great powers. In addition to the rise of China, multipolarity would require that the United States drop down a notch. As the Cold War ended, many Chinese analysts proclaimed that multipolarity was imminent. Contrary to their expectations, however, American strength did not flag in the 1990s. A new consensus emerged that U.S. predominance would not pass so quickly and that for a few more decades the world would feature "one superpower with multiple great powers," one of which would be China.[11] Periods of U.S. difficulty inevitably lead to new waves of Chinese speculation that the transitional period between unipolarity and multipolarity might be shortened. The financial crisis of the late 2000s convinced some Chinese analysts that America is in "collapse" or that "U.S. strength is declining at a speed so fantastic that it is far beyond anticipation."[12]

Accordingly, China began the post–Cold War era with its top leadership committed to nonaggression. Deng Xiaoping favored a cautious and restrained foreign policy while China builds up its core capabilities. In the 1980s, Deng laid out a set of guiding principles that became known as the "twenty-four-character strategy." The most talked about is *taoguang yanghui*. This phrase is often translated into English as "hide our capabilities and bide our time," which generates an ominous or even malevolent connotation by suggesting that China has a long-term plan to temporarily feign harmlessness and then suddenly shift to a more aggressive policy at an opportune moment. In fact, however, both halves of this four-character Chinese expression (literally "hide brightness, nurture obscurity") refer to keeping capabilities hidden, corresponding roughly to the biblically derived English expression "keep your light hidden under a bushel." Deng's intent seems not to have been to encourage sneaky behavior but rather to avoid threatening or boastful behavior. The full list of Deng's principles for Chinese foreign policy provides a more complete context:

lengjing guancha	observe calmly
wenzhu zhenjiao	stabilize [our] position
chenzhuo yingfu	handle matters patiently and confidently
taoguang yanghui	hide your capabilities; don't flaunt them
shanyu shouzhuo	keep a low profile
juebu dangtou	don't take the lead

The thrust of Deng's advice is that China should keep its emotions in check and avoid drawing unfavorable attention to itself so as to maintain an external political environment conducive to Chinese growth.

Deng's policy of remaining calm, cooperative, and conciliatory while building up the sinews of strength has served China well up to now. As China's relative strength continues to grow, the country draws closer to a reassessment of this policy. If the present trajectory holds, China will eventually be strong enough to raise its profile, take the lead, and demand that the world accommodate Chinese interests and preferences. A growing number of Chinese observers of international affairs believe China has already reached this point.

The mainstream Chinese view favors a cooperative and nonconfrontational foreign policy approach. According to this view, China's most pressing need is to address its internal problems such as economic development, corruption, and the uneven distribution of wealth. This requires a stable international environment. China should prevent Chinese nationalism from perturbing the external environment. When China acts on these nationalistic impulses, it suffers a foreign backlash that forces a Chinese retreat and makes the international community more suspicious of the consequences of China's rise. Furthermore, claiming international leadership is likely to bring China unwelcome costs and burdens. Rather, China should pursue its interests by working within the rules of the international system, avoiding conflicts with the major powers, assuring the world that China is not a threat, and promoting the Chinese model and Chinese principles nonaggressively through diplomacy and soft power. In other words, China should continue to follow Deng's advice. This view prevails in most of China's international affairs research institutions and has been the consensus approach of Chinese policy makers through the first decade of this century.

A more confrontational outlook in China takes a darker view of world politics and argues that China should more strongly assert its interests in international leadership, gaining control over Chinese sovereign territory and opposing U.S. domination, even at the risk of increased tensions between China and other major powers. This confrontational school of thought is common among Chinese military officers and PLA researchers. Adherents to this viewpoint tend to be strongly influenced by the modern Chinese ideologies of anti-imperialism and Marxism. The main features of the confrontational viewpoint are as follows: China has been a peaceful and nonaggressive country. Despite this, the United States and its allies have tried to contain China and have used the rise of China as an excuse for policies intended to prolong U.S. domination of the Asia-Pacific region. To maintain the desired image of a peacefully rising China, Beijing has assiduously avoided conflicts with the United States. These efforts, however, are becoming counterproductive: appeasing the United States encourages further domineering behavior by the Americans and misleads neighboring states into believing that China will not stand up for its own interests. Therefore China should stop worrying about its image and show more toughness in defense of its positions on international issues. For the Chinese who ascribe to this school of thought, Deng's advice is obsolete.

Many foreigners cringe at the thought of a bitter, vengeful China seemingly bursting onto the international scene as a major power with memories of its recent poverty and weakness still raw. To Westerners, a strong China is something new because China as a state was prostrate during most of the period in which Westerners have been familiar with China. What the West sees as China finally fulfilling its vast potential is to the Chinese a return to the natural order. For them, the descent of China from the ranks of the great powers was a historical anomaly, a temporary mistake awaiting inevitable correction. To Chinese, the rise of China is not an intrusion upon the international community; it is a rectification. Furthermore, Chinese fully expect a more powerful China to benefit the global community as a whole by promoting principles that will make international relations more peaceful. But if there is to be a peace dividend from the rise of China, many governments in the Asia-Pacific region do not yet see it.

Chapter Three

U.S.-CHINA RELATIONS UNDER HEGEMONIC TRANSITION

China's historical self-image impels the Chinese to aspire to regional leadership. Many international affairs analysts believe that the pressures of international politics, as well, will compel a strong China to try to dominate the Asia-Pacific region. According to this thinking, a state that is powerful enough will aspire to domination because this is the surest and most direct way to attain security. It is equally inevitable that other strong states, equally concerned about their own security, will resist. This is a controversial assertion. Some observers would argue alternatively that Chinese foreign policy as a whole has not fundamentally shifted toward a more assertive stance. Even if Chinese foreign policy has recently become more pushy in some areas as China has become stronger, in other areas China remains cautious and cooperative.

In my view, China's growing national power (especially China's economic capacity and technological prowess, which lead to Chinese military strength and political influence) relative to the other major countries will indeed increase pressure on the Chinese government to act more assertively in China's self-interest. The greater Chinese assertiveness visible lately on several important issues will persist and increase over the medium term. There may be a cycle of ebb and flow as Beijing follows strong thrusts with periods of pullback and damage control, but the thrusts will likely grow bolder over time. Many Chinese elites are calling for the Chinese government to take a stronger leadership role in world affairs and a more insistent position in defense of Chinese preferences in the region. The Chinese people expect that a stronger China will have more influence in shaping the rules, norms, and institutions that guide international affairs. In their view, to deny China increased international leadership would be an injustice.[1] As we have seen, in the Chinese view, increased assertiveness by the PRC is more than justified as a long-overdue redress of policies by foreign powers (mostly the United States) designed to repress China. The ancient Greek historian Thucydides is credited with the observation that in international politics, "the strong do what they will, and the weak suffer what they must." As a weak country, the PRC had little recourse against many policies by foreign governments to which the Chinese objected. For a strengthening China, however, resistance becomes increasingly feasible.

Expanding Chinese aspirations immediately clash with the agenda of the United States, which has been the strongest power in the Asia-Pacific region since World War II. Predictably, in recent years China has expressed its displeasure more forcefully about what the Chinese see as attempts by the United States and other countries to constrain China or encroach upon Chinese prerogatives. American activities such as surveillance missions by U.S. Navy aircraft and ships near China's coast, arms sales to Taiwan, joint military exercises with America's ally South Korea, and strategic cooperation with Southeast Asian countries have bothered the Chinese for many years, but in 2009–2010 the Chinese responses to these activities were noticeably tougher than they had been in years past. A major part of the explanation for this escalation is that the Chinese expect to be treated with more respect now that China is stronger. By proceeding with activities known to offend the Chinese, the Americans failed to meet this expectation, resulting in displays of Chinese anger.

As China becomes more relatively capable, two changes occur. First, Beijing's sense of having important interests geographically far from China will increase. For example, China's rapidly growing economy requires the Chinese to import larger amounts of resources from distant sources. In the scramble for global resources, which is as important to China as to any other country, Beijing is compelled to engage in economic cooperation with some countries that are prone to political instability and to rely on foreign supply lines subject to attack or disruption. Ships with Chinese flags or carrying Chinese cargo sail in seas where pirates lurk. Chinese laborers work on overseas projects. Since Beijing cannot trust the Americans or other foreigners to protect Chinese people, property, and interests around the world, the Chinese believe they need to develop their own capacities to do so.

Second, the Chinese realize they can do more than before to shape the external environment in ways that will make China more secure. New strategic opportunities are opening to China, and Chinese elites are debating how much and in what directions China should expand its external aspirations. There is agreement, however, that China should be more assertive now that it is stronger. The hawkish end of the spectrum contends that with America and the West in decline, China should grow out of its admiration for Western ways and prepare to take over global leadership from the United States, even at the risk of a confrontation. A more widely held opinion has been that China should be less passive in defending its interests and pointing out differences in Chinese and U.S. approaches but also that China should continue to cooperate with the United States and avoid taking a global leadership role for the foreseeable future.[2] China's expanded view of its interests and greater efforts to protect those interests—such as building a large blue-water navy to protect its oceanic supply lines—will push against the interests of other major powers, raising tensions. China and the United States could begin to see each other primarily as security competitors. This will leave U.S.-China relations vulnerable to a crisis, such as an international incident or a surge in nationalism stoked by one of the two governments. A crisis could devolve into a conflict.

Hegemonic Transition

The background context of today's U.S.-China relations is what international relations scholars call "hegemonic transition." Hegemonic transitions occur periodically through history and usually bring an increased risk of a major war. Countries constantly rise and fall, and they do so at different rates. Certain countries were great powers in the past but are minor powers today. One of the key determinants of a state's international ranking is the size of its economy, and this characteristic is relatively flexible. An individual state's rate of economic growth or shrinkage rarely stays the same for more than a few years. This alone guarantees fluctuation in any state's power level relative to the other states. At any given point in history, a few countries will be stronger than the rest. In international relations theory, "hegemony" means dominance, and a "hegemon" is a dominant state. A hegemon attains a leadership role because it is the strongest state in a region (regional hegemon) or in the entire world (global hegemon). The hegemon does not keep this position forever, however, because eventually another large country with a higher rate of economic growth will become stronger than the hegemon. According to power transition theory, when it becomes clear that the strength of a rising challenger is on track to attain and surpass the strength level of an established hegemon, a hegemonic crisis is likely. The mature dominant power has shaped the rules and norms of international affairs to suit its own interests and values, and it wants this version of the international system to persist. The rising challenger, on the other hand, is anxious to rearrange the international system, which it feels reflects an outdated situation. The rising state's people increasingly feel deprived because their influence is less than they deserve based on their new power level. The risk of war increases when the rising challenger is approaching parity with the established hegemon. The hegemon, concluding that continued relative decline and eventual subordination to the challenger is otherwise inevitable, considers starting a preventive war to undercut the challenger. Conversely, the challenger may start a fight because it loses patience with a system that disproportionately benefits a declining hegemon. Two additional factors might raise the risk of an outbreak of hegemonic war: (1) the declining hegemon believes its interests will suffer badly under the new system the rising challenger would put in place, and (2) the challenger is highly dissatisfied with the current system.

In a system where the dominant power has a huge lead over the next strongest power, the chances of war between the two tends to be low. The hegemon is satisfied with a status quo that reflects the hegemon's interests. The no. 2 power may be unhappy with the status quo or at least parts of it, but it is not strong enough to fight the hegemon for the right to reshape the system. This describes the U.S.-China relationship in the 1980s and the 1990s.

The situation changes, however, if China becomes a great power in the same league as the dominant power. China demands changes. U.S. willingness to accommodate China and allow those changes is tested. Such accommodation by the United States would require compromising American influence, leaving the United States with less control over its external security. A key issue in the hegemonic transition, then, is whether an equilibrium can be maintained throughout the transition period in which both players are satisfied enough that they choose not to fight. Such an equilibrium would be easy to maintain if the United States was confident that its interests would be protected under a Chinese regional hegemony and if China was completely happy with the current status quo and thus in no hurry to change it. Unfortunately, neither of these conditions applies. The United

States favors an international system that is conducive to the continued spread of democracy. China not only opposes pressing countries to change their domestic political systems; it also sees the American-sponsored democratization campaign as a direct and serious threat to China. Washington supports the norm that egregious behavior by outlaw governments, whether against the international community or against their own people, compels other states to stop this misbehavior, if necessary by force. China stands for nonintervention. The United States has demanded international pressure on countries such as Iran and North Korea to halt their objectionable policies, while China has argued against such pressure and tried to shield these countries from it. America insists that the people of Taiwan be allowed to choose their political destiny free from coercion by China. Beijing sees Taiwan as a domestic matter in which U.S. intrusion has prevented a settlement on China's terms. Beijing asserts that no country should have military bases on foreign soil. The United States considers its array of Asia-Pacific bases crucial to regional and U.S. security. Washington has even expressed an interest in keeping U.S. troops in Korea, historically part of the Chinese sphere of influence, after Korean unification. China's ideal Japan would be neutral and minimally armed. The United States has pulled Japan in the opposite direction, maintaining a formal alliance and encouraging Tokyo to lay aside many of the postwar restrictions on Japanese military capabilities and activities. While the United States and China share some important common interests, there are differences in values and interests between them substantial enough to guarantee that the power transition will be tense.

In keeping with the expectations of a hegemonic transition, China the rising power is becoming impatient. Senior Colonel Liu Mingfu, a PLA political officer, professor at China's National Defense University, and author of the 2010 book *China's Dream: Major Power Thinking and Strategic Posture in a Post-American Era*, argues that China should accept that international politics is a competition among militarily strong states for regional and world domination. The United States, he says, will struggle to maintain its position against a rising China. Therefore, both to defend itself and to claim the position of global leadership within its reach, China should strive to become the world's strongest military power as quickly as possible.[3] A recent editorial rant in *People's Daily* by General Luo Yuan, the deputy secretary general of the Society of China Military Sciences, captures some of the raw emotion at the heart of this viewpoint:

The United States claims, "Since I am the dominant player in the world, I can go anywhere I want and others have no rights to interfere. . . . [T]he American Nation is the most outstanding nation in the world. Its leadership in the world, which is bestowed by God, is undeniable. Therefore, Americans have the responsibility to handle world affairs and will appear wherever problems take place. Nevertheless, the results are usually the opposite—things become worse with the involvement of the United States. . . . [Americans] are convinced that the social system of the United States is the most advanced in the world. Therefore, they strive to sell their "democratic values" across the world, which sometimes means resorting to military action. . . . The United States will exercise its military power to punish the nations that do not follow its will. . . . [Americans believe] They do not need to pay attention to security concerns raised by any other country.[4]

"Containment" Versus Insurance

Most Chinese think the unspoken objective of U.S. policy toward China is captured in the term "containment." They believe the United States aims to keep China weak so that the Chinese cannot challenge America's accustomed power and privileges in Asia. Not surprisingly, Chinese who hold this belief harbor deep anger and outrage toward the U.S. government and in some cases toward Americans in general. It is a modern-day iteration of the Opium War: powerful and greedy Western barbarians, bent on further enriching themselves by exploiting Asia, show contempt for and cause harm to the Chinese people. When evaluating U.S. defense cooperation with other states in the region, Chinese observers are quick to assume that the main U.S. purpose is to keep China boxed in and thereby preserve U.S. domination. The Chinese are likely to see not only America's formal alliances with Japan, South Korea, and Australia in this light but also U.S. military cooperation with countries such as India, Vietnam, Thailand, Mongolia, and Taiwan. The U.S. government's recent emphasis on the relative importance of Asia and efforts to invigorate U.S. relationships with friendly countries in the Asia-Pacific region can be interpreted as increased American concern about China as a strategic competitor.[5] Various specific policies appear in Chinese eyes to be parts of a larger plan to encircle China more tightly: for example, American arms sales to Taiwan, the construction of a pier large enough to accommodate an aircraft carrier at a Singapore naval base, Washington's decision to remove the sanctions against India for its 1998 nuclear test and instead upgrade both nuclear and defense cooperation, and U.S. Navy ship visits to Vietnam. Chinese strategists believe that while North Korea is the pretext for U.S. and Japanese cooperation on a system to defend against ballistic missile attacks, the real target is China. From China's standpoint, the evidence for containment continues to pile up. Many Chinese elites believe the United States exploited the 9/11 terror attacks to expand U.S. global influence. Washington gained military bases in Central Asia close to China, tightening the perceived encirclement. U.S. military cooperation with the Philippines, much reduced since the Philippines decided to close major U.S. air and naval bases in the 1990s, revived because of U.S. interest in helping Manila fight the Muslim insurgency in the country's southern islands. The Chinese suspect that America's policy of supporting the spread of democracy throughout the globe is a Trojan horse designed to extend U.S. influence and to weaken countries that might challenge the superpower.

According to Chinese analysts, part of the containment strategy is to convince the international community that China is a threat, so that other governments will cooperate with U.S. efforts to suppress the growth of Chinese power and influence. This is the context within which Chinese view the expressions of concern about China's military buildup from U.S. officials. The U.S. Department of Defense produces a report to Congress on new developments in China's military modernization; this is the only annual, public, and widely disseminated report published by any government about another country's armed forces. From China's standpoint, the idea that the United States should fear China's military is ridiculous. The U.S. military has capabilities unmatched by China or any other country, operates globally from hundreds of foreign bases (China has none), and enjoys a budget nearly as large as the defense budgets of the rest of the world combined. Therefore, the Chinese suspect, U.S. complaints about Chinese military power must be based on a nefarious and unstated objective. Beside the obvious overarching strategic objective of maintaining American superpower status, there is the presumed influence of the often vilified military-industrial complex (a term made famous, ironically, by the retired five-star U.S. Army General Dwight Eisenhower). Chinese such as PLA General Peng Guangqian are among those who postulate that "exaggerating China's military power and regarding China as a strategic opponent can stimulate the research and development of U.S. military industrial enterprises and win high profit orders for U.S. military industrial enterprises."[6]

The Chinese belief in U.S. containment is wrong. Containment refers to the Cold War–era package of U.S. policies intended to check the spread of Soviet influence to other countries and regions. It included diplomatic, economic, and military elements. U.S. policy was based on the perception that the Soviet Union's objective was to pull as much of the world as possible into a rival international economic and political system fundamentally at odds with the system sponsored by the United States and the other prosperous democratic states. Washington and its European allies were part of an explicitly anti-Soviet military alliance, the North Atlantic Treaty Organization. The United States provided military assistance to governments under the threat of conquest or overthrow by pro-Soviet insurgents. The United States had a partial trade embargo against the Soviet Union during the Cold War that included comparatively high tariffs and denial of credit for the Soviet government and those of its allies. Heavy additional sanctions were added when the bilateral political relationship suffered a setback. (China was under embargo as well, until the normalization of U.S.-PRC relations in 1979). U.S. post–Cold War policy toward China is dramatically different.

What the Chinese see as containment the Americans see as insurance. Washington has conditionally acquiesced to the rise of China. U.S. power is arrayed in the Asia-Pacific region not to inhibit China's economic development, growth in prestige, or even its increase in military capabilities. Rather, U.S. military capabilities in the Asia-Pacific region and security agreements with other regional governments reflect a policy of preparing for adverse scenarios, including the possibility of aggression by China. U.S. policy also aims to persuade the Chinese that they will gain international prestige and influence as they use their power to uphold peace and promote global prosperity, although often the diplomatic signals of punishment and disapproval make a stronger impression on the Chinese than the signals of reward and approval. The U.S.-China strategic rivalry in the Asia-Pacific has been relatively restrained and exploratory. U.S. alliances in the region are not openly anti-China. There is no serious American effort to lure states such as North Korea, Burma, Laos, or Cambodia out of China's sphere of influence. America's post–Cold War posture toward China appears to have followed closely the statements of several presidential administrations to the effect that the United States welcomes a "strong and prosperous" China as long as it is "peaceful" and "responsible." China's gigantic trade surplus with the United States, which has exceeded $250 billion annually since 2007, is spectacularly inconsistent with the notion that America seeks to suppress China. Indeed, the United States has contributed more than any other single country to the rise of China since China's opening under the Deng regime.

Although the U.S. interest in opposing the rise of a peer competitor and the Chinese interest in becoming a great power appear to be on a collision course, up to now Washington has given peace a chance. The U.S. government demonstrated it will not go to war with China simply to prevent China's rise. Preventing China from becoming strong is not by itself a vital U.S. interest. In evaluating the interests of the U.S. and Chinese governments, we should consider not just what they want but also how badly they want it. Something a government is willing to fight over is commonly called a "vital interest." These are relatively few; most of the items on a government's foreign policy agenda are not compelling enough to lead to war. These can be called preferences. The chances of an outbreak of war are high when vital interests of two countries are in direct conflict—that is, the protection of one country's vital interest is only possible by denying or destroying the other country's vital interest. The outlook for a peaceful resolution is better in a case where a vital interest is pitted against a preference. Presumably, the country with a vital interest at stake will press forward, and the other country will back off and learn to live with the result. A dispute involving two competing preferences should be manageable without resort to hostilities.

If the U.S.-China rivalry is put into these terms, China's drive for prominence is a permanent, vital interest to Beijing. For the United States, keeping the field clear of great-power rivals *in the absence of hostile or aggressive intentions* is a preference but not a vital interest. A democratic China is also a U.S. preference, as is a China that is not a military great power. Opposing the rise of a potentially powerful rival in Asia would become a vital U.S. interest if a strong China attacked the norms upholding peaceful international economic and diplomatic activity in Asia, such as attempting to cut off U.S. access to the region, bullying U.S. allies, or carrying out armed aggression. This is how the United States ended up at war with Japan in the 1940s. Short of such a scenario, however, Washington would not pick a fight with a China that was rising through economic competitiveness and effective diplomacy rather than conquest or coercion. A non-great-power China has proven to be an American preference, not an American vital interest. As recently as 2006, the U.S. Department of Defense's *Quadrennial*

Defense Review said the United States will "seek to ensure that no foreign power can dictate the terms of regional or global security" or establish a "regional hegemony." The report also identified China as America's main military competitor. The 2010 *Quadrennial Defense Review* stepped back from this line in the sand, noting that a stronger China can contribute more to global stability and stressing the need for more U.S.-China coordination.[7]

The continued rise of China, however, will put further stress on this delicate equilibrium. The United States has strengthened its position on China's periphery since it has become clear that China is an emerging great power. U.S. strategic moves include revising and strengthening the alliance with Japan, adjusting the alliance with South Korea to make it more sustainable, seeking enhanced defense cooperation with India and Vietnam, and stationing bombers and submarines at bases on the western Pacific island of Guam. U.S. policy displays a commitment to raising U.S. military capabilities in the region to counter China's gains so that America can maintain its accustomed advantages. To the disappointment of Chinese observers, America's financial crisis did not seem to erode Washington's determination to maintain the U.S.-sponsored security order in the Asia-Pacific region. China saw the United States intervening in the South China Sea issue in 2010 and, in China's view, taking sides with the PRC's rival claimants Vietnam and the Philippines. Top U.S. officials announced in late 2011 that with the withdrawal of American troops from Iraq and Afghanistan, U.S. forces would "pivot" to Asia, suggesting an increase of American military strength in the region (or at least a continuation of forces levels in the Asia-Pacific amid cuts in other regions).

American and Chinese Fears

American fears about a stronger China stem from history, ideology, strategy, and latent racism. As an authoritarian (or, to many, a "communist") state, China is hostile to liberal political values and to the spread of democracy. China's support for norms and principles of international relations that the United States champions is dubious. Americans expect China to work to supplant U.S. influence and leadership in the region. China might replace the current economic and security arrangements in the Asia-Pacific region with a new order that would better serve PRC interests but would disadvantage the other countries. Chinese military power endangers American forces and limits U.S. freedom of strategic maneuver. The PRC is a potential menace to American allies, particularly Japan.

Specifically, a stronger China could contemplate actions that would directly threaten U.S. security and prosperity, such as attacking U.S. forces, preventing U.S. forces from entering theaters of battle to aid U.S. allies, blockading international sea lanes, or forbidding countries in the region from trading with the United States. There is currently no rationale for why the Chinese would want to carry out any of these acts except in the case of a war over Taiwan independence. Picking a fight with the United States, interfering with international maritime commerce, and encouraging the formation of regional trade blocs are policies that would be as harmful to China itself as to America. The immediate and visible danger that America fears from the rise of China is the loss of American influence in the Asia-Pacific region. The loss of influence would not automatically translate into a corresponding loss of American safety and prosperity. If Beijing kept its promises about a peaceful rise of China, it is conceivable that a dominant China would do as good a job as the United States now does preserving peace and stability in the region. Washington would be relieved of its costly regional policing duties while continuing to enjoy fair opportunities to compete for business in Asia. Clearly, however, the United States is not prepared to accept that American security and prosperity will be as well protected in a region under Chinese hegemony as in a region under American hegemony. In other words, America does not want to be in the position that China is now in.

For the Chinese, the United States is an eight-hundred-pound gorilla lurking in its front yard. A constructive relationship with Washington has been and continues to be vital to the Chinese achieving their economic development goals at a pace that staves off domestic discontent within China. The United States is a massive market for Chinese goods, a key supplier of education and technology, and an important gatekeeper in China's quest for greater international prestige and influence. At the same time, however, the Chinese government and its affiliated analysts portray the United States as the main impediment to China's rise. Chinese thus have a complex and somewhat conflicted view of the United States. On one hand, they envy America's wealth, power, and some aspects of American life. The United States is a valuable economic partner. On the other hand, China (like other countries) resents the exercise of U.S. power and influence in ways the Chinese believe are unfavorable to China. The Chinese have inflated views of alleged American malice toward China, of the reputed U.S. desire to dominate the region, and of an imagined U.S. intention to use democratization as a weapon for sowing chaos among America's enemies. The Chinese government also uses the United States as a negative example, highlighting unfavorable (and sometimes exaggerated) characteristics of the United States either to create a contrast that makes the PRC look good or to warn the Chinese public about the dangers of hankering after things Western. For example, Chinese officials and media often allege that the United States bullies other countries or tries to force its ideology upon them (which China claims not to do) and that democracy and unrestrained capitalism have generated awful social pathologies.

Most Chinese see the United States as "an insatiable domineering country that believes only in its own absolute power, one that would never allow any other country to catch up with it."[8] This view, more or less, prevails even among Chinese experts in global affairs who are familiar with the United States. Yang Jiemian, president of the Shanghai Institute for International Studies and one of China's leading experts on U.S.-China relations, writes,

> The U.S. international strategic goal is to maintain and intensify its superpower status, to keep the stability of the U.S.-dominated/led international system and to carry out the so-called "Pax Americana." Therefore, the U.S. will continue to watch out that no regional challenger to the U.S. appears in the Western-Hemisphere and other major strategic theaters, and to preserve its dominance in the international system of economy and values.[9]

The view of the average Chinese is that China should strive to make itself as wealthy as the United States, gain international respect, peacefully coexist with the United States, and end U.S. intervention in China's domestic affairs but that China should not try to challenge U.S. dominance or take over the United States' position of global leadership.[10]

There is a double historical layer of Chinese suspicion toward the United States. America is both capitalist-democratic and "imperialist." Although China's leaders have moved from the Marxist model toward capitalism (albeit with strong state involvement) in the management of the PRC's economic growth, vestiges of the Marxist outlook are still evident in the worldview of Chinese leaders. Accordingly, they view the United States as a neocolonial power committed to keeping Asia weak to facilitate American economic exploitation. Marxists expect that the capitalist powers will target the socialist states, seeing them as the vanguard of a global movement that must be stopped before it destroys capitalism. This Marxist worldview has increased the friction in the U.S.-China relationship by giving Chinese an additional reason to expect conflict between China, the leading socialist power, and the United States, leader of the capitalist bloc.

The Chinese do not particularly believe in American exceptionalism. In the nineteenth century, America was just another of the "eight imperialist powers." Its ascension to superpower status in the twentieth century intensified the usual great-power attributes of self-interested bullying and arrogance. Chinese view the U.S. government as being disingenuous and hypocritical, happy to use international organizations as vehicles for the support and legitimization of U.S. policies while brushing off international opinion and institutions to go its own way in the absence of foreign support.

With an inflated view of American malice toward China (as opposed to American antipathy toward the CCP), Chinese fear the rise of their country will cause the United States to strive harder to weaken China. Chinese political analysts recognize that there are different schools of thought in the United States about how to deal with China, ranging from a liberal position that advocates engagement and minimizing conflicts with China to a hawkish position that recommends openly confronting and threatening countermeasures against Chinese policies that cut against American preferences. The Bush presidency was a particularly worrisome time for the Chinese because it represented an unusual domination of U.S. policy by the "neoconservative" group. The Chinese perceive neocons as most likely to bring about a confrontation with China because of their perceived unilateralism and commitment to promoting global democratization. The Bush team entered office speaking of China as a strategic competitor and calling for greater support for Taiwan and a shift in emphasis from the U.S.-China relationship to the U.S.-Japan relationship. Yet the Bush administration ended up publicly rebuking Taiwan and bringing U.S.-China relations to a level that both countries described as the best since they normalized relations. In practice, the range of fluctuation in the United States' China policy in recent years has been narrow. While discussions of China among Americans outside of government are freewheeling, the weight of slow-changing geopolitical and economic circumstances usually forces policy makers to drive in the ruts in the road carved by their predecessors.

Some nonofficial U.S. commentary about China is highly alarmist and confrontational, sometimes even advocating that the United States should try to prevent China's economic growth. When the Chinese take note of such commentary, they often overlook or disregard the fact that these commentators do not hold positions in government and therefore are not directly involved in policy making. Rather, Chinese observers tend to fixate on these commentaries as unvarnished expressions of America's actual attitudes and intentions toward China, the hidden drivers of U.S. government policy. For example, the views of the U.S. international relations scholar John Mearsheimer are more frequently discussed and ascribed more weight among Chinese analysts than among Mearsheimer's countrymen who study U.S.-China relations. Mearsheimer is the dean of neorealist theory, which sees the political world as an inherently conflict-prone arena of struggle for relative power among nation-states that are primarily interested in their own survival, that can never fully trust other governments, and that must consider all other states as potential if not actual adversaries. Mearsheimer argues that based on the premise of his "offensive" variant of neorealist theory (i.e., that every state, if able, will try to dominate other states), a strong China will seek to control its neighbors and expel U.S. influence from the region. Thus, the United States should "abandon its policy of constructive engagement" and "do what it can to slow the rise of China."[11]

There are several reasons why the Chinese give undue attention to hostile nonmainstream views. The first involves differences between authoritarian and liberal democratic political systems. In a liberal democracy such as the United States, legal protections for free speech ensure the airing of an extremely wide range of views on all political topics, including opinions that are completely at variance from government policy. In the authoritarian system to which Chinese are accustomed, the government typically constrains political debate and does not tolerate challenges to official policy. Unfamiliar with political life in a democracy, the Chinese have difficulty believing that anti-China views can be promulgated in the United States without the support of a politically powerful individual or faction, an outlook that stems from the Chinese experience. Second, scholars at think tanks and universities are more closely connected to the state in China than in the United States. They are more likely to be close advisors to officials and purveyors of a prescribed official viewpoint than their U.S. counterparts. Again, however, Chinese transpose their experience onto American society, resulting in an exaggerated view of the linkage between nongovernment commentators and government policy. Finally, many Chinese find it easy to believe that strongly anti-China views are representative of mainstream American opinion because this confirms preexisting Chinese expectations.

Benign Versus Malign Subversion

Americans have a long history of trying to shape China's development. Originally it had nothing to do with hegemonic transition. Various groups with different motives—including missionaries, traders, strategists, educators, politicians, soldiers, investors, and activists—have shared the goal of making China more like the United States: economically developed, prosperous, democratic, Christian, and supportive of a U.S. global agenda. Attempts to foster democracy and respect for liberal international norms continue to pervade the U.S. government's approach to China. "Knowing that China has the potential for good or for bad," said Secretary of State Condoleezza Rice in 2005, "it is our responsibility to try and push and prod and persuade China toward the more positive course."[12] A common criticism is that Americans overestimate their ability to control the course of China's development. Interactions with the outside can certainly affect China, but often in ways foreigners did not predict or intend. Another criticism is that American officials are arrogant and intrusive to claim a responsibility to lift China to a higher plane of existence.

Americans hoping and working for certain kinds of change in China have suffered frequent disappointments. Only a few years after China earned the American public's sympathy as a resilient ally in the war against fascist Japan, the United States "lost" China to communism. The positive sentiments Americans developed for a pragmatic and market-oriented Chinese leadership in the 1980s crashed on the rocks of the government's violent suppression in 1989 of protestors demanding political reform. After an improvement in U.S.-China relations during the latter part of the George W. Bush presidency, the Obama administration entered office demonstrating a willingness to treat China as an equal and signaling that America would not let contentious issues such as the trade imbalance and human rights get in the way of cooperation on megaproblems such as climate change and the global economic crisis. The perceived payoff, however, was disappointing to Washington, as Beijing seemed to take advantage of Obama's conciliatory approach by asserting Chinese positions unusually strongly on several issues disputed between the United States and China.

With China emerging as a great power, the stakes involved in American efforts to shape China have greatly increased, even if the chances of success are no better than before. Washington hopes to steer China's development so that when China achieves great-power status, Beijing will be inclined toward friendly and cooperative relations with the United States and U.S. allies. The goal of channeling Chinese development in what the United States considers a positive direction helps explain why the United States tolerates such a massive trade deficit with the PRC; it is justified by the American belief that economic prosperity is fertile ground for democratization. The United States also administers myriad educational and training programs that directly or indirectly introduce Chinese to liberal values.

Americans and Chinese can agree on the basic proposition that the United States wants to subvert China's political system. Mainstream America has been inveterately hostile toward communist ideology since learning of it nearly a century ago. Communism as Americans understand it threatens the sacred cows of religion, liberal democracy, and private ownership of property. The "city on a hill" self-image has instilled in Americans a sense of mission to work toward democratization in other countries. Any government with the word "communist" in the name of its ruling party becomes a target. Where Americans and many Chinese differ is in their understanding of the intent behind U.S. support for political liberalization in China. Americans see democracy as a blessing that improves the quality of life of individuals, unlocks the productive potential of societies, and makes nations peace loving and law abiding. The CCP's argument, on the other hand, is that multiparty democracy is a proven destroyer of social order and economic progress. Knowing this, the Americans are intentionally employing democratization as a method for holding back China's development, says the CCP.

For Chinese, the internally focused counterpart to the U.S. policy of containment is "peaceful evolution," or attempting to undermine the current PRC political system through economic ties and cultural and ideological penetration. The objective is to encourage Chinese citizens to demand of their leaders more of the features that distinguish the Western democracies from the PRC, such as free-market economics, multiparty electoral politics, and civil and political liberties. If strong enough, these demands would transform China from a "communist" country (i.e., an authoritarian one-party state with a command economy) to a politically and economically liberal country that could be friendly with the West. The term "peaceful evolution" originated in statements made by U.S. Secretary of State John Foster Dulles in the 1950s. Dulles said the U.S. bloc should seek to use peaceful means to stimulate political changes in what was then the "Sino-Soviet bloc," changes that would result in the evolution of the USSR and China away from communism toward a more liberal form of government. Mao Zedong took Dulles's comments seriously and ordered top Party officials to study his speeches. In Mao's view, the peaceful evolution strategy was already taking effect in the USSR. This perception contributed to the Sino-Soviet split and to Mao launching the Cultural Revolution in 1966 to reinvigorate the Chinese communist movement. Mao saw peaceful evolution as a war against the newly emergent socialist powers waged by nonmilitary means, a view that Mao's successors in the CCP leadership continued to hold. Deng Xiaoping called it "smokeless war."

The breakup of the Soviet Union and other subsequent revolutions in formerly authoritarian states, which have left China as one of a small group of remaining "communist" countries, have magnified Chinese fears of subversion by the West. Chinese generally see the Soviet collapse as a successful demonstration of the peaceful evolution strategy: the West bombarded the Soviets with propaganda about the failings of socialism and offered economic and political support if Russia would liberalize. This undermined the authority of the ruling party. Gorbachev's government weakened the state, loosened the political system, and freed the empire, dramatically reducing Russia's international power and status. The West pocketed its strategic winnings without politically embracing the new Russia or providing the promised aid. Chinese believe the United States intensified efforts to bring down the CCP after the collapse of the Soviet Union and the Tiananmen Square incident of 1989. PRC leaders and media frequently alleged that the leaders of the protests in Tiananmen Square were stirred up by ill-intentioned foreigners.

Chinese official commentators use the term "peaceful evolution" broadly, using it to condemn activities (foreign cultural, economic, and social exchanges) that probably are not actually intended to overthrow China's political system as well as those that probably are. The peaceful evolution strategy includes negative foreign media reports about CCP policies, Western cultural exports, outside pressure on Beijing over human rights violations, and programs that bring Chinese students and scholars to Western countries for liberal brainwashing. The aim, say Chinese officials and their media outlets, is to undermine the Chinese people's respect for the CCP and sell them on the alternative ideology of "bourgeois liberalism," a disparaging reference to Western thinking, values, and lifestyle, and on the specific characteristics of Western-style political systems. The Chinese government is keenly sensitive to and resentful of U.S. calls for political liberalization in China. Since 1977, for example, the U.S. Department of State has annually published country-by-country assessments of the human rights performance of foreign governments. The PRC has always featured prominently as a human rights abuser. Beijing has met these reports with scathing criticisms that they are inaccurate, malicious, and hypocritical. In 1998, the Chinese government began publishing its own annual report, titled "Human Rights Record of the United States," to counter the State Department's report. The Chinese reports typically highlight American problems with poverty, racial inequality, gun-related violent crime, and drug abuse, as well as targets of opportunity such as the Iraq War Abu Ghraib prisoner abuse scandal.

Competition for Regional Influence

With the rise of China, the competition between China and the United States for influence in the Asia-Pacific region has intensified. A strong and rapidly developing China has become a credible global model and rival to American prestige. China's emergence as a potential great power heightens America's sense of vulnerability to the loss of U.S. influence both globally and regionally. Many recent commentaries have argued that China is beating the United States diplomatically, which will eventually undercut America's strategic position if Washington does not respond effectively. The Chinese inevitably view this discussion within the United States, and any U.S. actions that seem to stem from it, as evidence of American hostility to the rise of China and determination to keep China out of a regional leadership role.

As South Koreans became enthralled with the potential of a rapidly growing China to power a new era of Korean prosperity and to facilitate a North-South Korean détente, Seoul became more deferential to Beijing in the 2000s at the same time Korean dissatisfaction with the U.S. alliance increased. South Korea's President Roh Moo-hyun (in office 2003–2008) announced that he visualized South Korea as a "balancer" in the region. Many Americans judged that the ROK was gravitating toward China and called for stronger U.S. efforts to shore up the alliance.

Washington has deep ties in Southeast Asia, which it has developed over many decades, but in recent years Southeast Asians complained that the Americans were in danger of squandering their influence through insensitivity and inattention. Regional observers particularly chided the Bush administration for skipping important ASEAN meetings and for failing to accept that counterterrorism was not the highest priority concern of Southeast Asian leaders. Beijing, on the other hand, was making political gains through deft diplomacy and offers of deeper economic cooperation. Rising Chinese influence was an impetus for the Obama administration's determination to renew U.S. influence in Southeast Asia. The sense that the Americans were trying to reverse rather than accept what the Chinese saw as a natural shift in the geopolitical tide contributed to the indignant Chinese reaction when Washington publicly weighed in regarding the South China Sea dispute in 2010.

Somewhat ironically, Sino-U.S. competition spills over into multilateralism. The region features several multilateral organizations that partly overlap in membership and function. These organizations are potentially important because they make it easier for the governments in the region to discuss international issues together, to understand better each other's points of view, and to reach agreements on cooperation. Proponents of multilateralism argue that it could change the way countries have traditionally interacted by restraining self-interested behavior by the great powers, preventing conflict and facilitating joint economic and security activities. Skeptics argue that multilateral organizations do little to alter the age-old dynamic of great-power competition driving international relations.

Chinese officials were previously wary of participation in multilateral organizations. They feared China could be trapped into situations in which other countries ganged up against Chinese delegations. In the 1990s, however, Beijing came to believe that the advantages of multilateral participation outweighed the risks. China could use multilateralism as a means of extending China's influence over international affairs and defending China's interests, just as China had long accused the United States of doing. This Chinese change of attitude is a consequence of China's rise. It is because of China's increased relative strength that other members of multilateral organizations take China's views seriously, that regional organizations believe including China is essential, and that Chinese delegations can effectively veto many multilateral initiatives of which Beijing disapproves. Much of China's multilateral activity is directed toward resisting the United States. As a Chinese diplomat says, "we promote multilateralism to hold back U.S. unilateralism."[13] Consistent with the view of the skeptics, multilateral organizations are another arena in which U.S.-China competition is played out. Beijing has sought to increase Chinese influence and promote China's agenda in these organizations while undermining the participation of the United States and U.S. allies. Of the major regional multilateral organizations, China is most supportive of the ASEAN Plus Three (the Association of Southeast Asian Nations plus China, Japan, and South Korea), which promotes economic cooperation and does not include the United States. Indeed, most ASEAN members fear that China will dominate ASEAN Plus Three. Washington, on the other hand, is the chief supporter of the Asia-Pacific Economic Cooperation forum (APEC), which includes China among its twenty-one members. APEC was a response to West-bashing Malaysian Prime Minister Mahathir Mohamed's 1991 proposal for an East Asian Economic Caucus that would exclude the United States and Australia—a proposal that China strongly endorsed. When the idea of an "Asians only" East Asian Summit (EAS) emerged in 2004, China strongly supported it and maintained the position that membership should be restricted, while U.S. ally Japan favored including India, Australia, and New Zealand. Despite China's objections, the group agreed to let in these "outside" countries as a counterweight to Chinese influence. Beijing then tried to consign these countries to a peripheral role within the EAS by arguing that leadership and planning should remain with the ASEAN Plus Three states. This final gambit was controversial, and eventually Beijing flip-flopped and called for opening EAS membership to all countries with interests in the Asia-Pacific region. Since 2002, defense ministers and other officials from Asia-Pacific countries have met annually for a dialogue at Singapore's Shangri-La Hotel. Since the United States was an early supporter of the meeting, China tried to undercut the prestige of the Shangri-La summit by initially sending only low-level representatives. In 2010, the Chinese sent a relatively large delegation, headed by General Ma Xiaotian. The tension between China and the United States dominated the meeting. According to one observer, "the gulf between Ma's obfuscations and U.S. Defense Secretary [Robert] Gates' plain talking was disappointingly stark."[14] The United States supports ally

Tokyo's bid to become a permanent member of the UN Security Council. China, currently the only Asian member, opposes admitting Japan partly because of Japan's failure fully to make amends for its behavior during the Pacific War but also because "if an obsequious country dancing to the U.S.'s tune becomes a permanent member it is not different from giving the U.S. two seats."[15] The Obama administration touted the Trans Pacific Trade Partnership (TPP), a relatively far-reaching multilateral free-trade agreement that mostly attracted the region's democracies, as the economic arm of a resurgence of U.S. commitment to Asia. Taiwan's President Ma Ying-jeou expressed interest in joining the TPP, ensuring that the PRC would see the TPP as another vehicle for containing China.

Since the U.S.-China relationship is a mixture of cooperative and contention, observers who wish for peace have hoped the two countries can find areas of strategic common ground to offset their strategic disputes. In 2005, Deputy Secretary of State Robert Zoellick famously said the United States hoped China would to be a "responsible stakeholder" that "would work with us to sustain the international system."[16] Some Chinese analysts took Zoellick's speech as a positive sign, indicating that Washington was prepared to welcome a rising China and to treat the Chinese as equals. Other Chinese took the negative interpretation: that by labeling China a "stakeholder," the Americans would now hold China to a higher, tougher standard and would be more critical of Chinese policies that did not conform to the U.S. notion of "responsible" behavior.[17]

Some areas of potential partnership showed early promise but proved shallow or short lived. The terrorist attacks against the United States on September 11, 2001, for example, created an opportunity for improved U.S.-China relations. Washington drew a line in the sand for foreign governments: "Either you are with us, or you are with the terrorists," Bush famously announced. Beijing quickly moved to the U.S. side of the line. The Chinese government made supportive public statements, did not try to obstruct the U.S. invasion of Afghanistan or the establishment of U.S. bases in Central Asia, and agreed to share counterterrorism intelligence with the Americans. In doing so, Beijing bolstered its image as a globally responsible major power. In return, Washington agreed to list a Muslim separatist group in Xinjiang as a terrorist organization. The larger benefit for China was a deflection of U.S. strategic attention. U.S. strategists had recently begun to view China as America's chief potential adversary, the successor to the spot previously occupied by the Soviet Union. The new "war on terror" (WOT) changed America's strategic focus and made China and the United States allies against a more immediate threat. China made further gains by default as the United States expended blood, treasure, and international goodwill in the controversial wars in Afghanistan and Iraq. The post-9/11 improvement in bilateral relations, however, was superficial and limited. Although the Chinese have had their own problems with terrorism carried out by Islamic groups, the Chinese people were not uniformly sympathetic toward America's disaster. Strategically, the WOT gave the United States the opportunity to expand its influence in Central Asia and to reinvigorate some of its relationships with Southeast Asian states (through, for example, military cooperation with the Philippines against a Muslim insurgency in the southern islands). From China's point of view, the WOT accelerated the purported American campaign to encircle China. This downside rivaled China's gains from the WOT. Chinese analysts anticipated that when the war against terrorism ceased to dominate the thinking of U.S. defense policy makers and their attention returned to more traditional strategic issues, the Americans would again view China as an unambiguous adversary.

Can't China and America Just Get Along?

A bilateral relationship is a two-way street. Although it is accurate to say that the rise of China worsens tensions with the United States, this may seem to imply that China bears all the responsibility. Actually, the rise in tensions is attributable to a combination of Chinese activity and the U.S. *reaction* to that Chinese activity. We should therefore consider what might happen if the U.S. government chose to meet the rise of China with a response the Chinese would consider benevolent. Chinese officials and analysts have continually urged the United States to partner with China rather than build bulwarks against it. The Chinese are alienated, for example, by American efforts to maintain regional security (largely against China) through alliances with countries such as Japan, South Korea, and Australia, with additional efforts to engage other regional governments in less formal defense cooperation. A better approach, Chinese analysts say, would be to join with China in the co-managing of regional security. The Chinese would argue that they can contribute more to keeping regional peace than U.S.

allies can. Furthermore, a constructive U.S.-China relationship would settle the single most important regional security problem.

There is little doubt that China-U.S. tensions would plummet, as would the chances of a China-U.S. military conflict in the foreseeable future, if the United States acceded to the Chinese vision of an Asia-Pacific "partnership." There are, however, three problems with this idea. First, meeting Chinese expectations for a partnership would certainly require the United States to forfeit much of its influence and several important interests in the region. Beijing would demand the cessation of not only arms sales but any form of U.S. diplomatic or political support for Taiwan. Recent American moves such as the expansion of U.S.–South Korean military exercises in response to North Korean provocations and the U.S. statement in support of Southeast Asian countries attempting to stand up to Chinese pressure over disputed South China Sea islands would not be possible. Nor would U.S. surveillance of China from international air and sea space near the Chinese coast, since the Chinese would argue that "partners" must show trust by not spying on each other. The Chinese would also likely pressure the Americans to discontinue their alliances and withdraw from their bases in Asia as increasingly capable Chinese forces take over the role of regional policeman.

Second, security for the region as a whole might suffer if China succeeded the United States as the regional leader. Admittedly, some regional governments do not see the United States as a benign or welcome force in regional affairs and might prefer to see China replace America as the dominant power. Nevertheless, many Asia-Pacific governments openly wish for the United States to retain the key management role, seeing the status quo as more conducive to their interests than a new arrangement based on China's view of how regional affairs should be ordered.

Third, if America agreed to the concessions implied by a "partnership," China might keep asking for more. History shows some great powers have limited aims that can be satisfied with a reasonable amount of accommodation from their neighbors, while others have seemingly open-ended ambitions. Recalling the failure of pre–World War II "appeasement" policies to restrain Nazi Germany from launching an attempt to conquer all of Europe, many Cold War–era American leaders concluded that meeting an aggressive rising power's demand for concessions only whets the aggressor's appetite for additional concessions. Twenty-first-century China is profoundly different from Hitler's Germany, but we cannot rule out the possibility that a voluntary withdrawal of U.S. strategic influence would encourage the Chinese to raise their aspirations to a level the other major powers would find intolerable.

In short, the cost of avoiding the possibility of conflict with China would be the abdication of America's position as a great power in Asia. This is not likely until and unless Washington concludes that America cannot sustain this position either because China's relative advantages are overwhelming or because internal U.S. weakness forces an American retrenchment in its overseas commitments. This situation illustrates the tendency in international politics for security to be a zero-sum game: for one great power to have more security, a neighboring great power must have less.

It's Better to Dominate

While Americans have a wide range of opinions about the challenge posed by a rising China, most of those who have input into the making of U.S. foreign policy would share two beliefs. First, the United States has a special and widely accepted responsibility as a keeper of the peace in the Asia-Pacific region. The countries of the region, China in particular, have greatly benefitted from the stability that the United States helps provide. Second, it should be clear to China that U.S. military forces and partnerships in the region are not intended to prevent China's legitimate rise. Rather, they indicate U.S. determination to prevent threats to the United States and allied countries from rogue states—such as a China that decided not to obey international rules and norms. Therefore, there is no legitimate reason for China to oppose U.S. defense cooperation with the countries on China's periphery or to field military capabilities that could threaten U.S. forces.

Chinese, of course, would take strong exception to these beliefs. China does not accept a U.S. responsibility to keep the peace in Asia that justifies U.S. military bases, alliances, or surveillance activities in the Western Pacific. The Chinese fear these are manifestations of American resistance to the rise of China or least an American intent to place restrictions on China that the Chinese do not agree to. Today's "international" rules and norms reflect the sentiments and interests of a small group of Western powers during a small segment of history. Asian states led by a resurgent China have the right to frame their own norms for ordering regional affairs. The Chinese do not accept the premise that no other state may infringe on U.S. military supremacy. China maintains that unfettered U.S. dominance makes the region less rather than more secure and that China is more than justified in building military capabilities commensurate with its size and economic strength.

Washington has shown that while it may prefer to retain U.S. preeminence in the Asia-Pacific region and will defend its vital interests, the U.S. government will tolerate Chinese gains if they are achieved through peaceful competition within widely accepted international rules and norms. Active U.S. military resistance to China would not arise from China's increased capabilities alone but only from hostile Chinese intentions. Many Chinese believe America will go to war rather than accept outcomes such as the diminution of U.S. hegemony, PRC absorption of Taiwan, or the loss of Japan as an alliance partner, but this view is erroneous. In fact, Washington would not fight to prevent these developments if they came about without the use of force or coercion. In this sense, a war between China and the United States is less likely than some people think. This transition period remains tense, however, because Washington feels the need for an insurance policy, while China doesn't necessarily see it as only an insurance policy. The growth of Chinese capabilities alarms the United States, and U.S. responses alarm China.

Chapter Four

CHINA'S MILITARY RISE

The U.S. Department of Defense has divided the populated parts of the globe into several "areas of responsibility." China falls within the area of responsibility of Pacific Command, which describes its mission as "preserving the security, stability, and freedom" of the Asia-Pacific region as well as protecting "the territory of the United States, its people, and its interests."[1] After a century as a great power and nearly seventy years as a superpower, Americans are accustomed to thinking in such terms. This has become America's natural role. But would Americans feel the same way about a strong China claiming a "responsibility" to preserve conditions in North America that suited Chinese interests?

A large, rapid, and intensive upgrading of China's armed forces does not fit harmoniously into the American vision of world order. An openly stated goal of U.S. policy is to dissuade potential adversaries from building strong military forces with the intent to match U.S. capabilities. Washington does not want China to be a military great power. U.S. efforts to dissuade China, however, have largely failed. Despite the risks that go along with alarming the United States, the People's Liberation Army (PLA) is becoming more powerful.

Beijing would argue that a strong Chinese military contributes to world peace by ensuring the security of the Chinese people (a fifth of the earth's population) and by constraining objectionable foreign policies by the United States. But PLA modernization also negatively affects international peace and stability. First, increased PLA capabilities reduce the perceived security of other Asia-Pacific states, raising tensions between them and China. Second, powerful armed forces will open to China the option of seeking to dominate the region and forcing neighboring governments to act against their own interests in favor of China's.

Starting from a Low Base

Part of the reason for the size and speed of China's military modernization is that Beijing is playing catch-up. Throughout the Cold War, China had relatively weak and backward forces for a country of China's size, population, and perilous strategic situation. China usually had a tense relationship with at least one of the superpowers, and at times with both simultaneously. Because of its undersized industrial base and low technological level, China had to rely on the weak-country strategy of "people's war" (abandoning the cities and carrying out nationwide guerrilla warfare in the countryside) and the notion that the outcome of battle is decided by the troops' fighting spirit rather than by the weapons they carry. This was a familiar situation for the CCP leadership, which had started out vastly outmanned and outgunned by Chiang Kai-shek's Kuomintang army in the Chinese Civil War.

Another reason China's military forces were underdeveloped until recently is that they were chronically short on funding. China was relatively poor throughout the Mao era (he died in 1976). The Chinese government announced a grand plan in 1977 to carry out "four modernizations" in the areas of agriculture, industry, science, and the armed forces. The military had to wait for the other three. Funding for the PLA remained low in the 1980s even as the government made heavy investments in civilian sectors of the economy.

The circumstances of the PLA (which refers to all of the PRC's military, including the air force, navy, and strategic missile forces) had dramatically changed by the 1990s. China's economic growth was taking off under Deng's policies of marketization and engagement with the international economy. The cities were becoming too wealthy to abandon to an invader. In any case, with the Gorbachev reforms and the subsequent breakup of the Soviet Union and the Warsaw Pact, an invasion from Russia was no longer a serious worry. Chinese strategists shifted their thinking toward fighting and winning wars before the opponent entered Chinese territory. They closely observed how the United States and its allies fought during conflicts such as the 1991 Persian Gulf War, air operations against Serbia in 1999, and the post-9/11 campaigns in Iraq and Afghanistan. The danger of

Taiwan independence, which would require a PRC military response, appeared to be growing. Chinese military analysts concluded that the most likely future conflicts would be brief, regional wars with limited aims in which the skillful use of advanced technology weapon systems would be decisive. Substantially increased funding for military modernization was finally available. Furthermore, the PRC's new leader Jiang Zemin did not have a military background and needed to curry favor with the PLA to ensure its continued support. As a result, the Chinese military began to display the characteristics that worry Washington and other governments: large and continuing budget increases, a thorough modernization of weapons and military doctrine, and a greater orientation toward the capability to project military power beyond China's borders. "People's war" is still a touchstone of PLA doctrine, but it now refers to mass support for and assistance to Chinese military forces in times of war, such as military use of the civilian infrastructure, fishing boats harassing enemy shipping, and cyber attacks on the enemy's computer systems by civilian hackers.

Like other national militaries, the PLA is charged with defending the country's people, territory, and assets. The militaries of some nations strive to be apolitical, officially eschewing favoritism toward any particular party or faction. The PLA, on the other hand, along with its national security mission, is explicitly committed to protecting the CCP's position as the ruling party. As its name suggests, the PLA was formed during the Chinese Civil War as the military arm of the CCP. It has remained a party as well as a national army, which is reflective of the CCP's efforts to permanently conjoin the party and the state—the CCP doesn't plan to give up the reins of government to any other group. The Communist Party also expects the PLA to be subservient to the party's agenda. As Mao famously said, "the party must command the gun, and the gun must never be allowed to command the party." The PLA has mostly followed the party's orders. The military did a dirty job for the CCP in 1989 when it violently suppressed the Tiananmen protests, sacrificing some of its own national prestige to protect the Party leadership. The PLA leadership tends to be a bastion of ideological conservatism. It takes an expansive view of China's national interests, expects other governments to see Chinese security policies as defensive rather than aggressive, sees U.S. actions through the lens of containment, and demands that U.S. forces not operate near Chinese territory. PLA officers have great difficulty accepting the idea that Americans could wish China well while hoping for the ouster of the CCP. Although they ultimately follow direct orders from the top civilian rulers, PLA leaders often believe China's overall policies or some government organs, particularly the Ministry of Foreign Affairs, do not stand up to other countries strongly enough on behalf of China's interests and dignity. When they sense an opportunity, such as when there is no clear consensus in Beijing on a security issue, senior PLA figures may speak out in an attempt to sway the debate. On some occasions the PLA has withheld information from other parts of the Chinese government in order to gain more autonomy for itself or to push the civilian top leadership toward a tougher stance vis-à-vis a foreign government.

A Rich Country Needs a Strong Army

China is building strong military forces because this fits the Chinese conception of a great power, because the Chinese think a strong military will make them more secure, and because they can now afford it. The Chinese phrase "rich country, strong army" (*fu guo, qiang bing*), which goes back two millennia and remains Chinese shorthand for national success, neatly expresses the idea that economic development and a powerful military are naturally linked: a country cannot have one without the other. This historically inherited mindset is sufficient reason for a prosperous China to build strong military forces regardless of China's specific geopolitical circumstances of the moment. The insecurities over superior U.S. military power and Taiwanese nationalism add additional layers of reinforcement. The United States and Taiwan are perhaps most important not as factors convincing Beijing to build a strong military but rather as factors influencing the scope and shape of PLA enhancement. Beijing wants forces powerful enough to deter the United States from trying militarily to prevent China from pursuing important interests. The CCP leadership also needs the PLA to deter Taiwan from officially declaring independence from China and, if that deterrence fails, to win a war against Taiwan and, possibly, assisting U.S. forces.

Like other organizations, the PLA wants more prestige and a larger budget. The need to intimidate and if necessary defeat Taiwan is a powerful argument for PLA leaders lobbying the party leadership for more funds. The Taiwan war scenario also guides PLA modernization by prioritizing the weapons systems and tactics that the PLA would likely need in a cross-strait war and the accompanying need to ambush an approaching U.S. fleet. Even in the absence of the Taiwan issue, however, the PLA would still be building modern power-projecting capabilities, and much of what is needed for a Taiwan Strait war could be used in other conflicts in the seas off China's east coast.

The rise of China creates needs for a more outwardly oriented Chinese military. The PLA is increasingly active in operations outside China, such as UN observer and peacekeeping missions, military exercises with other countries, and protection of international sea lanes. In an important speech in December 2004, Hu told the PLA that in addition to its traditional responsibilities of defending Chinese territory, protecting the CCP, and backstopping internal security, the military must "play a major role in maintaining world peace" and "safeguarding China's national interests" by equipping itself to operate beyond China's borders.[2] In the first decade of the twenty-first century, the CCP leadership began urging state-run Chinese firms to "go out" and enter the global marketplace. These firms have been physically locating work sites overseas and building infrastructure in foreign countries. Tens of millions of Chinese annually now travel, work, or study abroad. The problems of Chinese citizens outside China being murdered, kidnapped, or requiring evacuation from dangerous locations are growing. In February 2011, for example, a Chinese warship that was already in the Gulf of Aden on antipiracy duty diverted to Libya to assist in the evacuation of Chinese nationals fleeing the uprising against the Gaddafi regime.

China's economic development also makes a strong military force more affordable. China's official military budget was $96 billion in 2011 and $106 billion in 2012.[3] This seems modest compared with U.S. defense spending, which was $671 billion in 2011 (over $100 billion of which was for the conflicts in Iraq and Afghanistan). But we must dig deeper. First, the numbers in China's official defense budget are intentionally deflated as part of Beijing's effort to assure the world that there is no need to fear the rise of China. This budget figure does not include several major expenses that in other countries are properly counted as part of the military budget, such as military research and development, purchases of foreign weapons and equipment, and funding for strategic (missile and nuclear) forces. Outside estimates of China's actual military spending vary widely, by everyone agrees it is higher than Beijing's announced figure. The respected Stockholm International Peace Research Institute used a figure of $114 billion for China's military spending in 2009. Estimates by the U.S. Department of Defense are higher. Second, if we set aside the United States and compare

China to the rest of the globe, we find that China has a great-power-sized commitment to its armed forces. China's military spending ranks second in the world, approximately doubling the amounts spent by each of the next tier of countries, represented by France, the United Kingdom, and Russia. Within the region, China looks imposing. Chinese defense spending far outpaces Japan's $51 billion, India's $35 billion, South Korea's $24 billion, and Vietnam's $2.4 billion. Third, many analysts argue that calculating China's military spending on a purchasing power parity (PPP) basis gives a more accurate picture. This method controls for the fact that things cost more in some countries than in others. A budget of $91.5 billion buys much more in China than it would in the United States. Employing the PPP conversion, China's official 2011 defense budget rises dramatically to $400 billion.[4] Finally, Chinese defense spending is rising rapidly. Throughout the past two decades, the average increase in the PLA's budget from one year to the next has topped 10 percent annually. Thus, we can expect that in the near future China's already robust defense spending will be much higher. But because of China's large and growing economic capacity, Beijing can manage large defense outlays without seriously straining the overall national budget. China spends only about 2 percent of its gross national product on defense (the United States spends between 4 and 5 percent).

Tensions with the United States

The PLA modernization, intended to make China more secure, makes the United States feel less secure. The commander of U.S. forces in the Asia-Pacific region, Admiral Robert F. Willard, said repeatedly that China's military development "appear[s] designed to challenge U.S. freedom of action in the region or exercise aggression or coercion of its neighbors, including U.S. treaty allies and partners."[5] Other U.S. officials and official policy documents echoed this assessment. A recent report from the U.S. State Department's International Security Advisory Board concluded that the PLA "seeks greatly enhanced military power and reach" with the specific goal of "checkmating U.S. military power" by deterring U.S. military action and by shaking the confidence of U.S. allies in American reliability.[6] U.S. allies, as well, see a growing Chinese military threat to U.S. forces. A 2011 Australian report with input from Australian officials concluded that as a result of China's military buildup, "the assumption that United States' operational bases in Guam, Japan, and elsewhere will enjoy high levels of security in future crises is crumbling. The assumption that U.S. and allied naval surface vessels can operate with high security in all parts of the Western Pacific is no longer valid."[7]

To back up these stated worries, there is evidence of increased U.S. strategic focus on the Asia-Pacific region since it became clear that China is becoming a great power. In the past decade, for example, the United States has moved attack submarines, B-2 bombers, unmanned Global Hawk surveillance drones, and stockpiles of precision-guided munitions to the U.S.-held Western Pacific island of Guam. Numbers of U.S. troops deployed in the Asia-Pacific region have declined since the end of the Cold War, but the declines are smaller than among the U.S. forces that were based in Europe. Deployments of U.S. naval forces into the Asia-Pacific region are increasing relative to deployments in other regions. The U.S. government's 2006 *Quadrennial Defense Review* signaled an intention to keep more U.S. naval forces in the Pacific than in the Atlantic. In late 2011 and early 2012, Washington committed to maintaining U.S. strength in Asia even as the U.S. Department of Defense implemented large budget cuts. The high priority given Asia is partly a result of tensions resulting from North Korean behavior, but it has much to do with the rise of China. (Many Chinese observers believe North Korea provides a convenient excuse for U.S. moves that are actually aimed at China).

Three specific issues heighten the tensions over a burgeoning PLA within a region with a strong U.S. military presence: the poor quality of U.S.-China military-to-military relations, the ongoing dispute over U.S. surveillance activities close to Chinese territory, and what the U.S. government alleges is a lack of transparency in the PLA buildup.

The U.S. military argues that the most important benefit of a robust military-to-military relationship with the Chinese is to help prevent unintended conflicts resulting from misunderstandings when U.S. and PLA forces encounter each other at sea or in the air in the western Pacific rim. Through visits and discussions, American officers can learn more about Chinese intentions and establish personal networks and lines of communication between personnel in the two militaries. There are at least two secondary U.S. goals: (1) to encourage the Chinese military to participate in constructive global activities (such as peacekeeping, disaster relief, or antipiracy operations), and (2) to dissuade the Chinese from trying to compete military with the United States by showing off U.S. capabilities. The

U.S. view is that military-to-military relations should be decoupled from bilateral political disputes, if for no other reason than to avoid an escalation of tensions. U.S. officials, however, are increasingly frustrated with the relationship. In what was hailed as an important breakthrough, the two countries established a "hotline" telephone connection between the PLA and the U.S. Department of Defense in 2008. To the chagrin of the U.S. side, the Chinese have on several occasions refused to pick up the phone when the Americans called. Presumably the PLA did not want to speak to the Americans without getting definitive instructions from the top Party leadership. More importantly, Beijing has repeatedly cancelled cooperative activities or (temporarily) severed the military relationship altogether to protest U.S. policies.

The PLA is frustrated as well. The Chinese have different expectations of the bilateral military relationship: for them, it is a way of working toward the discontinuation of U.S. military policies that the Chinese especially oppose, such as the arms sales to Taiwan or the congressionally mandated publication of the Department of Defense's annual report on the PLA (which the Chinese say is full of negative bias). Beijing emphasizes that the goal is developing "trust" but argues that American acts indicating distrust of China show that Washington is acting in bad faith. If the relationship is not bringing about the concrete results that the Chinese seek, it lacks intrinsic value for them.

The U.S. Department of Defense unapologetically claims for itself "a special responsibility to monitor China's military and to deter conflict."[8] Consequently, the U.S. Navy regularly sends ships and aircraft on tracking and surveillance missions near the Chinese coast. Here we can actually see the flying sparks as the edges of contrasting U.S. and Chinese visions for regional order scrape against each other. Chinese opposition to these missions has resulted in incidents in the South China Sea. These include the 2001 collision between a Chinese fighter jet and a U.S. EP-3 aircraft and the harassment of the USNS *Impeccable* by Chinese vessels in 2009. One aspect of this issue is a dispute between China and the United States over interpretations of international maritime law, but fundamentally the Chinese object to the U.S. military spying on them from within China's own neighborhood. The Chinese say these activities are provocative, destructive to attempts to build friendly bilateral relations, and disrespectful of China's "feelings." A common Chinese criticism is to assert that the U.S. Navy would not like it if Chinese ships loitered off American shores. The reaction of the U.S. Navy's Pacific Command is that close surveillance is normal great-power behavior and that the Chinese should learn to see it as a confidence-building measure. The Chinese take the opposite position that "friends should not spy on friends," meaning that surveillance is a sign of basic distrust and a lack of interest in improving the relationship.

U.S. officials say the problem is intentions as much as capabilities. Washington's argument in recent years has been that a PLA military modernization program is understandable given China's economic growth and increased technological competence. But the Chinese have not explained why they are moving so quickly, why they need such strong forces, and how they plan to use these forces. Since some of these military upgrades make the PLA more capable of threatening U.S. or allied forces in the region, the U.S. government argues that without Chinese clarification, America must prepare for the possibility that China is building the means to neutralize U.S. forces because Beijing plans to carry out actions the United States would oppose.

U.S. allegations that the PLA is not transparent enough are perhaps a useful way of pressuring Beijing to provide information and assurances. The validity of these allegations, however, is questionable for several reasons. Chinese officialdom is traditionally very secretive about the formulation of policy. National security issues are especially sensitive. Expecting the Chinese government to discard centuries of political culture and match the openness of the liberal democracies is not realistic. Historically, strategic deception in China was as much defensive as offensive—that is, it was not always to hide preparations for a surprise attack but also to conceal vulnerabilities that if known might bring on an attack by the enemy. The Chinese think that the United States, as a superpower with a lavishly funded military, can afford to be highly transparent about its forces and strategies as a way of intimidating its adversaries. China, on the other hand, needs to avoid revealing weaknesses or plans that would add to the already huge advantages the U.S. military holds over the PLA. Considering China's natural reticence to be transparent, many of Beijing's strategic intentions are surprisingly clear. The Chinese government has issued "white papers" (official policy statements) on national defense, the Taiwan issue, and arms control. The rationales behind China's drive to build air and naval power-projection capabilities are open to outsiders able to read Chinese journals. There is little mystery surrounding the CCP's commitment to preventing Taiwan independence and the strong possibility that this might require the PLA to tangle with the U.S. Navy. It is not clear what additional information Beijing would have to reveal to satisfy the U.S. demand for transparency or whether this standard of transparency is met by the United States or other countries of which Washington is less demanding.

Is the PLA Really a Threat to the United States?

Chinese defense experts argue that outsiders' fears about the growth of the PLA's budget are misplaced. Much of the increased spending goes toward salaries, allowances, and improved housing for the troops. As China develops, these costs rise. Analysts also point out that PLA spending per soldier is much lower than the same figure for many other countries. The United States, for example, spends ten times more per soldier than China does. Although China is modernizing its forces, the more developed countries are also moving ahead. Their technological lead over China might increase rather than narrow over time.[9]

Many U.S. analysts both inside and outside of government see China's military modernization as so big, fast, and sophisticated that it must imply illegitimate intentions. There is an implied dichotomy: China is either defensive, indicated by modest military forces, or aggressive, indicated by an interest in large military forces. This dichotomy, however, is false. From China's perspective, the military modernization is defensive and is justified by a security environment that includes a powerful U.S. regional military presence because the United States is a latent threat to the PRC. Nor does the PLA buildup imply a rejection of cooperation with the United States, only a desire to base this cooperation on what the Chinese would see as a more equitable basis. Chinese policy is not necessarily any more contradictory in this respect than an American policy of welcoming the rise of China while maintaining the insurance policy of military bases in the Western Pacific.

China is building forces that could project military power beyond the region. This raises the prospect of China becoming not only a great power that dominates its own region but a superpower with the ability to exert decisive force in far-flung parts of the world. Some observers argue this could lead to Chinese and U.S. forces clashing throughout the globe. While frightening, this scenario depends on the convergence of several uncertain factors. Chinese leaders are not hankering for superpower status, which they see as having mostly downsides: burdens, costs, international criticism, and an increased likelihood that other countries will join in anti-China cooperation. China would not necessarily achieve or even aspire to global power-projection capability comparable to that of the United States. Trying to match the capabilities of the U.S. Navy, for example, would be an unwise course for China unless the United States decided to retrench for economic reasons and left the field open. Instead of China trying to reach the superpower level, the more likely outcome is that outside of its immediate region the future China will have a military impact like that of today's Great Britain or France: able to accomplish a limited military task by itself far from home, or to contribute significantly to a multinational military campaign, but not strong enough to operate outside its neighborhood in the face of determined U.S. opposition. In fact, outside of the Asia-Pacific region China and the United States are more likely to cooperate than to fight each other. PLA forces pose a direct threat to U.S. territory only through China's nuclear-armed missiles, and this is not much of a worry for the United States because U.S. nuclear forces are much larger than China's. China has no reason to start a nuclear war in which the Chinese would be at a huge disadvantage.

For now and into the foreseeable future, the threat a stronger and modernized PLA poses to America is an indirect and geographically limited one: challenging U.S. military dominance in eastern Asia (which is, of course, China's backyard). Many of the PLA's new capabilities fit into what military analysts call an anti-access/area-denial strategy. In any foreseeable conflict in which China and the United States are at war, the Chinese armed forces won't need to invade California, bomb Washington, or keep American soldiers from capturing Chinese cities. Rather, the PLA must be prepared to fight off a U.S. aircraft carrier battle group steaming into the East China Sea, South China Sea, or Yellow Sea to intervene in a crisis. In the past, U.S. bases in the region were safe and U.S. fleets could sail into the Western Pacific and operate virtually with impunity. Chinese improvements in military technology, however, are forcing the United States to rethink some combat scenarios to factor in the increasing vulnerability of U.S. forces to PLA attack. American ability to protect friends and allies in the region is no longer assured. The Chinese are building their own high-technology networks—based on satellites and perhaps leading-edge science that in some areas could allow the Chinese to leapfrog ahead of current U.S. capabilities—to locate targets and strike them accurately from long distances. The PLA is acquiring modern, capable submarines, surface warships, and warplanes. China recently deployed a "carrier killer" ballistic missile with a range of up to 1,500 miles that can reputedly hit a moving warship and that U.S. shipborne defenses probably could not shoot down. The Chinese are also developing an electromagnetic pulse (EMP) attack capability: a nuclear explosion outside the atmosphere that kills no one through shock or radiation but creates an electrical surge over a large area below, disrupting all electronic equipment and disabling ships and aircraft. Both the carrier-killer missile and the EMP attack are examples of asymmetrical warfare, in which the weaker player does not try to duplicate every one of a stronger opponent's capabilities. PLA strategists are clearly thinking in such terms in their planning for a possible conflict with the United States. The Chinese recognize that the cost of trying to match every capability of the U.S. military would be prohibitive and perhaps impossible. The U.S. military's vulnerabilities include heavy reliance on sophisticated but relatively fragile satellite and computer systems. In January 2007 the Chinese destroyed one of their own weather satellites in orbit over five hundred miles above the earth with a ground-launched missile, demonstrating both an interest in and a capability for knocking out U.S. communication and sensor satellites. Chinese computer hacking skills pose a potential danger to some U.S. military activities. A cyber attack might, for example, impede a U.S. effort to intervene in a Taiwan Strait conflict. Another vulnerability that Chinese strategists impute to the United States is a weak stomach for casualties, especially in a conflict over something less than a direct threat to the American homeland (such as Taiwan independence or ownership of islands in the South China Sea). Thus the Chinese believe the psychological effect of a successful strike on a U.S. carrier (with its crew of over five thousand) could be as important as the military consequences.

China's armed forces, of course, have their own weaknesses and vulnerabilities. The PLA has not seen combat since 1979, when its forces performed poorly against overmatched Vietnamese units during the Chinese incursion into parts of Vietnam near the Chinese border. Chinese military analysts study other countries' wars, but the lessons they draw are often distorted by the need to remain within the boundaries of Chinese political correctness. While the PLA's improved capabilities reduce U.S. freedom of maneuver in maritime East Asia, American forces can still gain access to the region, even if in some cases U.S. warships might need to stay at greater distances from the Chinese coast in a time of war. The carrier-killing missile might be a "use it and lose it" weapon; PLA launch of a ballistic missile against deployed U.S. forces or a U.S. base in the region would immediately subject the Chinese satellite network to attacks that would destroy the systems that guide the missiles to their intended targets. Even if China was winning in an anti-access/area-denial campaign against U.S. forces in the Western Pacific, the U.S. Navy could use its global superiority to retaliate by blocking shipments of crucial supplies such as energy into China. Even if China was successful in its own neighborhood initially, U.S. forces could turn the conflict into a protracted war and eventually force the Chinese to surrender their gains. As the PLA strengthens itself with modernized capabilities, it also creates for itself some of the same vulnerabilities that Chinese planners see in the U.S. military. Chinese satellites are as easy to strike as U.S. satellites. Chinese warships are vulnerable to U.S. missiles and torpedoes. By incorporating information technology into its operations, the PLA increases exposure to cyber attacks. U.S. hackers are as clever as their Chinese counterparts, and Chinese defenses may be less effective than those in U.S. systems.

A Naval Challenge?

The Chinese navy's acquisition of modern oceangoing warships is the spear point of the PLA's challenge to the United States. The United States has the world's most capable navy, one that can project force to any of the world's oceans. The U.S. Navy already enforces the principle of free navigation throughout the globe. The PRC's entry into this field indicates, at best, a Chinese attempt to duplicate this American capability based on distrust for the United States. More ominously, some observers believe it may be the harbinger of a Chinese attempt to eventually displace the American navy from this role. A stronger Chinese navy also bolsters the PRC's anti-access/area-denial capability against the United States.

Up to the 1980s, the PLA Navy was a hybrid "brown-water navy" and "green-water navy": a force of small ships (patrol boats) unable to venture far from the coast, plus a few medium-size warships (such as frigates and destroyers) capable of short-term operations in the region adjacent to their home port. The PLA Navy has gradually broadened its vision, recently redefining its mission from "coastal defense" to "far sea defense." The potential for continued Chinese naval expansion is great. As China grows wealthier, more funds will be available for all branches of the armed forces.

Traditionally, China's ground forces have dominated the bureaucratic battle for funding, but the danger of an invasion of China or some other major conflict on the Asian mainland is much reduced today, while the need for air and naval forces is greater because security issues linked to tensions with the United States, Japan, Taiwan, and some Southeast Asian countries have become more prominent.

The Chinese leadership's decision to build a strong navy represents a victory for advocates of China acting unilaterally to protect its interests over advocates of China taking a cooperative and low-profile posture. The latter group believes international economic interdependence and globalization have made the trading nations dependent on each other to such a degree that maritime security must be multilateral, with the navies of the major powers sharing responsibility for keeping the sea lanes open and safe. This group believes that the Hobbesian view of international politics as "a war of all against all" is obsolete. Furthermore, if Beijing tries to build a strong enough navy to singlehandedly protect worldwide Chinese interests, China may worsen its own security situation by alarming the other major powers. The opposing view is that China's economic well-being depends on China's ability to control the sea lanes, and this requires a strong navy. China should not let the fear of alarming other countries deter China from building a strong navy. With a weak navy, China will leave the control of its destiny to other governments; if China has a strong navy, these governments will not dare to threaten China and Chinese forces can uphold Chinese interests without having to rely on foreigners—especially naval superpower America.[10]

Much of China's most vital imports, such as oil and natural gas, are transported to China by ship. Chinese analysts have for years wrung their hands over the "Malacca dilemma." The long and narrow Malacca Strait between Malaysia and the Indonesian island of Sumatra is the passage between the Indian Ocean and the South China Sea. Some 40 percent of the world's trade passes through it, and about 60 percent of the cargo ships and tankers in the strait are traveling to and from China.[11] The Chinese fear that a foreign power—most likely the United States—might block or restrict China's use of the strait. Chinese planners see a strong navy as a way to help mitigate the huge vulnerability of China's reliance on seaborne international trade. A Chinese navy with global reach might be able to intervene to prevent the molestation of ships sailing to or from China. Building an ocean-going PLA Navy does not necessarily mean the Chinese intend to compete with the US Navy for global preeminence. There are scenarios other than a conflict with the United States in which China would benefit from having a navy that is strong but not strong enough to defeat the U.S. Navy, including piracy against Chinese ships or a regional military conflict in which the United States chose not to get involved.

In fact, there is little reason for naval friction between China and the United States *outside* of the Asia-Pacific region. The U.S. Defense Department has recognized that PLA military expansion has the upside of enabling China "to contribute to the delivery of international public goods."[12] Washington praised Chinese participation in the multinational force conducting antipiracy patrols in the Gulf of Aden. One could easily imagine that such experiences could come to define U.S.-China relations if the United States opted to step back from being a major strategic player in eastern Asia.

Many observers have seen the aircraft carrier as a gauge of China's commitment to a blue-water navy. To be a naval great power with serious power-projection capability, China would need a fleet of carriers. (As a general rule, three are needed to keep one at sea at all times because the others will be occupied by training or maintenance.) Building and operating the carriers and their support ships would burn up a huge portion of the Chinese military budget. After years of speculation, the Chinese government recently confirmed its intention to build and deploy aircraft carriers. A renovated vessel purchased from the Ukraine is serving as the PLA Navy's first carrier, which will initially serve as a training platform. Aircraft carrier operations are extremely complex and may take decades for the Chinese to master. Eventually, the PLA Navy plans to build at least two and up to six additional carriers. The decision to build carriers was not an easy one for the Chinese leadership. The massive financial investment takes away from funding for missiles, submarines, fighter aircraft, and modern surface combatants. A PRC carrier also risks reinforcing regional fears that China intends to build up its military superiority over its neighbors in preparation for politically dominating them. A carrier would also be an easy target for American forces in the event of a U.S.-China war. Indeed, as far as the U.S.-China naval rivalry is concerned, the Chinese would arguably be doing the United States a favor by building carriers rather than spending the money on systems that are more threatening to U.S. warships. The downsides to the Chinese of deploying aircraft carriers are so onerous that, according to one theory, the decision to acquire them is not based on sober strategic analysis. Rather, it reflects the influence of public opinion, which sees the aircraft carrier as a symbol of great-power status and demands that China keep up with the other countries that have carriers.[13] Along with historical great powers such as Britain, France, and Russia, even Thailand, India, and Brazil have aircraft carriers, although they are considerably smaller and less powerful than the "supercarriers" (over seventy thousand tons) the United States operates. The deployment of Chinese aircraft carriers will probably do little to affect the supremacy of the U.S. Navy outside the Asia-Pacific region. Their main utility would be to strengthen China's military position in potential conflicts with its neighbors—but only if those conflicts did not draw U.S. intervention. Yet this advantage might be negated as China's neighbors, seeing the deployment of a carrier as a red flag, increase their defense cooperation with each other and with the United States.

China's Nuclear Forces

Consistent with the larger trend within the PLA, China is in the midst of increasing both the quality and size of its nuclear forces. The PRC is the only one of the original five nuclear weapons states (the others being the United States, the Soviet Union, Britain, and France) that is enlarging its nuclear arsenal. During the last few years, China has increased from twenty to fifty the number of its long-range missiles (called intercontinental ballistic missiles, or ICBMs) that can reach some part of the United States. The PLA has also more than doubled, to over one hundred, its stockpile of medium-range missiles, which could hit U.S. bases in Asia (most likely with conventional rather than nuclear warheads). The U.S. Defense Department says "China has the most active land-based ballistic and cruise missile program in the world": developing new variants for specific tasks, improving accuracy, and beefing up numbers of high-tech weapons.[14] Not surprisingly, this rapid growth in the most destructive category of weapons frightens Americans, convincing many that the United States is the target and Chinese domination of Asia is the aim. The increases in hardware appear all the more ominous because of the usual concerns about a lack of Chinese transparency. Indeed, the Chinese government is even more secretive about its nuclear forces than about the other branches of the PLA. In China's view, the main purpose of China's nuclear weapons program is to prevent bullying and blackmail by the other nuclear powers. This is not merely a hypothetical scenario for the Chinese. U.S. officials repeatedly threatened to use nuclear weapons against China during the 1950s, when China did not have the bomb. Chinese even argue that theirs is "the country most frequently threatened by nuclear attack," although this seems disrespectful of Japan, which suffered two actual atomic attacks during World War II.[15]

China is building more ICBMs and refusing to reveal where it will stop, even as the United States and Russia are reducing their arsenals. This leads to speculation that the Chinese are trying to achieve nuclear parity with the world's two leading nuclear powers. Indeed, this fear has been an obstacle in negotiations between Washington and Moscow to make further cuts. Both have encouraged China to join in the nuclear arms reduction talks. China has declined, saying the two former superpowers should first make deep cuts since their nuclear arsenals are so much larger than those of any other country.

From the point of view of the United States, the fewer nuclear weapons a potential adversary has, the better. Americans may take it for granted that the United States can be trusted with nuclear superiority because the United States is the global peacekeeper and the sustainer of an international system from which all countries benefit. China, of course, does not accept these assumptions. The Chinese also see hypocrisy in Washington's vigorous pursuit of nonproliferation against unfriendly countries such as Iran and North Korea coupled with a more relaxed American attitude toward the nuclear programs of countries such as Israel and India. In this instance, the Chinese argue that balance brings peace. Unbalanced and decisive U.S. nuclear superiority, Chinese would argue, actually makes conflict more likely, as overly aggressive U.S. policies would require a determined Chinese response.

At the end of 2010, China had an estimated 175 immediately usable nuclear warheads, plus another sixty-five in reserve.[16] China is expected to deploy at least one hundred nuclear warheads, with some estimates as high as three hundred, on ICBMs between 2015 and 2020.[17] The PRC has developed the ability to load multiple, independently targeted warheads on a missile. This gives one missile the ability to destroy several cities. The Chinese have been slow to implement this capability, perhaps because they need more nuclear testing to perfect smaller but sufficiently powerful warheads. To provide some perspective, the United States' nuclear arsenal includes 450 ICBMs and about two thousand deployed warheads, plus another three thousand in reserve and 4,600 awaiting dismantling. France has about three hundred warheads, and Britain 225.

Deterrence between two countries armed with nuclear weapons is based on each believing that it could not launch an attack without suffering unacceptably destructive retaliation. During the Cold War, this was called "mutual assured destruction." Somewhat perversely, holding each other's civilian populations hostage to nuclear annihilation can provide stability and peace between two adversaries. If one country achieved the ability to launch a nuclear surprise attack capable of wiping out the other country's means of striking back, there would be a dangerous imbalance in security. One country would gain near-invulnerability and the other would be subject to extortion. Until recently, China's retaliatory capability has been vulnerable because its relatively small number of ICBMs were in immobile launch silos. Early Chinese ICBMs also used liquid fuel, which required a lengthy preparation before the missiles could be fired. The newer types of Chinese nuclear missiles, however, cannot be so easily destroyed. They use solid fuel, allowing the missiles to remain in a constant state of readiness. They are mobile, making their locations unpredictable. The PLA is building a network of tunnels in the mountains of Hebei province totaling over three thousand miles in length. Dubbed the "underground Great Wall," these facilities will enable missiles to be stored, transported, and prepared for launching while thousands of feet underground, safe from attack and invisible to spy satellites.[18] Some of China's nuclear missiles can be launched from submarines at sea, which are not only invisible to satellites when submerged but also mobile, and they can even shorten the distance of the missile flight by sailing close to the U.S. coastline. Through these upgrades to their nuclear forces, the Chinese have now attained survivability for their retaliatory capability.

Beijing has tried to make its nuclear forces appear less threatening. Under pressure from the United States and other governments, the Chinese for the first time addressed the complaints about nontransparency in their nuclear strategy by including a few sentences on this topic in their 2009 defense white paper. This goes against Chinese instincts. Beside the traditional Chinese inclination to be secretive about sensitive military planning, Beijing believes it gets more deterrence for its money by maintaining a degree of uncertainty in the minds of opponents about China's nuclear forces. Outside analysts generally saw the discussion in the white paper as not very enlightening but at least a positive step toward greater openness.

A more important concession by China is its "no first use" (NFU) policy: Beijing pledges not to use nuclear weapons against non-nuclear states and not to use them against a nuclear-armed state except in response to a nuclear attack on China. The Chinese are proud to repeat that they are the only nuclear weapons state to make such a commitment. This stance places China on a moral high ground from which Beijing calls on the other nuclear powers to follow China's example. NFU is so magnanimous, however, that Chinese nuclear strategists have seriously questioned this policy since the 1990s. NFU does not distinguish between tactical (small, battlefield-sized) and strategic (capable of destroying enemy cities) nuclear attacks, unilaterally limiting China's options. The United States and other nuclear powers remain free to consider employing tactical nukes while exploiting the assurance that China will not. With the United States already superior to China in both conventional and nuclear capabilities, China cannot afford to saddle itself with an additional disadvantage, many Chinese argue. Some Chinese have raised questions about what counts as a first use. One line of argument, for example, is that a U.S. attack *using conventional weapons* on Chinese nuclear weapons sites is equivalent to a first use because it would threaten China's nuclear retaliatory capability; therefore China would be allowed to respond with nuclear weapons. Another argument is that NFU would not forbid the Chinese from exploding a nuclear device to cause an electromagnetic pulse, because the nuclear explosion would not directly kill anyone. Pushing this argument a little further, one might argue that a nuclear "demonstration" strike on a sparsely populated piece of enemy territory as a warning or show of resolve would not count as a first use, even if a small number of people were killed or harmed. NFU is such a large concession by the Chinese that many outside observers believe China will eventually renounce or modify it.

The Chinese say their forces require modernization to remain credible as a deterrent because of new developments in the regional security environment. The United States is strengthening its offensive nuclear capabilities. During the Bush administration, the United States demonstrated interest in developing new types of nuclear weapons. Since the 1990s, the risk of a war with the nuclear-armed United States over Taiwan has increased. Chinese analysts argue that it was Russia's large nuclear arsenal that prevented the American military from intervening in the Russian campaign to subdue Chechnya during the 1990s. This argument may seem specious to Americans, but it is based on the notion, believable to Chinese ears, that the main U.S. interest in both Chechnya and Taiwan is to use separatism to weaken a rival major power. The Chinese believe U.S. strategists are open-minded about using nuclear weapons in wartime. India has recently deployed nuclear weapons and declared that China is the main reason. North Korea's acquisition of the bomb might lead to South Korea and Japan doing the same.

The Chinese now have more money and a higher level of technology with which to upgrade their forces. But despite having the motive and means to build a very large force, the Chinese continue to believe a small retaliatory force is adequate. Even if the United States has enough warheads to destroy China many times over, the Chinese do not see the need to match these numbers. A small force buys a lot of deterrence if it threatens the adversary's large population centers. As a PLA general puts it, "What is the difference between a person dying one hundred times and dying just once?" The presumed American intolerance of casualties allows the Chinese to get by with even less, says the general: "In China's view, the United States cannot stand an attack by even one bomb." The Chinese political analyst Zhang Baohui reasons that if the PRC deployed six missile-carrying submarines during a war with the United States and U.S. forces took out four of the submarines, the remaining two could send seventy-two warheads toward U.S. targets. Even with the very generous assumption that a U.S. missile defense system could stop 60 percent of the incoming warheads, twenty-eight would still get through. Thus, says Zhang, even a medium-sized Chinese nuclear force is sufficient to deter a nuclear attack from the United States—assuming that the expectation of losing over twenty U.S. cities would be unacceptable to American political leaders.[19]

Chinese willingness to accept a much smaller nuclear force than that of the United States is premised on the expectation by both sides that Chinese nuclear missiles are able to destroy U.S. cities. The ballistic missile defense system proposed by the United States, however, throws a spanner into the works. Washington portrays the proposed anti–ballistic missile shield as a purely defensive system to which there could be no legitimate objection because it affects only a rogue government or organization planning a missile attack against the United States. In warfare, however, a strong defense can facilitate a more aggressive offense. China sees ballistic missile defense as a U.S. attempt to negate China's strategic nuclear retaliatory capability, which would make a U.S. nuclear strike on the Chinese homeland feasible. Chinese fear this vulnerability would carry over into any non-nuclear military conflict between China and the United States as well. U.S. forces could act more boldly against China both in wartime and in peacetime if the possibility of Chinese nuclear retaliation was removed.

A U.S. system to destroy incoming ballistic missiles, a task described as "trying to hit a bullet with a bullet," has yet to prove practical. If it does, the most direct Chinese countermove would be to build a much larger number of ballistic missiles that can target the United States. Even if a U.S. antimissile system could stop a small number of missiles, stopping a large number approaching at the same time would be a much greater challenge and might overwhelm U.S. defenses. Chinese analysts conclude that a U.S. missile defense system will probably never be able to stop all incoming missiles. The consequences of even a small amount of "leakage" would be dire, as every missile that got through might be able to destroy several cities.[20] Another Chinese response to an American missile defense system would be to make Chinese missiles harder to shoot down. The Chinese have already been working for at least a decade on measures to increase the survivability of warheads in flight, including jamming a defensive system's radio transmissions, reducing the radar signature of missiles, employing decoys to distract the system, and increasing the maneuverability of missiles.[21] Motivations for the proposed U.S. missile defense system go beyond China. The strongest argument for it is the threat of a small-scale missile attack launched by a "rogue" regime or a nonstate terrorist organization. With regard to China, however, the system looks like a poor bargain for the United States: it is uncertain to work yet certain to push the Chinese toward developing the even more robust nuclear force Washington does not want them to have.

China's opposition to a ballistic missile defense system evidently does not prevent the Chinese from building one of their own. Officially, China is opposed to the "militarization" of space. Beijing has called for a prohibition on the presence of antisatellite weapons and other antimissile system components in space and for a general ban on "experimenting" with the use of outer space to gain strategic advantages. The Chinese antisatellite test in January 2007, however, violated these principles. The test also drew international criticism because the destruction of the satellite created a cloud of debris that will pose a hazard to other countries' satellites and spacecraft for years to come. Beijing did not notify the international community prior to the test and did not acknowledge the test until several days afterward. In another test in January 2010, apparently timed to signal Chinese displeasure over the latest U.S. arms sale to Taiwan, a similar Chinese missile successfully intercepted a Chinese medium-range ballistic missile. The second test demonstrated a vastly greater Chinese capability than the first.

The Chinese are expanding and improving their nuclear forces because they want to ensure that they have a credible nuclear retaliatory capability and because they don't want a sense of unmatched nuclear superiority to embolden U.S. military action against Chinese interests in the Asia-Pacific. They are content, however, to field nuclear forces that will remain considerably smaller than America's even after the Chinese buildup and the U.S. drawdown are complete. China's nuclear forces have been, and will continue to be, undersized. As a medium-sized power, China maintained only bare minimum force levels. As a great power, China is projected to have the nuclear strength of a middle power, roughly equivalent to France.

One Country's Security Is Another Country's Insecurity

China views its own military buildup and modernization as overdue, proportionate to China's size and new wealth, and beneficial to the region. The United States sees the size and speed of the PLA buildup as unnecessary and ominous. China's long-term threat to global U.S. military supremacy is still unproven. What is undeniable is that China's emergence as a military great power challenges the status quo of American military preeminence in the region. U.S. forces can no longer assume they can prevail in every regional battle scenario with minimal losses. For the smaller countries in the region that see an increasing PRC capability to project military power outside of China's borders, continuing to resist China over bilateral strategic disagreements is becoming less tenable. From the American point of view, a massive increase in Chinese military strength is on balance a deterioration of the security environment. For the Chinese, it is the opposite. But the actual security benefit the Chinese realize from stronger military forces might be reduced by the countermeasures taken by the United States and its friends in the region. The PLA buildup reinforces the suspicions of governments worried about the rise of China, increases the likelihood of unintended military clashes between China and other Asia-Pacific countries, and sets off alarms in the countries that have serious strategic or political disputes with Beijing.

Chapter Five

JAPAN AND CHINA

A Long Struggle with Bitter Resolve

Japan-China relations are famous for the awkward combination of a deep and growing economic relationship and a stunted, often tense political relationship. Bilateral economic relations have rapidly expanded in the last two decades, even during periods of especially poor relations such as the early 2000s. China is Japan's top trading partner and is crucial to Japan's continued prosperity. The PRC is also, however, Japan's most formidable security problem.

Since ancient times, China has been both a source of knowledge and wealth and an adversary to Japan. Japan borrowed heavily from Chinese culture and philosophy. Ancient Japanese deeply respected China and at times paid tribute to the Chinese monarch. During part of Japan's history, rival samurai leaders tried to control the trade with China, seeing it as a means of amassing funds for the fight against their domestic enemies. Competition with China influenced the development of the Japanese state as much as respect for China did. A rivalry between the two countries for greater influence in Asia repeatedly played out in wars over control of Korea. The ancient Japanese gradually developed a sense of superiority over the Chinese owing to the fact that China's monarchy periodically saw dynastic change (i.e., one family group lost control of the throne to another) while the same dynasty reigned in Japan since 660 b.c.e. The technological prowess demonstrated by the Western powers in Asia during the nineteenth century convinced both Japanese and Chinese of the need for self-strengthening. China's efforts were partial and disjointed. In contrast, the political, economic, and industrial transformation Japan underwent in the Meiji era beginning in 1868 laid the foundation for Japan to become the first Asian great power.

Japan's defeat of China in the 1894–1895 Sino-Japan War clearly established in Japanese minds that Japan was thoroughly superior to a China that was anciently glorious but had become a flaccid and backward country in the modern era. Japanese contempt for China was a major contributing factor to the atrocities that invading and occupying Japanese troops committed against Chinese civilians. During the Cold War, when Chinese military capabilities were relatively modest, Japan had little concern about a security threat from China. The United States, Japan's ally, provided sufficient protection even after China acquired nuclear weapons in 1964. Japanese were as worried about the consequences of a weak China—such as boatloads of Chinese economic refugees arriving on Japan's shores—as they were about the dangers posed by a strong China. Tokyo's China policy concentrated on rebuilding trade ties with China and encouraging stability and reform within China. Japan became the largest donor of foreign development assistance to China. As Japan progressed from "miraculous" economic success story to economic superpower, Tokyo envisioned China as a secondary cog in a regional economic system led by Japan. In the 1990s, it became clear that China's rapid economic growth gave the country potential to quickly reach great-power status. At the same time, Japan slipped into a long recession, its population began to decline, and the previous decade's "Japan as Number One" craze faded. In historical terms, the period during which Japan was stronger than China is anomalous and brief. Beginning in the late 1800s, the era of Japan's ascendancy over China arguably ended in the year 2010, when China surpassed Japan as the world's second-largest economy.

The bilateral political relationship improved in the late 2000s after hitting a low point during the Koizumi Junichiro years. The prime ministers who succeeded Koizumi did not openly visit the Yasukuni Shrine, which the Chinese believe glorifies Japanese guilty of war crimes against China. Abe Shinzo visited China and upgraded economic and technological cooperation. Beijing reciprocated by reducing the usual criticism of Japan over the history issue and making statements that emphasized looking optimistically toward the future of bilateral relations. During a visit to Japan in 2007, Wen Jiaobao acknowledged Japanese apologies and expressed appreciation for Japanese economic assistance to China. Beijing has placed new controls on anti-Japan media reports, which pleased Tokyo. The movement toward Japanese military normalization slowed, which pleased Beijing.

During this period of political recovery, however, the basic strategic problems between Japan and China remained in place and even quietly worsened. The steady buildup of Chinese military capabilities continued, as did Chinese naval probes into the waters near the Japanese islands. China continued to regard Japan as a partner in American military hegemony over eastern Asia. The dispute over the Senkaku Islands flared up again. These strategic barriers continued to prevent a breakthrough in Sino-Japan relations. In 2009–2010, Japan's new prime minister Hatoyama Yukio tried to move Japan a step closer to an accommodation with China. His government said Japan should rely less heavily on its relationship with America and strengthen its ties with Asia. He called for a more "equal" U.S.-Japan relationship, signaling that he would not do everything the Americans wished. Japan's security predicament, however, made this agenda difficult to carry out. Hatoyama tried to revise a previous agreement with the U.S. government concerning the U.S. Marines' Futenma air base on Okinawa. According to the plan, the base would move from a densely populated area to a less crowded site on the Okinawan coast. Siding with Okinawan residents who wanted to lighten the burden of hosting U.S. bases, Hatoyama promised instead to relocate the Marine units outside of Okinawa. U.S. officials insisted on sticking to the original plan, arguing that alternatives would undercut the combat effectiveness of the alliance. North Korean military provocations, combined with China's tolerance for Pyongyang's misbehavior, raised the perceived value of the American security umbrella. After less than a year in office, Hatoyama resigned in June 2010, citing his inability to keep his campaign promise to move the base off Okinawa. The new prime minister, Kan Naoto, quickly affirmed his support for the original base realignment plan.

Making a Bad Situation Worse

Several issues, most of them with deep historical roots, bedevil the Japan-China strategic relationship. This creates a context of bilateral insecurities and suspicions that the rise of China intensifies.

The Pacific War History Issue

The Pacific War set the parameters for today's China-Japan relations. It was by no means the first war between China and Japan, but it was the most recent, and it was a particularly bloody one. The PRC government claims the Japanese invasion killed twenty million Chinese.

The war is the basis for the Japanese assertion that the Chinese government fosters anti-Japanese sentiment. There is considerable merit in this accusation. Prior to the 1980s, Beijing suppressed research into and discussion of Japanese war crimes because the Chinese government hoped to improve relations with Japan. To allow for the establishment of normal diplomatic relations between China and Japan in 1972, the Japanese prime minister offered a weak expression of regret for the "unfortunate period" of the war, while Beijing agreed not to ask for war reparations with the understanding that Japan would provide generous aid to Chinese economic development. In 1982 the CCP needed a new means of rebuilding its prestige and mobilizing public support for Deng's economic reform and modernization campaign. The Japanese media reported that Japan's Ministry of Education was demanding that Japanese history textbooks be revised to describe Japan's Pacific War invasion of China in innocuous, nonjudgmental language—a "sanitization" of history. Soon thereafter, the Chinese government embarked on a "patriotic" education campaign centered on sanctification of what the Chinese call the War of Resistance Against Japan (*KangRi Zhanzheng*). The main points of the campaign were that China won the war in a "miracle," that the CCP deserves the credit, and that this victory was a turning point in world and Chinese history, in particular setting China on a path to "liberation" and development. In this narrative, Japanese villainy was counterposed against CCP heroism. The message was that the Chinese people should get behind the Party and work for economic development so China can be strong and secure. Chinese media offered increased coverage of Japanese war crimes. Many museums and monuments appeared that commemorated the war and Japanese atrocities. The government allowed Chinese scholars, legal activists, and advocacy groups to engage in research, publicity, and campaigns for redress for Chinese victims of the war. Beijing's play of the history card culminated with PRC President Jiang Zemin lecturing his hosts during a visit to Japan in 1998. This played badly in Japan, and thereafter the Chinese leadership decided to ease up on the Japan bashing. Not so the Chinese public. Several large, spontaneous anti-Japan protests occurred in China during the 2000s, with the heaviest concentration in 2005. The Chinese government was often squeezed between its desire to limit the damage to its relations with Japan and its fear of offending Chinese public opinion by restricting displays of "patriotism."

Japan pushed back. Koizumi made annual visits to the Yasukuni Shrine in defiance of specific Chinese warnings. Koizumi argued that the Chinese government had no right to dictate how the Japanese should honor their own war dead. Japanese society too began to show signs of guilt fatigue. By the end of Jiang's 1998 visit to Japan, many Japanese had come to believe that China was cynically using the history issue as a tool to extract concessions and to suppress Japan's international leadership potential and felt that Japan's good-faith efforts to satisfy the Chinese were wasted. In important ways Japan had been a model international citizen since the removal of its fascist government at the end of the war. Tokyo was a major donor to the United Nations and a leader in peace and anti-nuclear-weapons activism. Japanese were keenly aware that until Wen's speech in Japan in 2007, the CCP never openly acknowledged the extent of postwar Japanese financial aid to China. Japan was the main provider of foreign aid to China through its official development assistance (ODA) program beginning in 1979. This aid reached over $2 billion annually in the 1990s. The Japanese continued making loans to China until 2008, the year China hosted the Olympic Games, China's unofficial coming-out party as a developed country. Subsequently, Tokyo continued giving China grants and technical assistance, mostly for projects to protect the environment.

Japanese are also dismayed that although several Japanese prime ministers, many other officials, and even the Japanese emperor have apologized to China and other victimized countries about Japan's aggression during the Pacific War, these apologies have not satisfied the Chinese (or the Koreans). There are two reasons why the effect of the apologies has been limited. First, the particular words used in these apologies are not strong enough; they denote regret but not admission of responsibility for serious crimes. Second, prominent Japanese continue to make public statements in support of the conservative, nationalistic Japanese view that Japan had good intentions and acted honorably during the Pacific War and that the claims of Japanese atrocities are fabricated. Chinese and Korean observers argue that a Japanese prime minister's apology for the war is negated if the following week a Japanese businessman or politician says the Nanjing Massacre didn't happen or that the "comfort women" were not coerced.

From the Japanese point of view, the Chinese government's overemphasis on present-day Japan's guilt for the crimes during the first half of the previous century has several consequences. First, it contributes to Japanese businesses in China suffering "politically motivated harassment."[1] Second, it indicates an intention by Beijing to suppress Japanese military and international political power. Third, it increases Japanese insecurity by fueling the perception that when China becomes more powerful it will seek vengeance against Japan.[2]

The Alliance

From China's point of view, the U.S.-Japan alliance unites China's most deadly enemy of the recent past with China's main rival of the present and future.

China's view of the alliance, however, has always been somewhat ambivalent because the alliance has the additional feature of strategically restraining Japan. The Chinese understand that the alliance "contains" Japan by keeping Tokyo's policies closely tied to America's Asia strategy. The United States, which fought the Pacific War at great cost, does not want to see the reemergence of a powerful, independent, and chauvinist Japan any more than China does. The Chinese comfort level with the U.S.-Japan alliance has tended to fluctuate according to the general state of U.S.-China relations and also with China's sense of whether or not Taiwan is moving toward formal independence from China (since Beijing considers both Washington and Tokyo to be accomplices of the Taipei government). In the 1950s and 1960s, Beijing characterized the alliance as a vehicle for Japanese remilitarization and U.S. hegemony in Asia and strongly opposed it. As Chinese relations with the Soviet Union soured and Sino-U.S. relations improved in the early 1970s, China's view of the alliance softened. Beijing became more appreciative of aspects of the alliance that were positive from China's standpoint: Japanese alignment with the United States kept Japanese militarism in check and was preferable to Japan allying with the Soviet Union.

Despite assurances from Washington and Tokyo, Beijing sees U.S.-Japan military cooperation as mostly anti-China. The Chinese also object to the United States urging Japan to become militarily stronger and more active so Japan can contribute more to the American security agenda in the region. During the 2000s, the balance may have tipped permanently toward the Chinese viewing the alliance primarily in a negative rather than a positive light because of Japan's steady march, at U.S. urging, toward breaking free of the postwar constraints on its armed forces.

Rearmament

The so-called rearmament issue stems from the "pacifist" constitution that was part of the victor's peace imposed on defeated Japan after World War II. Ironically, soon after writing or overseeing the writing of Japan's constitution, the U.S. occupation authorities began pushing the Japanese government to lay it aside and build larger military forces because of the Cold War, which Tokyo proved reluctant to do. The pertinent section of the Japanese constitution is Article 9, which reads:

> Aspiring sincerely to an international peace based on justice and order, the Japanese people forever renounce war as a sovereign right of the nation and the threat or use of force as means of settling international disputes. To accomplish the aim of the preceding paragraph, land, sea, and air forces, as well as other war potential, will never be maintained. The right of belligerency of the state will not be recognized.

Taken literally, this seems to forbid Japan from having armed forces. But the *interpretation* of Japan's constitution matters more than the actual text. The interpretation has been that Japan has the same right to self-defense as any other country, so the constitutional prohibition kicks in only if Japan contemplates weapons or policies that go beyond self-defense. This has not prevented Japan from building armed forces that are quite formidable. So the issue is not rearmament; Japan began rearming even during the U.S. occupation. Rather, the question is whether Japan's armed forces should remain bound, and how much so, by unique political restrictions.

Japan's annual defense spending has been limited to about 1 percent of GDP, a modest level. Spending above this level would be politically difficult. Since Japan's "Self-Defense Force" can only have "defensive" and no "offensive" weapon systems, Japan has no aircraft carriers, long-range strike aircraft, or land-attack missile forces. Despite U.S. wishes to the contrary, the Japanese government has taken the position up to now that the commitment to using force only in self-defense precludes Japan from participating in collective defense with the United States. While America is obligated to help defend against an attack on Japan, the Japanese military cannot help fight back against an attack on America. The Japanese public continues to be reticent about fielding a military that goes much beyond a police and disaster response force.

Nevertheless, within these constraints Japan has gradually expanded the capabilities and missions of the Self-Defense Forces. Japan has periodically taken key steps toward strengthening its armed forces, undermining several important principles and assumptions that have upheld the notion of a "pacifist" Japan. Understandably, Beijing has complained about each of these steps. The pace of Japanese remilitarization, and the strength of Chinese complaints, increased beginning in the 1990s. Beijing particularly objected to the revised guidelines for the U.S.-Japan alliance, which specified that Japan's defensive perimeter includes "areas surrounding Japan" (overlapping areas that surround China) and that the Japanese military would provide logistical support for U.S. forces engaged in combat. To the Chinese, this appeared to institutionalize Japanese participation in a hypothetical war to prevent Chinese forces from capturing Taiwan.

Until recently, China has been one of several factors influencing Japanese remilitarization but not necessarily the dominant factor. One of the key steps by Japan, for example, occurred in 1981, when China's Dengist economic reform period was just beginning and there was not yet widespread recognition that China was rising quickly toward great-power status. In that year Japan's Maritime Self-Defense Force (the Japanese Navy) took responsibility for patrolling the sea lanes up to one thousand nautical miles from the Japanese coast. Oscillations in the drive toward remilitarization are partly a result of developments in Japanese domestic politics. Japan's economic recession of the 1990s weakened support for the preeminent faction within the ruling Liberal Democratic Party, which wanted economic cooperation to be the main feature of Japan's China policy. This faction lost ground to a group of LDP leaders who believed sufficient time had passed since the end of Pacific War for the constraints on Japan's military to be removed. These more nationalistic Japanese leaders also had strong ideological objections to Chinese authoritarianism and were tired of Chinese criticism over the history issue. At the same time, the influence of the political left, which opposed a strong Japanese military and the alliance with the United States, declined. This political shift led to the election of Koizumi as prime minister and a downturn in Sino-Japan relations. International pressures *other than* China have also been influential. Foreigners taunted Japan for conducting "checkbook diplomacy" during the 1991 Gulf War. Tokyo provided a substantial financial contribution of $13 billion but no troops. Some Japanese politicians have argued that to keep the alliance with the United States viable, Japan must expand its military forces to meet U.S. demands that the Japanese take a greater role in maintaining international security. North Korea has emerged as a more immediate (and probably shorter-term) threat to Japan than China. The North Korean regime is virulently hostile toward Japan and is developing a capability to mount nuclear warheads on ballistic missiles that could reach Japan. The test flight of a North Korean missile high above Japan in 1998 deeply affected Japanese public opinion and increased support for a stronger Japanese defense force. Nevertheless, many observers believe North Korean provocations provide a pretext for Japanese steps toward a stronger military posture that are really aimed at China but cannot be openly described as such for fear of worsening relations with Beijing.

The North Korean threat is tied to a dying regime. China, on the other hand, is permanent. With its growing capabilities and assertive behavior, the PRC has become the strongest motivation for Japanese rearmament.

Competition for Regional Leadership

Tokyo and Beijing have competed for centuries for regional leadership. For most of history, China was the region's predominant country. During Japan's Pacific War hegemonic moment, the Japanese empire included Southeast Asia as well as Korea, Taiwan, and Eastern China (plus many Pacific islands). Defeat stripped Japan of its Asia-Pacific empire and left a legacy of regional mistrust of Japan. Ironically, Japan's recent foe the United States helped Japan return to prominence in the region through economic power, as Washington encouraged the revival of Southeast Asian business ties to Japan and provided assurance that postwar Japanese influence need not be feared. China, on the other hand, was a sponsor of communist insurgencies in Southeast Asia and had little to offer the region economically during the first decades of the Cold War. That situation has now completely changed, with regional countries viewing trade with China as the engine of their future economic growth. From Tokyo's standpoint, China is usurping Japan's previous position in Southeast Asia. The race between Tokyo and Beijing for free trade agreements with Southeast Asian countries is as much about political leadership as it is about enlarging economic opportunities. Japan helped establish the ASEAN Regional Forum and is a key member of

ASEAN Plus Three. Tokyo's goals in both are to counter China's regional influence and to support the regional effort to constrain and socialize Beijing to prevent domineering Chinese behavior. Tokyo has struggled to dilute China's influence in regional multilateral organizations by trying to include outside and democratic countries such as India and Australia.

Another arena of Sino-Japanese competition is the United Nations. Japan has a clean foreign policy record since 1945 and is the world's second-largest financial contributor to that organization. Tokyo has unsuccessfully asked for the removal of the obsolete clauses in the UN Charter that refer to Japan as an "enemy state." More importantly, Japan has campaigned hard for a permanent seat on the UN Security Council, the body that makes decisions on international peacekeeping, sanctions, and the use of force under the UN mandate. There are five permanent Security Council members with the power to veto proposed actions. They are the five major countries that were on the winning side of World War II: the United States, Russia, Britain, France, and China. The Council has ten other seats, without veto powers, that other UN countries occupy for two years at a time on a rotating basis. There is widespread recognition that the membership arrangement should be changed. The problem is gaining agreement on a new arrangement. Along with Japan, other contenders for permanent membership are Germany, India, Brazil, plus one representative country each from Africa and from the Arab League. Among the many aspects of the debate, Beijing has openly opposed giving Japan permanent membership, arguing that Japan must first do more to acknowledge its Pacific War crimes.

Disputed Territories

Territorial disputes between countries tend to be highly volatile and difficult to solve because the perception of another state trying to take away national territory usually brings out a strong, emotional, and uncompromising attitude from the mass public. A squabble over territory is enough to strain seriously what would otherwise be a friendly bilateral relationship. Unfortunately for Japan and China, a maritime territorial dispute is an additional and potent source of tension between them, and one that is intensified by the rise of China. There are two major components of the dispute: ownership of the Senkaku Islands (Diaoyutai to the Chinese) and disagreement over demarcating the two countries' exclusive economic zones (EEZs) in the middle of the East China Sea.

Beside the pressure on the two governments to defend what is perceived as national territory, the economic stakes are substantial. Both countries badly need the resources the East China Sea offers. The East China Sea is an important food source for populous China and seafood-loving Japan. The seabed contains oil, natural gas, and minerals. International estimates of the hydrocarbon reserves in the entire East China Sea are about one hundred billion barrels of oil and about seven trillion cubic feet of natural gas. Chinese estimates, unfortunately, tend to be higher: up to 170 billion barrels of oil and two hundred trillion cubic feet of natural gas. The higher value the Chinese attach to the potential resources in the disputed areas diminishes hopes of Beijing compromising its claim to reach a peaceful settlement.

The Senkakus don't look like they are worth going to war over. The group includes five small uninhabited islands and three rocks, with a total area of about four square miles. According to Beijing, Chinese discovered the islands and for centuries used them as navigational aids. The islands were Chinese territory until Japan seized them, along with nearby Taiwan, after defeating China in the Sino-Japan War of 1894–1895. Since the Chinese link their loss of the Diaoyutai with the loss of Taiwan, they maintain that the post–World War II return of Taiwan to China implicitly includes the Diaoyutai, even though these islands are not specifically mentioned in the 1951 San Francisco Peace Treaty. Japan, on the other hand, argues that no country owned the Senkakus until Tokyo's decision to annex the islands in 1895 and that this decision was unrelated to the acquisition of Taiwan as a spoil of the Sino-Japan War. Temporarily under U.S. administration after the Pacific War, the Senkakus returned to Japanese sovereignty along with Okinawa in 1972. China did not challenge Japan's claim to ownership until 1970, following the publication of research findings suggesting large deposits of oil in the bed of the East China Sea. Tokyo officially does not consider the Senkakus disputed territory, and Japan's de facto administration of the islands is unchallenged internationally. An ancillary dispute is whether or not the owner of the islands can also claim exclusive economic rights to a large swath of the sea surrounding the islands under international law; Japan says yes, but China says no.

The basis of international maritime law is the 1994 United Nations Convention on the Law of the Sea (UNCLOS), signed and ratified by the governments of most of the world, including China and Japan. (The United States has not ratified UNCLOS but abides by most of its provisions.) UNCLOS allows a coastal state to claim an EEZ that can extend up to two hundred nautical miles into the adjacent ocean. An EEZ gives the coastal state exclusive rights to the resources in that part of the sea. The East China Sea is bordered by the coast of China on the west and Japan's Ryukyu Island chain on the east. This sea is not wide enough to accommodate two-hundred-nautical-mile EEZs on both the Chinese and Japanese sides, as its width at its widest point is only 360 nautical miles. This requires Japan and China to reach a compromise on fixing the boundaries of their respective EEZs. UNCLOS does not provide a definitive answer to the question of how to settle overlapping EEZ claims. One principle the law supports is drawing a dividing line halfway between the coasts of the two claimant countries. Another principle UNCLOS supports is the right of a state that is on the edge of a continental shelf to extend its EEZ to the end of the shelf. According to this concept, that coastal state has rights over the continuation of its land mass under water until there is a clear break in that continuity indicated by a steep drop in the depth of the seabed. UNCLOS says the continental shelf principle can extend a coastal state's EEZ from the usual two hundred nautical miles to as much as 350 nautical miles. Appeal to the Law of the Sea does not settle this dispute between Japan and China. Tokyo uses the midline principle to set the boundary for its EEZ, taking half of the sea and leaving the other half to China, arguing that this is a fair compromise. (Some Japanese elites outside the government say this is too accommodating because Japan's median line proposal was never official and that Japan should push for a two-hundred-nautical-mile EEZ.) Beijing, on the other hand, claims an EEZ that extends to the end of the continental shelf. The shelf underlies most of the East China Sea, its edge formed by the Okinawa Trough, which is just west of the Ryukyus. Beijing's claim would give China exclusive rights to almost all of the recoverable hydrocarbon resources (oil and natural gas) in the bed of the East China Sea. This leaves a large portion of the East China Sea covered by overlapping Chinese and Japanese EEZ claims.

An example of how Sino-Japanese competition for the resources in the bed of the East China Sea can cause political tensions involves the Chunxiao gas field. Chunxiao is completely within China's claimed EEZ but straddles the midline that Japan claims as the divider between the Chinese and Japanese EEZs. Thus, the Japanese feared that drilling on the Chinese side could draw off resources from the Japanese side. Japan's trade minister Nakagawa Shoichi memorably demonstrated Japan's objection during a meeting with a Chinese negotiator. Nakagawa placed two straws in a glass of orange juice and said China was planning to "suck out Japan's resources with a straw."[3] In 2005 both sides took steps that escalated the dispute. Seeing the Chinese begin production at Chunxiao, Tokyo authorized Japanese drilling as a response. Chinese naval vessels appeared near the Chunxiao field in a show of force. When a Japanese P-3C patrol aircraft arrived to investigate and overflew the Chinese ships, a PLAN destroyer aimed its guns at the plane. An agreement to develop the area jointly temporarily defused the crisis, but the agreement foundered. To Tokyo's chagrin, the Chinese announced in 2011 they had resumed unilateral drilling.

Since 1978, acts by the Chinese or Japanese governments or by nationalistic private citizens (from Japan, China, Taiwan, and Hong Kong) have periodically caused the question of sovereignty over the Senkakus to flare up into a crisis between Tokyo and Beijing. In the past, the Chinese government has sometimes tried to contain these crises. In 1996, for example, a group of Japanese nationalists erected a lighthouse on one of the Senkaku islands to reinforce Japan's claim to ownership. Chinese in the PRC, Hong Kong, and Taiwan protested. But while activists from Hong Kong and Taiwan sailed to the islands and planted flags onshore, Beijing held its citizens back.

As China becomes more relatively powerful, Beijing has less incentive to hold back. In 2001, Beijing and Tokyo agreed to give each other advance notice before sailing ships into the waters of each other's claimed EEZ. Thereafter, however, China frequently violated this agreement. December 2008 saw a subtle escalation when the PRC sent ocean survey vessels into the territorial waters (twelve nautical miles from the coastline) of the Senkakus for the first time. The Chinese response to the September 2010 incident near the Senkaku Islands was extraordinarily strong, suggesting that the danger of an East China Sea crisis between China and Japan escalating into a larger conflict is increasing. The Japanese Coast Guard approached a Chinese fishing boat captained by Zhan Qixiong about ten miles south of one of the Senkakus. Zhan's boat intentionally collided with two Japanese Coast Guard (JCG) patrol ships. The JCG then boarded and seized the Chinese boat and its crew. It is not clear why the JCG originally targeted Zhan's boat. At the time there were over one hundred other Chinese boats fishing in the area. A previous bilateral agreement allows both Japanese and Chinese fishing boats in the disputed area. That agreement did not include the territorial waters of the Senkakus, within which this incident took place, but by tacit agreement Japan had not been preventing the Chinese from fishing within the territorial waters limit of the Senkakus. The arrest of the crew, as well, suggested that the Japanese intended to enforce their sovereignty claim more vigorously than in the past. If the waters around the disputed islands were to be unofficially treated as the high seas, under international law the proper response by the JCG would have been the prompt deportation of the Chinese crew and insistence that they face prosecution in China. Instead, however, Tokyo detained the crew for six days and kept Zhan for an additional eleven days.

Then it was China's turn to assert its own sovereignty claim vigorously. The Chinese government suspended ministerial-level meetings with Japan as well as discussions of joint extraction of East China Sea hydrocarbons. Beijing announced it was detaining four Japanese nationals in China, employees of a Japanese construction firm, on suspicion of spying on Chinese military facilities. China moved to curtail its export to Japan of rare-earth elements, upon which Japan's electronics industries were highly dependent. Tokyo buckled, announcing it would release Zhan to prevent further deterioration of bilateral relations. Many Japanese severely criticized the decision as surrendering to Chinese bullying. After Zhan's release, Beijing demanded compensation and an apology, both of which Japan refused. The 2010 Senkakus incident caused a shift in Japanese attitudes toward China. Many Japanese began to believe for the first time since the end of World War II that their territory is under threat from a foreign power. The episode increased pressure on Tokyo from the public and the media, even those on the political left, to stand up to the challenge. It was a climate in which the Japanese prime minister could compare China to Nazi Germany, as Abe likened China's assertive posture toward the disputed areas to Hitler's seizure of neighboring territories to fulfill Germany's need for *Lebensraum*.[4] China's muscle flexing came at a cost. The United States has tried to keep itself out of the Senkakus/Diaoyutai dispute by saying it takes no position on the question of which country ultimately has sovereignty over the islands. The 2010 incident, however, drew from the U.S. government a public reaffirmation that the U.S.-Japan treaty obligates American forces to help defend all Japanese-administered territory, which includes the Senkakus. This alarmed Beijing. U.S.-China relations suffered along with Japan-China relations.

Solutions to the East China Sea disputes are nowhere in sight. Incidents and crises will continue to occur. China's willingness and ability to project force into the East China Sea to protect Chinese sovereignty claims has steadily grown. As China's capabilities and expectations increase, the Chinese (both government and mass public) will increasingly believe that China should move beyond managing the East China Sea sovereignty issue toward permanently resolving it in China's favor. The rise of China raises the risk that an incident in the East China Sea will escalate into a conflict.

Taiwan

There is no issue about which the Chinese are more sensitive and insecure than Taiwan. The notion of foreigners interfering with China's plans to unify with Taiwan draws an angry and indignant response from the Chinese as intense as the perception that foreigners are trying to suppress the rise of China. Japan is a target of this Chinese anger and indignation because China suspects, for historical reasons, that Japanese want to keep Taiwan outside of the PRC's control. Japan demanded that China hand over Taiwan as part of the rewards of Japan's victory in the Sino-Japan War of 1894–1895. Tokyo administered Taiwan for fifty years. During that time, as mainland Chinese are well aware, Taiwan's Japanese-run government did its best to get Taiwan's inhabitants to think of themselves as subjects of the Japanese emperor rather than as Chinese nationals. Japan's surrender to the Allied forces at the end of the Pacific War forced Tokyo to hand Taiwan over to the Republic of China in 1945. Some Taiwanese of that generation would later say they preferred Japanese rule to the mainland Chinese rule that followed. Taiwan's first Taiwan-born and first democratically elected president, Lee Teng-hui, famously said he considered himself as much Japanese as Chinese. Many Japanese politicians and societal groups are supportive of the Taiwan government because of the shared colonial experience and because the Japanese respect Taiwan's democratic political system. Exchanges and links between Taiwan and Japan have increased over the last decade.

Although Japanese officials are cautious about making statements that might rile the Chinese, many retired or nongovernment Japanese strategists argue that PRC possession of Taiwan would seriously threaten Japan by placing an unsinkable Chinese aircraft carrier amid the sea lane that carries most of Japan's energy supply. The solution to that problem is to work against the PRC ever gaining control of Taiwan. Tokyo has had many chances to assure Beijing that Japanese military forces would never support a symbolic formal breakaway from China by Taiwan's government. Instead, the Japanese have repeatedly left open the possibility that they might be involved in defending Taiwan against PLA forces. In Beijing's eyes, the 1997 revision of the guidelines for U.S.-Japan security cooperation seemed to be made with this intent. The revision broke new ground by codifying a role for the Japanese military in a regional war: the Self-Defense Forces will provide logistical assistance for U.S. forces engaged in hostilities as part of vaguely defined "situations in areas surrounding Japan" that are "important" to Japan's "peace and security."[5] The joint statement from the February 2005 U.S.-Japan Security Consultative Committee Meeting, which included the top officials for both defense and foreign affairs from both countries, listed "the peaceful resolution of issues concerning the Taiwan Strait" as a "common strategic objective."[6] The mere acknowledgement that Japan and the United States were jointly thinking about Taiwan as a strategic issue drew a strong rebuke from China. Subsequent statements from this committee omitted any explicit reference to Taiwan.[7]

Despite efforts by Tokyo and Washington to keep their planning discrete, the Chinese understand that Japan's military would likely furnish behind-the-lines support for American units fighting to defend Taiwan from a PLA attack and that some of the U.S. combatants would operate from bases in Japan. Japanese participation might include components of the anti–ballistic missile system. The arsenal of hundreds of PLA missiles positioned across the strait is perhaps Taiwan's greatest strategic fear. Japan's *Kongo*-class destroyers, however, are equipped with radar and missiles designed to shoot down ballistic missiles. Tokyo could send these destroyers to the waters near Taiwan in the event of a conflict there, potentially compromising one of the PLA's best weapons against an independence-minded Taiwan.

If Japan's Taiwan policies generate Chinese hostility toward Japan, the reverse is also true. Tokyo, along with the rest of Asia, officially accepts Beijing's position that Taiwan is part of China. In a legal sense, China-Taiwan relations are a "domestic" issue and thus are in a different category than the "international" relations between China and other state governments in Asia. This allows China to continue to reiterate its commitment to peaceful behavior in Asia while simultaneously making bellicose threats toward Taiwan. Implicitly, the Chinese are arguing that Asians need not worry because the PRC only goes to war against its own people, not other people. Neither

Japan nor other regional countries accept this logic. Rather, the Japanese have seen belligerent Chinese policies toward Taiwan as a bellwether of how a stronger China might treat Japan. What the Japanese have seen up to now is troubling. The missile exercises China carried out to intimidate Taiwan before its presidential election in 1996 were especially bad. One PLA missile landed within forty miles of Japan's Yonaguni Island. This Chinese saber rattling was the major impetus for the revision of the guidelines for U.S.-Japan security cooperation.

Japan Perceives Aggressive Intentions—and Responds Accordingly

With China's advantages in population size and resource endowments, Japan cannot hope to match up with the Chinese military in quantitative terms. Even the downsized PLA has about ten times the manpower of Japan's armed forces. China lags behind Japan qualitatively in some areas, but China's technological sophistication is improving. The Chinese have long enjoyed total superiority over Japan in areas such as the capability to strike an adversary's territory with either nuclear or conventional weapons. Like China, Japan is heavily dependent on maritime trade, including the sea lanes that pass through the Malacca Strait and the South and East China Seas. Most of the oil that Japan uses, for example, travels this route from exporters in the Middle East. The PLA Navy buildup ostensibly undertaken to make China's supply lines more secure makes Japan feel less secure about its own supply lines. A strong Chinese military makes Japan vulnerable to the cutoff or blockade that the Chinese fear from the U.S. Navy. To Japanese worries about Chinese capabilities are added the signs of aggressive Chinese intent that Japanese see in some Chinese policies and activities. The Japanese military's main policy research organization observed in early 2011 that "China in 2010 began to take an assertive approach in pursuit of its own national interests, disregarding friction with the United States and neighboring countries." Tokyo's 2011 defense white paper broke new ground by characterizing Chinese actions as "overbearing."[8] To make matters worse, China is highly undersensitive to Japan's China-related security worries. From China's point of view, given what Japan did to China last century, anyone who accuses China of threatening Japan is being disingenuous. The Chinese see their behavior as morally justifiable and defensive. Chinese naval forays into and beyond the East China Sea stem from China's right as a large, strong country to build a large, strong navy. The Chinese would also turn the accusation of aggressiveness back on Japan by arguing that the Japanese are encroaching on (disputed) Chinese territory in the East China Sea and harbor designs on keeping Taiwan from unifying with the PRC. China appears completely unsympathetic to Japanese concerns about China's nuclear weapons, against which the Japanese have no counterbalancing capability. Any Japanese concerns, the Chinese would argue, should be assuaged by China's "no first use" policy. When Japanese Foreign Minister Okada Katsuya told Chinese Foreign Minister Yang Jiechi during a 2010 meeting that China should cut or at least not increase its stockpile of nuclear weapons, Yang reportedly became "incensed" and nearly walked out of the meeting. A *Washington Post* report added that Yang "shocked" Okada by screaming that Japanese troops had killed Yang's relatives during the Pacific War.[9]

Japanese are at least as disturbed as Americans by the speed with which Beijing is upgrading the PLA. When Beijing announced that its 2011 military budget would include yet another large increase over the previous year (in this case 13 percent), Japanese Defense Minister Maehara Seiji spoke for many of his countrymen when he said, "It is an extremely high ratio for defense spending" and "We are gravely concerned over what China has in mind for modernizing its armaments."[10]

In the first decade of the twenty-first century, increased incursions by Chinese warships into the waters near Japan have rattled the Japanese. In some of these cases, Chinese vessels did not break international law, but Japanese officials suspect the Chinese had adversarial purposes such as spying, testing the response time of the Japanese defense forces, or mapping the seafloor for future operations by Chinese submarines. In April 2010, the PLA Navy sent an unusually large force of ten ships through the East China Sea to train in the Pacific Ocean. The ships twice passed through the Ryukyu Islands and Japan's EEZ. This was lawful, since UNCLOS allows warships the right of "innocent passage" through another state's EEZ. Nevertheless, the size and course of the Chinese fleet compelled the Japanese Maritime Self-Defense Force to muster its own ships and aircraft. As Japanese warships shadowed the Chinese fleet, Chinese helicopters flew dangerously near to the Japanese ships. The Japanese government formally protested against the helicopter flyovers. A PLA spokesman parried that the Japanese ships "should not have interfered with our ships by conducting a pursuit over so many days and at such close range."[11] In other cases,

Chinese incursions violated international law. On at least two occasions, in 2004 and 2008, a Chinese submarine has passed through Japanese territorial waters submerged. International maritime law requires that foreign submarines in territorial waters must surface and fly their national flag. The incursions include Chinese aircraft as well as naval vessels. According to the Japanese Defense Ministry, during 2011 alone Japanese fighter aircraft scrambled 156 times to meet Chinese aircraft approaching Japan.

In reaction to the rise of Chinese capabilities and the perceived assertiveness of Chinese policies, Tokyo has tried to bolster its security in ways that the Chinese are prone to interpret as threatening to China. While seeking the benefits of economic cooperation with China, Tokyo is also procuring insurance against aggressive Chinese behavior through "active, if quiet, balancing against China"—paralleling China's military buildup with a complementary (but not identical) Japanese buildup, maintaining close cooperation with the United States, and seeking stronger security ties with other countries.[12] China's military policies contributed to the Japanese decision to cut ODA to China. Tokyo is already planning for the possibility that Chinese forces will try to seize Japanese-claimed islands in the East China Sea. The potential threat from China is the main reason the Japanese remain interested in the remarkably durable U.S.-Japan alliance even long after the end of the Cold War. Polls in Japan show that public support for the alliance exceeded 75 percent in the late 2000s.[13] Japan shrugged off opposition from China to join in the U.S. effort to build an anti–ballistic missile system and has been spending about $2 billion annually as part of this effort. As a start, Tokyo decided to purchase Patriot PAC-3 and SM-3 missiles from the United States. Japan has had its own spy satellites since 2003. In 2005, the Japanese Air Self-Defense Force (the Japanese Air Force) began moving some of its F-15J fighter aircraft to Okinawa to strengthen defenses against a possible Chinese air attack. The Japan Defense Agency upgraded to the cabinet-level Ministry of Defense in 2007. Japan recently bought four Boeing KC-767 tanker aircraft for in-flight refueling. This capability is controversial because it could extend the range of Japanese fighter-bombers, making it possible for Japan to attack another country. Tokyo has argued that the purpose of in-flight refueling is defensive rather than offensive: it will allow Japanese fighters to remain in the skies near Japan for longer periods.

Japan's National Defense Program Guidelines is a government report usually issued every five years that gives a broad overview of national security strategy for the near future. The latest report, published in December

2010, reveals a fundamental shift from the Cold War posture of defending against an invasion from the north (i.e., by Russia) to strengthening defense in the south—an adjustment that clearly stems from growing Chinese strength and activities in the East China Sea. The announced plans included deploying more submarines, transferring more fighter aircraft to Okinawa, and building a new radar station in the Ryukyus. The plan to increase submarine numbers from sixteen to twenty-two represented a substantial change, since Japan's submarine force had not exceeded eighteen for the previous twenty years.

To get around political constraints on the Japanese military such as the unwritten rule that the military's budget is capped at 1 percent of the national GDP, the Japanese government has expanded the size, firepower, and mandate of the Japanese Coast Guard, making it into what scholar Richard J. Samuels terms the "de facto fourth branch of the Japanese military." Since a domestic civilian ministry oversees the Coast Guard, its budget does not count against the national defense budget. The role of the Coast Guard has grown from law enforcement (such as antismuggling) to the national security mission of defending Japanese sovereignty claims over the offshore islands and their surrounding waters. Japan's Coast Guard ships are large (up to 150 meters long) and oceanworthy, they are equipped with guns that can tear up a vessel that is not armored, they can themselves stand up to small arms fire, and some carry helicopters. Under newly amended rules, Japanese Coast Guard ships have the authority to shoot first under certain circumstances, while Japanese Navy warships must wait until they are fired on before they can shoot. The Coast Guard ships are not naval warships in disguise. They don't have several key capabilities that define modern frigates and destroyers, such as antiship missiles, antisubmarine warfare equipment, and robust antiaircraft defenses. They make it possible, however, for Japanese Navy ships to concentrate on missions other than patrolling Japanese-claimed waters. Using Coast Guard vessels to confront Chinese and other foreign ships is also less provocative and less likely to create an escalation than using naval warships. This is the same reason the Chinese employ large and well-armed Fisheries Enforcement ships in disputed waters.

Japan has courted the other major regional democracies. Japanese international affairs scholar Soeya Yoshihide, a member of the advisory group to the Japanese Foreign Ministry, says Tokyo's increasing interest in developing security cooperation with other states in the region "is a recent development and the rise of China is a driving force."[14] Late 2000s Japanese prime ministers Abe and Aso spoke of closer security cooperation within a "concert of democracies" and an "arc of freedom," which obviously excluded China. This yielded a joint military exercise including Japan, the United States, Australia, and India (plus Singapore) in the Bay of Bengal in 2007. Bilateral security dialogues began with Australia in 2005. In March 2007, Japan and Australia announced an agreement to expand bilateral defense cooperation. Their Joint Declaration on Security Cooperation notes that the two countries have "shared security interests" and provides for exchanges and cooperative activities. This was far from a formal military alliance, but it was the first agreement of its kind between postwar Japan and a country other than the United States. Although the agreement does not mention China, the Chinese response was that it represented the first step in building an Asian version of the U.S.-Europe NATO alliance and was highly threatening to China. Tokyo reached a similar agreement with India a few months later. Japan has tried to engage Russia in discrete balancing against China, although this effort has met little success because of political obstacles such as the dispute between Tokyo and Moscow over ownership of the southern Kuril Islands.

A New Cold War?

If present trends continue, China's seemingly limitless potential, combined with its rapid rate of economic and technological growth, will likely raise China to a predominant position in the region. Under these circumstances, would Tokyo give up balancing against China and seek instead to accommodate China? In the past, modern Japan mostly aligned itself with the dominant powers—the Anglo-American camp from the Meiji Restoration until the Pacific War, and the United States after the war. The only exception was when Tokyo perceived that the international system had broken down as a result of the global economic crisis of the 1930s. Establishing their own regional hegemony through military conquest proved catastrophic for the Japanese. This lesson was seared into the national psyche by the extensive U.S. bombing of cities in the Japanese home islands during the war. Perhaps it would be harder for the Japanese to accommodate the dominant power if that country is historical rival China rather than Britain or the United States. On the other hand, younger generations of Japanese tend to be less attached to the United States and less negative toward both China and South Korea.

While appeasement of China cannot be ruled out, today it is not part of the mainstream strategic debate among Japanese about their country's future. At present, only small minorities advocate either appeasement or the other extreme alternative, which is openly attempting to contain China. Most Japanese accept the premise that Japan should maintain strong economic cooperation with China. Within this mainstream, the most important debate is over the security policy that should accompany economic engagement with China. The "soft" view is that the alliance with the United States is still essential and that the Japanese government should reinterpret its constitution to allow Japan to participate in collective defense if this is necessary to preserve the alliance. The "hard" view goes further, arguing that Tokyo should develop defense cooperation with additional partners in the region, expand Japan's own military capabilities, and welcome U.S. nuclear weapons or at least nuclear-powered U.S. Navy ships in Japan. The latter point is controversial because one of the Japanese government's "Three Non-Nuclear Principles" is to forbid the introduction of nuclear weapons into Japanese territory. Many Japanese also oppose the presence of nuclear-powered American warships. Some observers argue that if the alliance with the United States became inadequate or unavailable as a protection against China, the next most likely alternative would not be accommodation but rather full Japanese rearmament and a cold war with China. Funabashi Yoichi, one of Japan's most authoritative commentators on foreign affairs, has been an advocate of constructive Japan-China relations. Reacting to the 2010 Senkakus rare-earths episode, however, Funabashi wrote, "If China continues to act as it has, we Japanese will be prepared to engage in a long, long struggle with China. . . . Japan would be prepared to deal with China with bitter resolve tinged with a form of resignation."[15]

Chapter Six

PRESSURE ON CHINA'S NEIGHBORS

China's neighbors feel the effects of the rise of China most directly and heavily. All see opportunities to benefit economically from China's growth, but they also face the prospect of increasing vulnerability to political domination by China. If the focus is limited to security, we can say that none of these countries is better off with China as a military great power. A stronger China intensifies what Indians perceive as a PRC effort to contain India by arming India's nemesis Pakistan, seeking influence with other South Asian governments, demanding Indian submission to Chinese claims over disputed territory, and building up a PLAN presence in the Indian Ocean. A relatively more powerful China bodes ill for Vietnam's attempts to avoid Chinese domination and is particularly bad news for Vietnam's claims over disputed South China Sea territory. China's increasing economic, political, and military heft in the region is closing the space for Russia's desired reemergence as a great power and may eventually rekindle traditionally serious Sino-Russian tensions. Although China represents opportunity as well as potential danger to South Korea, since the turn of the century, a rising China likely offers Korea fewer benefits and more strategic challenges than Koreans have hoped. These challenges will likely include pressure to end the alliance with the United States and interference with Seoul's plans for reintegration with North Korea. Burma seeks to escape from its overdependence on China, but this will be increasingly difficult with the growth of the PRC's power combined with Beijing's interest in controlling Burmese affairs.

India

India and China are similar not only in that both are large, populous, and rapidly developing countries, but they are also both great civilizations. Their empires were largely separated during premodern times by the natural barriers between them formed by Tibet and the Himalayan Mountains. Historically, India had influence that reached from Central Asia through the subcontinent and into Southeast Asia. Their interactions became more intense during the postwar era with Indian independence and the establishment of the People's Republic of China. China and India began a new era in their relationship in the 1950s with a celebration of their purported brotherhood. Newly independent India under Prime Minister Jawaharlal Nehru and the newly revolutionized PRC saw themselves as coauthors of an international system reoriented toward fair treatment of the developing countries. At the same time, however, the PRC government moved to solidify Chinese control of territories along the Indian frontier, including Tibet. Sino-Indian cordiality quickly evaporated. When the Dalai Lama fled Tibet amid a doomed uprising against Beijing's rule, India allowed him and his followers to establish a Tibetan government in exile at Dharamsala. In 1959, Nehru reflected on the birth of the PRC ten years earlier. He said that considering China's large population and drive toward industrialization, "taken also with the fact of China's somewhat inherent tendency to be expansionist when she is stronger, we realized the danger to India."[1]

That danger emerged early and prominently in disputes over the lengthy Sino-Indian border. The dispute includes two chunks of territory that are the size of small provinces: Aksai Chin, occupied by China but claimed by India; and Arunachal Pradesh (or "South Tibet" to the Chinese), occupied by India but claimed by China. In 1962, skirmishes in some disputed sections of the China-India border led to an organized Chinese incursion. PLA troops pushed out Indian forces before declaring a ceasefire and then unilaterally withdrawing. Although the fighting did not settle the border dispute, both sides saw the short war as a victory for China and a humiliation for India. It left Indians with deep animosity, distrust, and a desire for revenge toward the Chinese. For a generation after the war, bilateral relations remained tense. The two countries did not restore diplomatic relations until 1976.

Negotiations over the disputed border have dragged on for over three decades. It remains an obstacle to improved relations as well as a potential powder keg. Both countries have in recent years increased the pressure in the dispute over Arunachal Pradesh. Beijing tried to block India from getting a $2.9 billion loan from the Asian Development Bank on the grounds that India would use part of it to build water projects in the disputed province. India accuses the Chinese of hundreds of border violations. The Indian government moved additional troops into Arunachal despite warnings from Beijing that this would worsen bilateral tensions.

Beijing moved toward a rapprochement with India (as well as with other states in the region) in the 1990s. China took Pakistan's side less frequently than previously in political disagreements between India and Pakistan. The Chinese offered additional concessions to improve relations with India from 2000 to early 2006 in an effort to lure India away from cooperating with the United States in the encirclement of China. Beijing expanded India-China military ties, recognized Sikkim as part of India, and voiced support for India becoming a permanent member of the UN Security Council. India, however, continued to move closer to Washington with the "New Framework for the US-India Defense Relationship" and the U.S.-India nuclear cooperation agreement. India also remained unsatisfied with China's position on the issue of disputed territory.

China was unsatisfied as well and shifted to a tougher policy to show displeasure with India (while simultaneously improving relations with Japan). Beijing became less compromising with India on the border issue. In 2006–2008, the PRC government allowed Chinese media to indulge in a campaign of sharp rhetoric against India, including criticism of India's perceived hostility toward China, denigration of India's aspirations to be a great power comparable to China, and threats to teach India another lesson like the one in 1962. The perception among the Chinese public of India as an enemy soared accordingly. The Indian media was quick to respond with a flood of reports about a heightened Chinese threat. The two countries sounded like they were indeed on the verge of another war. The analyst Mohan Malik believes the Chinese India-bashing campaign reflects PRC insecurity over Tibet and over Indian cooperation with other countries to balance against China.[2] This episode was a sobering reminder of how quickly the bottom could drop out of the Sino-India relationship.

China is India's top trading partner. Many observers have touted the potential of deep economic cooperation that would yield an amalgamated "Chindia" by, for example, joining India's computer software expertise with China's prodigious hardware manufacturing capacity. The problem with this vision is that China aims to become a world leader in software and is likely to achieve this goal before becoming dependent on a partnership with Indian technicians. India-China trade has risen rapidly in recent years to reach a modest level (equivalent to the amount of trade between China and Brazil, but only about a quarter of the trade between China and South Korea). The nature of this trade, however, does not suggest a partnership of equals: India mainly exports raw materials to China while mostly buying manufactured products from China. India suffers a large trade deficit with China and is uncomfortable with heavy reliance on Chinese imports. Competition between China and India for energy supplies is already apparent and likely to grow. In short, the bilateral economic relationship does not provide much in the way of a "safety net" to prevent a conflict over strategic disputes.

While superficially China and India engage in talks and even make agreements to reduce tensions and build trust, the sources of distrust and bilateral tensions persist or even increase. For example, although Beijing and New Delhi have agreed to reduce troop numbers along their border, both countries are busy improving the military infrastructure in these areas and replacing conventional troops with elite soldiers or units with specialty training such as in mountain warfare.

Beijing attempts to carry out the same policy toward India that the Chinese indignantly accuse the United States of implementing against China: containment. India's sense of encirclement grows along with the rise of relative Chinese capabilities because Chinese encirclement is more feasible and threatening from India's point of view as China grows stronger. A militarily robust, politically influential, and economically bulked-up China has more powerful tools with which to contain India, including a larger PLA Navy presence in the Indian Ocean, trade and investment with the other states on India's borders, military support for India's nemesis Pakistan, and diplomatic pressure on India's potential allies. Within the shadow of China's rise, India is rising as well. Chinese opposition is a potential obstacle to India's aspirations. In the minds of India's top strategic planners, China has become the primary adversary. The PRC replaces Pakistan, which India increasingly sees as a short-term manageable threat, in contrast to China. India responds to perceived Chinese encirclement with a policy of "countercontainment."[3] In short, the rise of China makes China's containment of India more threatening to India; consequently, India's perception of China as an adversary increases, and India's countercontainment becomes more vigorous, stiffening China's posture toward India.

Containment and Countercontainment

Beijing believes that outside of its immediate subregion of South Asia, India is a minor-league country. Chinese have often disparaged India's aspirations to become a great power as delusional. The Chinese believe India lacks China's national power and international influence. Although international observers often group together or compare China and India as two large and populous rising powers, Chinese find this demeaning and prefer to compare their country with the United States. Chinese see evidence of their superiority in their defeat of India in the 1962 war and in China's faster economic development during the post-Mao reform era. India underwent major economic reforms of its own, but over a decade later than China and with less spectacular results. Chinese have a much larger average annual income than Indians, and the Chinese economy is more than double the size of India's. Furthermore, Chinese view India's democratic political system and the ethnic, social, and religious cleavages within the Indian polity as serious obstacles to efficient national development.

Although the Chinese do not take India seriously as a potential great power, India gets Chinese attention as a strategic troublemaker. Beijing is sensitive and highly adverse to India cooperating with other countries to try to constrain China. PRC observers see the strengthening of Indian relationships with Southeast Asian countries within this context. Chinese analysts agree that the United States wants to partner with India in the containment of China, although many believe Washington will not succeed because of India's deep historical aversion to becoming a U.S. ally. The Chinese think India is prone to overplaying this card by expecting concessions from China (on the border negotiations or support for Pakistan, for example) under the threat of India joining an anti-China alliance with the United States or Japan.

China dislikes India's increasing naval strength in the Indian Ocean because this poses a challenge to China's objective of securing Chinese use of the Indian Ocean sea lanes. India's harboring of Tibetan exiles and alleged support for Tibetan independence activism is a major bilateral sore point. India seemed to command greater regard from the Chinese after India's 1998 nuclear weapons tests, although the Indian government angered China by saying the PRC's nuclear arsenal was the reason India acquired nuclear weapons.

China employs a collection of tactics at multiple levels to limit India's external influence. Beijing has tried hard to reduce India's profile in international organizations if not exclude India altogether. Indians blame China for trying to impede Indian membership in important organizations such as the ASEAN Regional Forum, the Shanghai Cooperation Organization, and Asia-Pacific Economic Cooperation (APEC). Although the Chinese government publicly pledged to support India's bid for a permanent seat on the UN Security Council in 2005, this was part of a double game: Beijing also worked behind the scenes to ensure this would not happen.

More directly threatening to New Delhi, Beijing has attempted to replace Indian with Chinese influence in the territory surrounding India. The PRC's military occupation of Tibet in 1950 was an unwelcome expansion of Chinese control over an area that in recent history had been under heavy Indian influence. In Burma, China took advantage of the international outcry over the Burmese military's suppression of the democratic uprising in 1988. India, traditionally close with Burma (which was previously a province of India), joined in the condemnation of Burma's ruling military junta. In contrast, China moved in to cultivate a relationship with the isolated junta by selling arms and investing in the extraction of Burma's natural gas. China is the main arms supplier not only to Burma but also to Pakistan, Nepal, Bangladesh, and Sri Lanka, as well as to insurgent groups in northeast India. In India's view, even the ostensibly economics-driven Chinese investments in new infrastructure linking China with India's neighbors have the strategic purpose of containing India by extending China's influence to India's doorstep.

China's close relationship with India's longtime enemy and neighbor Pakistan is the clearest example of Chinese containment. During a visit to China in 2005, Pakistani President Pervez Musharraf said the China-Pakistan relationship was "deeper than the oceans and higher than the mountains."[4] The PRC has indeed been a consistent, and sometimes sole, supporter of Pakistan since the 1962 Sino-Indian border war. China gave military support (but no soldiers) to Pakistan in its 1965 and 1971 wars with India. After the military coup d'état in Islamabad in 1999, Chinese officials praised the military government for improving Pakistan's economic performance. China has supplied Pakistan with both nuclear and missile technology as well as with a wide range of conventional arms. Beijing blamed India's 1998 nuclear test for Pakistan's subsequent deployment of nuclear weapons. The two countries share intelligence about India's military. When U.S.-India relations were improving during the Bush administration, China and Pakistan countered in early 2006 with a bilateral Treaty of Friendship, Cooperation, and Good Neighborly Relations. When the United States threatened to cut financial aid for Pakistan's antiterrorist military campaign during the downturn in U.S.-Pakistan relations in 2011, some Pakistanis said they could turn to their friend China instead.

China's recent approach to official comments on India-Pakistan disputes, especially since both countries obtained nuclear weapons, has moved from solidarity with Islamabad to a more balanced stance. Beijing did not endorse Pakistan's military action in Kargil in 1999 and has stopped echoing the Pakistani call for a plebiscite in Kashmir. Nevertheless, the two countries continue to uphold an unofficial alliance. Pakistan reciprocates Chinese support by keeping up the positive example of a Chinese relationship with a Muslim country to enhance China's image in the Muslim world. Islamabad also promises to crack down on Islamist militants who train anti-PRC Uighurs and kill Chinese workers in Pakistan, even though this can be hard for the Pakistani government to deliver because it antagonizes communities within Pakistan. The main basis of their relationship, however, is their shared hostility toward India. Chinese support strengthens Pakistan in its struggle with a much larger enemy. For the Chinese, this is a way of harassing India by proxy. Chinese arms sales and political support to Pakistan sustain a conflict that India might otherwise be able to win decisively. The effect is to force India to expend much of its attention and resources within its immediate neighborhood, weakening India's ability to play a major strategic role outside South Asia. Indians believe the Pakistan threat would be greatly diminished without Chinese assistance to Islamabad. The China-Pakistan relationship also presents India with the possible problem of a two-front war if a conflict breaks out between India and either of the other two.

China has a strong interest in limiting Indian strategic cooperation with countries outside South Asia. This could be interpreted as an offensive policy by Beijing: holding India down and restricting its freedom of action. It could also be interpreted as a defensive Chinese policy stemming from Beijing's own fear of encirclement. Sometimes Beijing sends hostile signals to India to punish New Delhi for getting too close to the United

States or another potential Chinese adversary. This, however, is something of a catch-22 for the Chinese. They risk accelerating the same anti-China cooperation they want to preclude, because a perceived rise in hostility from China increases support within India for defense partnerships with the other major democracies.

India attempts to counter what it perceives as Chinese encirclement by marshalling its own strength and by seeking defense cooperation with other states. India doubled its defense spending during the first decade of the twenty-first century. New Delhi recently announced a major military modernization program that will include expensive acquisitions of new military platforms such as advanced aircraft and aircraft carriers. The number of Indian Navy ships will increase by 25 percent. In 2010 India announced an unprecedented upgrade of its forces along the border with China and the assignment of a squadron of aircraft to the Assam region adjacent to the disputed area of Arunachal Pradesh. In mid-2011 India's air force began a major reorganization of its forces to shift emphasis away from Pakistan and toward countering the capabilities of an improved PLA Air Force. In April 2012 India successfully tested a new missile capable of carrying a one-ton nuclear warhead to any city in China. These adjustments will not necessarily bring the Indians a sense of security anytime soon, and indeed they may fall further behind the PLA over time. India's defense industries suffer deep structural problems and have underperformed for decades. An additional problem is efforts by India's civilian government to limit the influence of the armed forces because of fear of a military coup d'état. Indian's forces have struggled in conflicts with smaller opponents such as Pakistan, the "Tamil Tigers" of Sri Lanka, and various domestic insurgent groups.

Clear upgrades are visible in Indian strategic cooperation with other countries that share India's apprehension about rising Chinese strength. This decade has seen New Delhi seek a deeper and broader relationship with the United States after a long period of reticence. The Indians have taken this path despite PRC attempts to both woo and coerce them. A critical mass of the Indian elite has accepted the idea that India needs a strategic partnership with the United States to offset China's growing power. The George W. Bush administration talked up the potential of such a partnership. Washington moved from economic sanctions against India in 1998 in retaliation for India's nuclear weapons program to significant defense cooperation and even an offer of partnership on nuclear energy less than a decade later. Not surprisingly, China criticized this deal as indicative of an American double standard on nuclear nonproliferation (i.e., it's okay for countries friendly to the United States such as Israel and India but not for countries such as Iran and North Korea). The bilateral 2005 defense agreement opened the way for U.S. weapons technology transfers to India, joint training, and Indian participation in the anti–ballistic missile defense program. The United States assented to Israel selling Phalcon AWACs aircraft to India after blocking a similar proposed sale to China in 2000. Whether this partnership can meet high expectations is questionable. India has a proud tradition of nonalignment and many Indians remain wary of closely cooperating with Washington. During the Obama administration, India opposed U.S. positions on climate change and international trade, resisted implementing a proposed deal for U.S.-Indian cooperation on nuclear energy, and passed on an opportunity to buy U.S. warplanes.

Prominent Indians have recommended stronger defense cooperation with Japan, Vietnam, and Taiwan to counter China's strength. India held its first joint naval exercise with Japan in 2004. India and Australia agreed in 2006 to pursue cooperation in training, military-related research, and maritime security. New Delhi cooperates with Mongolia to monitor Chinese military activities, and the two countries have held several joint military exercises. In an attempt to impede Chinese dominance of the South China Sea, India has helped strengthen Vietnam's armed forces by providing training, maintenance and repair, discounted weapons sales, and spare parts for military equipment. In recent years New Delhi has tried to undermine China's (historically recent) preeminent position of influence in Burma. India has supplied weapons and other military aid to the Burmese junta, sent in engineers to help rebuild Burma's infrastructure, and offered loans with low interest rates. Large-scale demonstrations led to another antidemocracy crackdown by the junta in 2007. This time India's government stayed relatively quiet. Burma seemingly welcomes the opportunity to reduce its dependence on China. India has even developed closer defense ties with the small Indian Ocean countries of the Maldives and Seychelles to counter China's activities in the Indian Ocean.

Worsening Flashpoints

An issue related to China-India border tensions is the problem of fresh water scarcity. India and China are, respectively, the world's largest and second-largest consumers of fresh water. Both will face severe water shortages in the near future. According to an authoritative 2009 report, India will have a 50 percent shortfall between the water it needs and the water that is available by the year 2030. China will have a 25 percent shortfall.[5] As PRC deputy prime minister in 1999, Wen Jiabao warned that water shortages threatened "the survival of the Chinese nation."[6] China has the advantage of ten of Asia's major rivers originating in the Tibetan plateau. China's problem is that the southern part of the country has too much water (chronic flooding), while the arid north, home to half of the population, has too little. This imbalance, combined with a desperate need for hydroelectric power, has led China to build more large dams than any other country.

This has important consequences for China's neighbors, including India. The Yarlung Tsangpo (Yalu Zangbu) River flows across southern Tibet before making a hairpin turn and crossing into India, where it is known as the Brahmaputra River. Since at least 1990 the Chinese have considered damming or diverting water from the Tsangpo. In the late 2000s a project to divert the waters of the Tsangpo seemed imminent. Scientists pointed out that this would threaten the livelihoods of millions of people in India and Bangladesh by causing higher salinity levels, increased silting, and losses of irrigation and fishing for the inhabitants downstream. "If Beijing goes ahead with the Tsangpo project it would practically mean a declaration of war against South Asia," said one observer.[7] The PRC government eventually dropped this project because of an assessment that existing dams would not be able to cope with the water diverted from the Tsangpo. Instead, the Chinese changed the project to a hydroelectric dam across the river that would not divert or store its waters. Addressing the near-panic in India, Chinese officials promised to be responsible and to consider the effects of Chinese projects on downriver countries. Indian commentators expressed distrust toward Beijing and dismay that the Chinese had found a new means of constraining India's development. Some analysts anticipate a future military conflict between China and India over water resources. A "water war" can perhaps be dismissed as an extreme scenario, but continued population growth (until about 2030 in China and longer in India), the thirst in both countries for more resources as part of their economic development, and the possibility of reduced river flows because of climate change will magnify the bilateral tensions stemming from the water shortage issue.

India and China are engaged in a quiet naval arms race in the Indian Ocean. Indians believe it is, as the name suggests, *their* ocean. They are sensitive and strongly averse to the increasing PLA Navy forays into the Indian Ocean. They often accuse the Chinese of seeking to turn it into a "Chinese lake." But China, as well, has an interest in the Indian Ocean because much of China's oil imports pass through it. Thus the Indian Ocean is becoming another arena for Sino-Indian territorial friction.

Fears of Chinese encroachment into the Indian Ocean have led to the allegation that the PRC is pursuing a "string of pearls" strategy. Some analysts understand the "pearls" to be de facto Chinese military bases: ports, airfields, or surveillance posts in the Indian Ocean region to which the Chinese military has access either because the Chinese built the facilities or because Beijing has curried favor with the host government. Others describe the "pearls" more broadly to include dual-use or nonmilitary infrastructure such as pipelines and important highways. The "pearls" form a "string" because they line the Indian Ocean littoral on both sides of India, reinforcing the idea that the PRC is boxing India in.

China has indeed built or improved ports in Pakistan, Burma, Bangladesh, Sri Lanka, Madagascar, the Maldives, and the Seychelles. Some strategists, however, have concluded that the "string of pearls" notion is a myth. In their view, China's assistance to governments building port facilities along the Indian Ocean is based on economic rather than strategic concerns. The Chinese intend for these facilities to expedite the delivery of energy imports to China. These will be commercial ports rather than military bases, and the PLA is not involved in their development. While some analysts assert that the Chinese have built military listening posts on islands owned by Burma, others dispute that claim. Furthermore, some interpretations of the "string of pearls" are less nefarious than the alleged PRC plan to strangle India. The Chinese might be acting defensively. They want to monitor possible threats to their key oceanic supply lines and feel compelled to develop alternative delivery routes that reduce their vulnerability to a naval blockade at a key choke point. Beyond the imperatives of commerce and reducing the risks to energy supplies, the various Chinese activities along the Indian Ocean may not be parts of an explicit strategy dictated by the central government. If they are, the driver may be a soft-power strategy rather than a military-power strategy: not an attempt to lay the groundwork for domination or colonization but rather to buy regional goodwill, thereby strengthening Chinese prestige and undercutting interest in joining a campaign to contain China. It is not clear how militarily useful these "pearls" would be in a time of conflict. The countries hosting the ports might think twice about antagonizing

China's adversary by welcoming Chinese warships. And even with the use of ports and intelligence-collection stations in the Indian Ocean, the PLA Navy would be at a massive disadvantage in the Persian Gulf relative to the navies of the United States and other major Western countries.

The most prominent of the "pearls" is the port at Gwadar, Pakistan. Relatively deep, the port can accommodate the largest classes of ships. The Chinese helped build a commercial port at Gwadar that is now operated by a Singapore state-owned company. China also plans to build a pipeline with a terminal at Gwadar that will carry oil brought in by ships from Africa and the Middle East to China's Xinjiang province, bypassing the sea lane through the Strait of Malacca. Many media reports up to 2011 said the Chinese were building a base at Gwadar for the Pakistani Navy. Some observers were prematurely describing it as a Chinese naval base and even a "Chinese Gibraltar" that would allow the PLA Navy to maintain a presence near the Persian Gulf. The most convincing assessments, however, anticipated Gwadar would be a primarily Pakistani base at which Chinese warships could dock and resupply. Development of the port at Gwadar is of great interest to the Pakistani government as an alternative to Karachi, which has processed up to 90 percent of the shipping trade into and out of Pakistan but is vulnerable to blockade because it is close to India.

While Chinese intentions regarding Gwadar and the other "pearls" are debatable, most Indian observers fall into the group that believes Chinese activity along the Indian Ocean is largely in the service of Chinese military and strategic goals and directly impinges upon India's security. China and India are simultaneously beefing up their respective capabilities to project naval power into the Indian Ocean. China does not recognize this sea as an Indian preserve. India does not accept China establishing a strong or permanent naval force there. The situation is ripe for incidents at sea and for each side to interpret the other's actions as illegitimate and threatening. In January 2009, for example, a tense confrontation reportedly occurred when an Indian submarine shadowed two Chinese destroyers passing through the Indian Ocean en route to the waters off Somalia for antipiracy duty. During this incident, the Chinese dispatched a helicopter armed with antisubmarine torpedoes and forced the submarine to the surface. It was ironic and ominous that such an incident could result from a Chinese military operation that the international community saw as constructive. Regardless of the PLA's ostensible mission, it may be difficult for the Indians to see Chinese warships in the Indian Ocean with anything but suspicion and hostility.

Vietnam

Historically, the China-Vietnam relationship is a story of Vietnam trying to avoid domination. Vietnam has been more successful when China is relatively weak. Otherwise, the Vietnamese have been willing to accommodate China up to a point but have resisted when China encroaches too closely on Vietnam's independence.

From ancient times, China weighed heavily on Vietnam's world. On one hand, Chinese culture strongly influenced Vietnamese civilization. On the other hand, the struggle against Chinese control shaped Vietnam's national identity. Vietnam's methods of managing China ranged from outright warfare to showing deference and paying tribute. China ruled Vietnam during most of the first millennium. After finally breaking out of annexation by China, Vietnam tried to manage the threat of Chinese dominance by accepting a tributary relationship that acknowledged China's regional leadership. China tried unsuccessfully to reconquer Vietnam three more times. Nevertheless, Vietnam repeatedly returned to tributary status, seeing this as its best security strategy. When the relationship was stable and China allowed Vietnamese autonomy, Vietnam could turn its attention to expansion of its political control over peoples to the south. The French colonization of Vietnam beginning in the late 1800s coincided with Western intrusion into China, ended Vietnam's status as a tributary of China, and made the Vietnamese and Chinese anti-imperialist comrades. Post–Pacific War communist revolutions in both countries deepened the bond. Beijing quickly recognized the new Democratic Republic of Vietnam (DRV) regime in the northern half of the country and supported Ho Chi Minh's campaign to conquer the French- and U.S.-supported governments in the south. Equipment, training, intelligence, and advice from the PRC were crucial to the DRV's decisive victory over the French at Dien Bien Phu in 1954. When the Americans took up the fight to defend the South Vietnamese regime and the Soviets countered by supplying the DRV with heavy weapons, the Chinese were obliged to continue aiding Hanoi to retain their influence, even though Beijing feared being dragged into another war with the United

States (the Korean War had ended only a few years earlier). Dependent on Chinese assistance, Vietnam felt the need to be deferential toward Beijing. Hanoi did not, for example, challenge China's claims to islands in the South China Sea. Relations between North Vietnam and China became strained, however, because of Hanoi's relationship with China's rival the USSR, because the Hanoi government disapproved of China's hard-left ideological turn that led to the chaos of the Cultural Revolution, and because Hanoi suspected that China's hidden agenda was to prevent the reunification of Vietnam.

The Vietnam War was sustaining the Vietnam-China relationship. With the end of the war and the reunification of Vietnam under the Hanoi regime, the relationship collapsed. The Vietnamese government suspected that its ethnic Chinese population might cooperate with the PRC and even sabotage the Vietnamese economy under orders from Beijing. Hanoi implemented policies that harassed Vietnam's ethnic Chinese and encouraged them to leave the country. This infuriated Beijing, which terminated economic assistance to Vietnam. Growing bilateral tensions culminated in the border war of 1979. The immediate cause was Vietnam's invasion of its neighbor Cambodia in 1978 to oust the murderous and ultraradical Khmer Rouge regime, which Beijing supported as part of a strategy to keep Vietnam from dominating Indochina. The deeper issue was that Vietnam, now unified and confident after its victory in the long war against the French, American, and South Vietnamese forces, believed it could finally stand up to China, perceived as treacherous, in defense of its own interests. Beijing, on the other hand, expected Vietnam to show continued deference and gratitude for Chinese aid. Instead, the Chinese perceived that Vietnam was cooperating with the Soviet strategy of trying to seal off the region from Chinese influence.[8]

From this, its lowest point in the modern era, the relationship gradually recovered. Vietnam's new policy of economic modernization contributed to a withdrawal of Vietnamese forces from Cambodia in 1989, without which a rapprochement with China was not possible. Russia stopped offering beneficial trade terms. Vietnam began to see increased trade with southern China as essential. Europe's abandonment of communism gave the Chinese and Vietnamese ruling parties a sense of increased solidarity. China was on a campaign to lower tensions with countries throughout the region. The two countries restored normal diplomatic relations in 1991. When Vietnam joined the Association of Southeast Asian Nations in 1995, Hanoi insisted this was not aimed at China (although undoubtedly it partly was).

After a period of Western (and briefly Japanese) regional preeminence that disrupted the age-old pattern of Sino-Vietnam relations, China's rise has led to the reemergence of Vietnam's historical strategy of bending to Chinese power but not breaking. This involves Hanoi acknowledging Chinese hegemony, making significant sacrifices to accommodate Chinese interests and to avoid offending China, and publicly affirming enthusiasm for cordial Sino-Vietnam relations, and this despite deep suspicion and hostility toward China among the Vietnamese mass public and many elites. Vietnamese leaders try to keep tight control over anti-China sentiment because in many areas they value cooperation with China. For example, Hanoi jails some Vietnamese nationalists who criticize the government for not being tough enough toward China.

The increase of China's power relative to Vietnam leads China to expect greater deference from Hanoi. Instead, the Chinese see that Vietnam discreetly courts an American military presence in the region as a balance to Chinese power. Furthermore, on certain fundamental interests, such as the maritime territorial dispute, Hanoi digs in its heels and signals a determination to avoid outright Chinese domination. Dissatisfied with Vietnam's incomplete accommodation, Beijing pressures Hanoi to meet more fully China's expectations, and Hanoi makes a stand against that pressure, resulting in an increase in bilateral tensions.

As with other neighbors of the PRC, the rise of China makes Vietnam desirous of an American insurance policy. The fact that Vietnam, which recently fought a war against the United States and is aware of American hostility toward socialist one-party authoritarian regimes, wants America to wield strategic influence in the region says much about Hanoi's view of China. Since normalizing relations with the United States in 1995, Vietnam has played a delicate game of quietly building a military relationship with America at a pace that would not draw serious Chinese objection. A visit to Vietnam by the U.S. secretary of defense was postponed twice during the 1990s, eventually occurring in 2000. In 2001, Hanoi cancelled at the last minute a preplanned visit by Admiral Dennis Blair, the commander of U.S. forces in the Pacific, saying the government was too busy to host him. The analyst Ian Storey predicts that Vietnam will never enter into a close strategic partnership with Washington because of the aversion to antagonizing

Beijing, because some Vietnamese elites still distrust the United States, and because recent history has made Vietnam wary of depending too heavily on one country for protection.

Since it wants the United States to balance against China but does not want to be seen by China as joining with the United States in this balancing effort, Hanoi's main strategy is an indirect one: encouraging the United States to do more.[9] Vietnam sent a subtle signal that it welcomes a U.S. naval presence in the South China Sea by hosting port calls by U.S. Navy vessels beginning in 2003. Hanoi sent a slightly stronger signal by participating in a "fly out" of Vietnamese visitors to a U.S. aircraft carrier off Vietnam's coast in 2009. The Chinese understand what is happening and express their displeasure. "Vietnam is the major advocate of inviting the U.S. into the South China Sea as a 'balance,'" said one PRC newspaper. "Vietnam has been trapped in an unrealistic belief that as long as the U.S. balances out the South China Sea issue, it can openly challenge China's sovereignty, and walk away with huge gains."[10] Vietnam has not participated in military exercises with the United States. The closest U.S.-Vietnamese military cooperation to date took place when the U.S. destroyer *John S. McCain* made a port call in Da Nang in 2010. According to the U.S. Navy, the *McCain*'s crew hosted Vietnamese Navy personnel for "shipboard damage control and search and rescue demonstrations, as well as exchanges in culinary arts."[11] The Chinese apparently felt that the swapping of recipes between U.S. and Vietnamese naval cooks crossed the line; a *People's Daily* editorial by Li Hongmei warned, "It is advisable for Vietnam to give up the illusion it can do what it likes in the South China Sea under the protection of the U.S. Navy."[12]

If welcoming a balancing U.S. presence is one of the areas in which Hanoi is willing to brave a certain amount of Chinese disapproval, the South China Sea territorial dispute is an area where the Vietnamese openly defy the PRC.

South China Sea: Rising China Versus Defiant Vietnam

Several territorial disputes complicated attempts by China and Vietnam to rehabilitate their relationship after the 1979 war. The disagreement over the Sino-Vietnam land border was settled in the late 2000s. The disputes over maritime boundaries, however, persist. The Tonkin Gulf is formed by the coast of northern Vietnam on the west side and by China's Leizhou Peninsula and Hainan Island on the east. Although both sides accepted a division of the waters in the Gulf of Tonkin in 2004, incidents in the gulf still occur. On one occasion in 2005, Chinese patrol vessels fired on Vietnamese fishing boat crewmen, killing nine.

Prior to Vietnamese reunification, South Vietnamese troops garrisoned some of the Paracel Islands. Both Vietnam and China claimed the islands, but Hanoi kept quiet about the dispute to avoid straining its relationship with Beijing. Shortly before the end of the war between North and South Vietnam, after the American forces had pulled out and it was clear Hanoi would win, the Chinese took the opportunity to seize the entire Paracels group. After unification, Vietnam openly claimed sovereignty over the Paracels despite the Chinese occupation. Vietnam regularly protests Chinese moves to develop tourism and to prospect for resources in the Paracels.

Since 1999, China has unilaterally declared and tried to enforce a ban on fishing for several weeks in the northern part of the South China Sea, ostensibly to give fish populations a chance to recover from overfishing. Vietnam refuses to recognize the ban, resulting in countless confrontations between Vietnamese fishing boats and Chinese patrol vessels. Chinese patrol ships arrest hundreds of Vietnamese fishermen every year and sometimes detain them for several weeks.

In Beijing's view, Vietnam has escalated the dispute by expelling Chinese fishing boats and unilaterally taking steps to extract resources from disputed areas. China also blames Vietnam for "internationalizing" the South China Sea dispute in 2010 while Vietnam occupied the rotating chairmanship of ASEAN. Hanoi did this by successfully encouraging Washington to state its interest that the South China Sea disputes be resolved without coercion, multilaterally, and on the basis of international law—all direct or implicit criticisms of Chinese positions. Even if the Chinese believe their actions are defensive and reactive, the rise of China has stoked Sino-Vietnamese South China Sea tensions in two ways. First, China's claims to ownership of waters that are much closer to Vietnam than to China are a legacy of the Middle Kingdom's preeminence in the region during premodern times. Beijing's attempt to force its uncompromised will upon the Vietnamese in a question of disputed territory reflects a Chinese expectation that with the rise of China's relative power, Vietnam will assume a deferential posture as in centuries past. Second, increased PRC naval power-projection capabilities—partly through proxies such as quasi-military patrol vessels and occasionally fishing boats—have made possible the specific acts that comprise the rise in tensions in the South China Sea.

Despite the buildup in Chinese naval power, Hanoi shows no signs of backing down. The Vietnamese public insists the government protect what the Vietnamese claim as national territory and resources. In recent years, Vietnam has demonstrated an increased willingness to assert its interests in the South China Sea and to criticize China over this issue. Vietnam's government plans to rely even more heavily on fishing and the harvesting of offshore energy resources in the country's economic development over the next decade. Hanoi has accelerated the modernization of its military forces that might be involved in defending its South China Sea claims, including the purchase of frigates, SU-30 jet fighter aircraft, and *Kilo*-class submarines from Russia.

A series of events in May and June 2011 suggested a decision by Beijing to signal a Chinese willingness to move closer to using force in defense of China's claims (and in disregard of Vietnam's). The events involving Vietnam were preceded by three incidents involving the Philippines, another claimant in the South China Sea territorial dispute. These incidents help fill out the context. On February 25, 2011, three Filipino fishing boats anchored at Jackson Atoll, 140 nautical miles west of Palawan (within what the Law of the Sea would support as the Philippines' EEZ). A Chinese patrol vessel approached and radioed an order for the boats to leave immediately, saying they were in Chinese territory. One of the boats had trouble pulling up its anchor and asked for more time. The Chinese ship reportedly responded, "I will shoot you," and fired three warning shots. The Filipino crew, believing they were in danger, cut their anchor line to escape.[13] On March 2, a Philippines-contracted survey ship sailed near Reed Bank (again, within what would be the Philippines' EEZ). Two Chinese patrol vessels ordered the ship to leave. The Chinese made aggressive maneuvers that appeared to be threats to ram the survey vessel. On May 24, Chinese ships unloaded building materials in a reef off Palawan within the Philippines' claimable EEZ, a violation of a 2002 agreement signed by China and the other claimants.

Vietnamese vessels had a similar series of run-ins with the Chinese. Hanoi reported that on May 26, three Chinese patrol vessels swarmed a Vietnamese exploration ship within what Vietnam claims as its EEZ and cut a submerged cable towing the ship's underwater survey equipment. Vietnamese sources also revealed this was not the first time the Chinese had cut a

Vietnamese survey vessel's cable. On June 1, Vietnam's Ministry of Foreign Affairs reported that three Chinese patrol vessels "used guns to threaten" a Vietnamese fishing boat near the Spratly Islands. On June 9, Hanoi reported that a Chinese fishing boat escorted by two Chinese patrol vessels cut the cable of a Vietnamese-contracted survey ship, again within two hundred nautical miles of Vietnam's coast. The Vietnamese government said the sabotage was premeditated because the Chinese boat carried a "cable cutting device." The ability of armed Chinese patrol craft to operate in waters far from China but close to Vietnam (and the Philippines) was crucial to these Chinese operations.

Vietnam's government-controlled press vigorously condemned China. Vietnamese authorities took the unusual step of allowing mass anti-China protests in Hanoi and Ho Chi Minh City. A few days after the two publicized cable-cutting incidents, Hanoi announced that it would conduct naval live-fire exercises off its central coast and warned other countries' ships to avoid the area. This was the first time the Vietnamese government publicized such an exercise. The CCP-connected newspaper *Global Times* issued an ominous threat: "If Vietnam insists on making trouble, thinking that the more trouble it makes, the more benefits it gains, then we truly wish to remind those in Vietnam who determine policy to please read your history"—an apparent reference to China's punitive 1979 invasion of Vietnam.[14]

By 2011 China was in effect using a "good cop, bad cop" approach toward Vietnam. High-ranking Chinese officials exuded firmness combined with restraint, as if trying to persuade the other claimants to give up while simultaneously keeping up the desired image of China as a peaceful and responsible great power. The attempt by the Chinese Ministry of Foreign Affairs to recast the June 9 cable-cutting incident as a Vietnamese victimization of Chinese fishermen suggested Beijing wanted to distance itself from allegations of belligerence. According to a spokesperson's version of the incident, "armed Vietnamese ships" illegally drove away Chinese fishing boats, after which the net of one Chinese boat got caught in the cable of the Vietnamese survey vessel. This dragged the Chinese boat backward for an hour and endangered the crew. To free their boat, the Chinese crew cut the cable.[15] While the Foreign Ministry tried to appear reasonable, Chinese government-controlled media played the bad cop, making unvarnished threats. A *Global Times* editorial on June 21, 2011, said, "If Vietnam wishes to create a war in the South China Sea, China will resolutely keep them company. China has the absolute might to crush the naval fleets sent from Vietnam. China will show no mercy to its rival due to 'global impact' concerns."[16] Chinese patrol vessels and in some cases fishing boats did the physical dirty work of harassing and intimidating rival claimants, which took a rougher form than the statements coming out of Beijing. It is possible the variety of signals was not part of a carefully executed master plan but rather was unintentional, indicating a lack of coordination or differing agenda among various agencies and levels of government.

Consistent with the historical pattern, Vietnam has tried to compartmentalize the territorial dispute to prevent it from fouling the overall relationship with China. In the midst of heightened South China Sea tensions in June 2011, as Vietnamese crowds were marching in the streets shouting denunciations of China, the Chinese and Vietnamese navies went ahead with a planned joint naval patrol in the Gulf of Tonkin. But with the Chinese increasingly capable and confident of settling the issue on their terms and the Vietnamese unwilling to capitulate, another lethal incident at sea between the two countries is all too easy to foresee.

Russia

Media commentators and some analysts commonly describe the relationship between China and Russia as an "alliance." This is inaccurate. The two countries have no formal alliance. Beijing officially describes the relationship with Russia as a "strategic and cooperative partnership," but the Chinese government has also used the same phrase to characterize China's relations with India and South Korea. China and Russia are cofounders of the Shanghai Cooperation Organization, but members insist this organization is not an alliance. Nevertheless, recent Sino-Russian relations display close political and economic cooperation in some ways reminiscent of allies. Americans feel this keenly because much of the cooperation between Beijing and Moscow appears aimed at opposing the U.S. global agenda.

Such a level of cordiality between Russia and China is a historical abnormality. History has taught Russia neither to be confident in its own strength nor to be trusting toward strong neighbors. Although the Russian state has controlled vast territory and resources, maintaining this control has been difficult. The sheer size of Russia makes it nearly indigestible to attackers but also dilutes the strength of the Russian bureaucracy and armed forces. The country's borders have not been defensible against various powerful

Eurasian nations, leading to frequent invasions. These included the Mongol "Golden Horde" that invaded Russia from the east during the thirteenth century. The Mongols burned Moscow and established two centuries of rule over southern Russia and tribute taking from northern Russia. The loyalty of parts of the Russian empire to the central government has been questionable. Twice during the twentieth century Russia fell from great-power status into national collapse, creating a deep sense that the country remains vulnerable even when it appears powerful.

Nor are China and Russia natural allies. Chinese have not forgotten that in the nineteenth century, when Russia was stronger and the Chinese Qing dynasty was declining, the Russians took territory and other concessions from China. Russia and the PRC cooperated during the twentieth century when both perceived a common dire threat from the U.S.-led capitalist powers. Yet this threat was not enough to prevent Beijing and Moscow from a political and ideological falling out. The Sino-Soviet relationship dissolved acrimoniously in the 1960s. Mao was displeased that Moscow balked at his request for nuclear weapons. The Soviets were unhappy with Mao for picking a risky fight with the Taiwan-based Kuomintang over the offshore islands without consulting Moscow. The PRC and Soviet governments disagreed about which political and economic strategies to promote internationally in the struggle of socialism against capitalism. The Soviet invasion of Czechoslovakia in 1968 made the Chinese fearful they might be similarly attacked and led to armed clashes on the Sino-Russian border. By the late 1980s China and Russia were headed in different directions. Russia was liberalizing its political system while declining economically and geopolitically. China retained an authoritarian political system but was demonstrating dizzying economic dynamism. From China's viewpoint, a Russia that had reached rapprochement with the West might join them in opposition to China.

The outlook for China-Russia relations, however, soon changed dramatically. In the early 1990s, Russia's view of the West soured with the perception that the West was systematically humiliating Russia, most seriously through the expansion of NATO into Russia's former sphere of influence. At the same time, China needed powerful friends to compensate for post-Tiananmen ostracism by the industrialized democracies. Bilateral relations unexpectedly blossomed. Russia went from ideological enemy to political and strategic partner. Moscow has helped protect China from formal UN criticism for failure to protect human rights while serving as China's main source of modern foreign armaments. The embargo by Western countries on military sales to China imposed after the crackdown on protestors in and around Tiananmen in 1989 led to Russia selling China as much as $2 billion worth of arms annually during the 1990s. A 2004 agreement settled the three-hundred-year-old bilateral border dispute. In 2005 the two countries had their first joint military exercise. Russia supports Beijing's sovereignty over Taiwan; Beijing maintains that Moscow's management of the troubled republic of Chechnya is a Russian internal affair. China and Russia band together in opposition to U.S. policies such as building a missile defense system and adding new Eastern European member states to NATO. In addition to counterbalancing U.S. influence so as to bring about a more "fair" international system, Moscow and Beijing share common interests in thwarting the spread of separatist and terrorist activities into their territory, promoting stability in the newly independent Central Asian states, averting a conflict on the Korean Peninsula, and preventing Japan from becoming militarily powerful. Beijing has gone so far as to say it will "support the renaissance of Russia as a great power."[17]

While the rise of China clearly raises tensions with regional rivals such as Japan and India, the effect of a stronger China on relations with Russia is more ambiguous. Some analysts expect that Russia and China will build on their present relationship and eventually establish a bilateral alliance. Others believe Russia will accommodate China and settle for a subordinate regional position. Both of these scenarios are plausible. Another possibility, however, is that the fundamental bilateral differences will never be overcome and will eventually drive the two countries apart.

Although a common interest in resisting Western pressure revived the Sino-Soviet relationship again in the post–Cold War era, the resilience of this bilateral relationship in an era of rising Chinese relative power is questionable. A fundamental Russian compulsion is to become a great power again. China's rise indirectly threatens this Russian goal by limiting the political and economic space available for a Russian resurgence. Led by its massive economic influence, China rather than Russia is becoming the hub and manager of regional affairs. China's rise is also a potential long-term threat to Russian security because conflict between a strong China and a Russia that aspires to greater national prominence cannot be ruled out. With this in mind, we might take a more skeptical view of what is currently a friendly and cooperative Sino-Russian relationship. On one hand, there are firm limits on the scope and depth of bilateral strategic cooperation between Russia and China. On the other hand, bilateral differences and tensions have ample potential to grow.

After 1999 it seemed possible there was enough momentum in China-Russia relations to produce an alliance. This momentum petered out quickly, however, because of the lack of depth in bilateral trust and shared interests. The Russians feared they would be the junior partner in such an alliance. The Chinese still had hard feelings over the acrimonious Sino-Soviet breakup in the 1960s. Since then neither country has seen their partnership as a rival bloc challenging the United States and its allies. Rather, the relationship has been a defensive one. Both China and Russia use their relationship with each other as a means of strengthening the position of each in its bargaining with the West, particularly with the United States. As Russian President Boris Yeltsin said in 1995, "We can rest on the Chinese shoulder in our relations with the West. In that case the West will treat Russia more respectfully."[18] Indeed, the two countries have often disregarded each other's interests while independently seeking improved relations with the West. Neither China nor Russia has done much to assist the other beyond making statements of solidarity. The Chinese have shown little willingness to make sacrifices on behalf of Russian interests such as preventing the expansion of NATO or forcing the Japanese to accept Russia's position on the Northern Territories. Nor has Russia exerted itself to pressure Taiwan toward reaching a political settlement with China. Beijing and Moscow both have interests in restraining what might otherwise be excessive U.S. power. But both also have influential groups of elites who benefit from globalization and are averse to estranging themselves from the West. The desire to avoid seriously jeopardizing their relationships with Washington is stronger than the desire of either Moscow or Beijing to form a true alliance. The relationship is thus vulnerable to weakening through Washington improving relations with one or both of the two partners.

Suspicion and quiet rivalry underlie much of Chinese-Russian relations, even in areas of apparent cooperation. Beijing and Moscow are coleaders of the Shanghai Cooperation Organization (SCO), which unites them and the newly independent Central Asian states against the "three evils" of "terrorism, separatism, and extremism"—plus the more recently added evils of illegal immigration and drug smuggling. The Russians see Central Asia as part of their historical sphere of influence. SCO member states Kazakhstan, Uzbekistan, Tajikistan, and Kyrgyzstan were parts of the Soviet Union before its breakup in 1991 and remain members of the Russian-led Commonwealth of Independent States. Moscow has been cool toward the Chinese idea of using the SCO to promote a free trade area, fearing the expansion of Chinese influence in Central Asia. Privately, officials involved in discussions between China and Russia over the SCO reveal constant bilateral tensions.[19]

Russia is one of the world's top energy exporters and wants to reduce its reliance on customers in Europe. China is one of the world's top energy consumers and wants to diversify away from dependence on Middle East suppliers. It seems a match made in heaven. Yet the China-Russia energy supply relationship has been slow to develop because of conflicting economic interests as well as Russian fears about the rise of China. To increase its economic health, Russia must deepen its reliance on China. But this increased reliance pushes Russia further into a subordinate position within regional Chinese hegemony. Moscow faces a dilemma between prosperity and autonomy.

The relationship between China and the eastern region of Russia, known as the Russian Far East (RFE), epitomizes this dilemma. Russia's population is about one-tenth the size of China's and is shrinking; China's continues to grow. The RFE is especially sparsely populated, averaging about one person per square kilometer. During the last twenty years, the Russian population in the RFE has declined by one quarter. The RFE is also rich in resources including oil, natural gas, diamonds, gold, and timber. Since the bordering provinces of China are much more populous, Russians fear Chinese migrants will swamp and peacefully "conquer" the RFE. A visa waiver program beginning in 1992 led to a huge influx of Chinese job seekers, traders, investors, and smugglers into Russia. According to credible estimates, the number of Chinese immigrants in the RFE probably peaked in the 1990s at between one and three hundred thousand. Some of these later left the RFE, and in any case these numbers are lower than the number of Chinese in the RFE during the first two decades of the twentieth century.[20] Nevertheless, a "yellow peril" panic broke out among the Russian public, with alarmists claiming the number of illegal Chinese immigrants in Russia was as high as five million.[21] The Russian authorities feel deep anxiety about losing control of the RFE to China, although they rarely speak openly about this anxiety lest they offend their Chinese partners. On one occasion, however, Prime Minister Vladimir Putin said the influx of foreigners into the RFE from neighboring states combined with the decline of Russian citizens in the RFE constituted the "biggest threat to Russia."[22]

As a storehouse of energy resources, the RFE is a potential source of Russian influence in energy-hungry Northeast Asia. To realize this influence and remain a major power in the region, Russia must economically develop the RFE, including building the infrastructure necessary to extract and transport hydrocarbon resources. Russia tried but failed to develop the RFE largely without foreign assistance. In 2009 the Russians resorted to seeking Chinese investment for building pipelines and agreed to link development of the RFE with Chinese plans to develop the neighboring Chinese province of Heilongjiang. As the Russians well understand, this is a step toward Chinese domination of the RFE and toward greater Chinese influence over the economies of both Russia and the region.[23] Additionally, China gets oil directly from Kazakhstan and natural gas directly from Turkmenistan through pipelines. This challenges Russia's former great-power prerogative of controlling the outflow of energy resources from the former Soviet republics of Central Asia.

A close look at the bilateral military relationship also reveals cracks in the edifice. The Russians have mixed feelings about selling advanced military equipment to China. Many Russian strategists, including high-ranking generals, have questioned the policy of arming a strong neighbor that could be an adversary in the future. The counterargument is that these sales help sustain the Russian defense industrial sector, which might wither without a steady flow of orders, with serious consequences for Russian security.

China originally bought one hundred Russian Su-27 fighter aircraft and agreed to produce two hundred more under a licensing agreement. But the Chinese built only 105 of these before reneging on the agreement. Instead, the Chinese began producing their own unlicensed copies of the Su-27, designating it the J-11 and fitting it with reverse-engineered Chinese knockoffs of the Su-27's avionics and radar systems. The Chinese not only stopped buying Su-27s from Russia; they also began exporting their J-11, taking business away from Russia in the Third World. The Kremlin angrily considered legal action against China for violation of intellectual property rights.

The peak of the Russia-to-China arms trade appears to have passed by the end of the first decade of the twenty-first century. With the revived Russian economy, Russian defense industries were less dependent on Chinese purchases for survival. And the Chinese were clearly moving toward producing more of their own advanced weapons rather than buying them off the shelf. What was once a strong bond between Russia and China is disappearing. The natural suspicion between two strong neighbors, however, persists. Strategists in each country view the other country as a potential security challenge. The Russian Navy's plans for shipbuilding and refurbishing in the period from 2011 to 2020 indicate a subtle shift in the designated primary potential adversary from NATO to China, with a move away from aircraft carriers and other large warships toward frigates that will operate in the seas to Russia's east and south.

Instances of Russian acquiescence to Chinese power, such as arms sales and development of the RFE, may suggest that the rise of China will not increase the chances of Sino-Russian conflict but rather will force the Russians to accept subordinate status that will preclude serious tensions with Beijing. At the same time, however, we must wonder if the Russians can so easily abandon their aspiration to return to great-power status. Dissonance with that aspiration grows as the Russian government takes steps that cede greater powers over regional affairs to the Chinese. China-Russia relations cannot be considered fundamentally stable because Russia has an extremely mixed view of China. The emergence of a *moderately* powerful China—the level China reached at around the turn of the century—arguably improved the prospects for peace with Russia as compared with a weak China that Moscow might be tempted to bully. With China capable of defending itself, Russia must conclude that cooperation and reducing tensions are the preferable courses of action. A *very* powerful China is a different matter. In that case, the question for the Russians changes to whether they can avoid sinking into such a degree of subordination to Beijing that Russia's independence and perhaps even its territorial integrity is threatened.

South Korea

Although Koreans recognize that Chinese culture heavily influenced their society in ancient times, a major point of Korean identity is that Koreans have maintained their distinctiveness despite the designs of powerful neighboring countries. South Koreans see themselves as culturally, technologically, and politically more advanced and sophisticated than mainland Chinese. During the Cold War, Seoul considered China an adversary. Chinese troops fought alongside North Koreans against South Korean and UN forces during the Korean War (1950–1953). Subsequently, Seoul's conservative, authoritarian regimes stayed firmly within the camp of their

American ally. South Korea even contributed troops to the Vietnam conflict. Nevertheless, South Koreans still saw China as a potential partner. By the 1980s, the U.S. rapprochement with China and doubts about the permanence of America's commitment to defend the Republic of Korea (ROK) caused South Koreans to rethink their relationship with China. Seoul had two main motivations for improving the relationship with China. The first was to stabilize and gain leverage in South Korea's relations with Chinese client state North Korea. The second was to increase economic interaction with China in support of South Korea's plans for its own economic development. Seoul and the PRC established normal diplomatic relations in 1992. This was something of a sellout by China in the eyes of North Korea, as during most of the Cold War Beijing had supported Pyongyang as the sole legitimate government on the Korean Peninsula. China welcomed the new partnership because Beijing wanted to trade with the ROK, saw that South Korea was destined to be the stronger power on the peninsula, and had grown weary of North Korean intransigence. ROK-PRC trade has increased briskly since the early 1990s. As with the Japan-China economic relationship, there is great complementarity between the PRC's low labor costs and South Korea's technological and managerial expertise.

Thus, the apparent trend of recent decades suggests that the PRC and the ROK are drawing closer together, cooperating more, and moving beyond their formally adversarial posture. The continuation of this trend, however, is in doubt. The rise of China creates or deepens security problems for the ROK. As a "shrimp" living next to a "whale," Korea has always been vulnerable to domination by China except during periods of Chinese weakness. South Korean analysts suspect that a stronger China will be more domineering toward the ROK and other regional governments. They are uncomfortable with the Chinese military buildup and already feel China has become too pushy in offering "advice" to Seoul.[24] Although many Koreans have described the presence of U.S. bases as an American military occupation of Korea, the rise of China supplies a rationale for continuing the ROK's alliance with Washington aside from the North Korea issue. As the regional great power, however, Beijing will eventually demand that Seoul abrogate the alliance. South Koreans resented a warning in 2006 by the Chinese ambassador that the ROK should not allow Korea-based U.S. forces to get involved in any conflicts outside the Korean Peninsula (such as a Taiwan Strait war).

Seoul's strategic view of China is complicated by the division of the Korean Peninsula. The South Korean government relies on China for help in moderating North Korean policies hostile toward the South. For dealing with the immediate problem of managing North-South tensions, Seoul sees Chinese influence in North Korea in a positive light. When they think beyond the current situation to the future unification of the two Koreas, however, South Koreans see Chinese influence differently. They suspect the Chinese would try to retain undue control over northern Korea after reunification, if not attempting to obstruct reunification altogether. What one analyst calls China's "*de facto* economic colonization of the DPRK" indicates a sizable and permanent Chinese stake in North Korea, the loss of which would be costly.[25]

The difference in political systems between South Korea's liberal democracy and the PRC's ham-fisted authoritarianism increases friction and distrust between the two societies. Bilateral incidents periodically erupt in which the mass public in one or both countries pressures its government to take a nationalist stand that at least temporarily damages Sino-Korean relations.

Both countries worry about territorial irredentism. Ethnic Korean communities span the border between China and North Korea. The land and history of this area is still contested. This is clear from the smoldering controversy over Koguryo, an ancient (37 b.c.e.–668 c.e.) Korean kingdom that covered northern Korea and part of what today is northeastern China. Koreans consider it the beginning of the Korean state. A group of Chinese scholars commissioned by the PRC government in 2002 published several papers arguing that Koguryo was a vassal of the Chinese empire. In 2004, the Chinese Ministry of Foreign Affairs deleted references to Koguryo in its website's summary of Korean history. The apparent Chinese goal was to prevent future Korean claims to territory on the Chinese side of the border, where between two and three million ethnic Koreans reside. South Korean media extensively covered these activities, which Koreans interpreted as China trying to steal their history. The issue threatened to damage permanently South Korean perceptions of the agenda China intended to pursue as a great power. China's image in the ROK plunged from mostly positive to mostly negative.

Another territorial controversy over Gando (Jiandao in Chinese) turns the tables on the PRC. Gando lies in what is today PRC territory just north of China's border with the DPRK. It is populated by as many as a million ethnic Koreans. In 1909 the Korean government, then under Japanese control, ceded Gando to Qing-dynasty China. The Japanese used the transfer of Korean territory to China as part of a deal that included the Chinese granting Japan rights to build railroads in Manchuria. Koreans maintain that the land transfer was illegal because a Japanese administration that had invaded Korea did not have the right to give away Korean territory. The South Korean government has publicly stated it believes the Gando Convention is invalid and has resisted Chinese pressure to retract this position, which leaves open the possibility that Korea will assert ownership over what is now part of China.

Seoul has not pushed for Korean ownership of the Chinese side of Baekdu Mountain, which straddles the PRC-DPRK border, but the Chinese are aware that this is the wish of many Koreans, who hold the mountain sacred. To the chagrin of their hosts, a group of Korean athletes at the 2007 Asian Winter Games in Changchun, China held up signs during an award ceremony that read "Mount Baekdu is our territory."

The potential for disputes with China is evident. It was also clear throughout the first decade of the twenty-first century that China was on track to become East Asia's strongest economic and military power. Yet the ROK did not appear particularly worried about China during that decade. Many South Koreans harbored fears of Chinese domination, but these fears did not drive South Korean foreign policy. The ROK did not openly balance against the PRC. Prior to the North Korean incidents that caused losses of South Korean lives in 2010, Seoul did not strengthen the alliance with the United States during the decade. Instead, Seoul and Washington made plans to withdraw U.S. troops gradually from the peninsula and to reduce the U.S. leadership role within the alliance. South Korean military strengthening was cautious and restrained. Absolute ROK defense expenditures rose from 1999 to 2011, but expenditures as a percentage of gross domestic product fell from the beginning to the middle of the decade before rising slightly by the end of the decade. This is explained by robust ROK economic growth. Some of the ROK's military acquisitions and deployments during this period were applicable to the North Korea threat. Others appeared to address other possible contingencies that might involve China or Japan. At the same time, however, defense cooperation and military exchanges between South Korea and China increased. All things considered, the ROK's approach to China during the first decade of the twenty-first century looked like hedging rather than balancing, indicating that Seoul was not treating China as a serious threat. Seoul made a considerable effort to accommodate and to avoid antagonizing Beijing. The ROK has avoided partnership with the United States on policies that anger China, such as support for Taiwan and criticism of human rights practices in China. The Roh Moo-hyun administration said it favored moving toward a more equidistant position between the United States and China despite South Korea being a formal U.S. ally. South Korea's government blocked proposed visits by the Dalai Lama. Seoul politely turned down the U.S. request to participate in joint development of a ballistic missile defense system—which China strongly opposed—saying it would be too expensive and technically difficult. In 2008, Beijing rewarded South Korea by announcing that the PRC-ROK relationship had become a "strategic cooperative partnership," the same designation China used for its relations with quasi-ally Pakistan.

The reason the ROK has been accommodating a rising China rather than openly attempting to offset China's growing strength is that economic hopes have outweighed nagging security fears. South Koreans see business with China as the key to their country's future prosperity. "China fever" swept South Korea in the early 2000s. Up to around 2005, surveys of both elite and public opinion showed that South Koreans thought China represented more of an economic opportunity than a security threat. Some Korean opinion leaders argued that improving relations with China rather than maintaining the relationship with the United States should be the ROK's top foreign policy priority. Unquestionably, China's importance to South Korea relative to that of the United States has grown. The United States, long South Korea's largest trading partner, yielded this position to China in 2004. The number of South Korean students studying in China has risen steadily, reaching about seventy thousand in 2010 and expected soon to surpass the number of South Koreans studying in the United States. In the strategic realm as well as the economic realm there was an argument for treating China as a partner. Seoul believed Beijing could play a constructive role in helping the ROK achieve its short-term goals in relations between North and South Korea by pressuring Pyongyang toward détente and reform.

Worries about the rise of China will be more prominent in ROK foreign policy in the years following the first decade of the twenty-first century. The ROK view of China shifted in the latter part of the decade because of two factors. First, the exuberance over the prospect of China-driven prosperity calmed down. Second, the ROK government changed ruling parties. Progressive leaders were ascendant in South Korea during the period from

1997 to 2007. They held relatively benign views of China and emphasized cooperation over strategic anxiety. When conservatives gained control of South Korea's government, Seoul's policies reflected greater skepticism toward China. This recent period of the ROK approaching a rising China with partnership and accommodation may have been a brief honeymoon that will give way to a more hard-nosed Korean assessment of the PRC. China's unwillingness and inability to restrain provocative acts by North Korea in 2010 caused South Koreans to rethink the notion of Beijing as a constructive influence on ROK-DPRK relations. In the late 2000s Seoul sought to improve relations with the United States to counterbalance its relationship with China. The ROK stopped describing its position as one of political equidistance between Beijing and Washington. Seoul sent three thousand ROK troops to Iraq in support of the U.S.-led campaign, despite the opposition of the South Korean legislature and public. The South Korean government negotiated a free trade agreement with the United States that required unpopular compromises. The ROK also put aside its reservations about joining the U.S.-sponsored Proliferation Security Initiative.

Even in the economic side of the relationship, South Koreans are increasingly aware that a strong China brings problems along with opportunities and that greater economic interdependence with China may not deliver the benefits Koreans initially expected. After 2006 the euphoria over trade with China subsided. The South Korean business community more frequently expressed concerns about such issues as losing overseas market share to rival Chinese suppliers, excessive ROK dependence on the Chinese economy, and the stiff challenge China would present in sectors where Koreans have been successful, such as semiconductor manufacturing and shipbuilding. China's effort to nurture indigenous innovation generates policies that discriminate against foreign businesses in favor of Chinese firms. Foreign companies operating in China are required to share their technology, and Chinese enforcement of intellectual property rights is notoriously weak. Both of these conditions are helping China quickly overcome the gap with higher-technology economies such as South Korea's. The pressure of over a billion people hungering for prosperity will escalate the competition with the ROK for scarce resources. As an example, South Koreans complain that illegal Chinese fishing in South Korea's exclusive economic zones in the seas west, south, and even east of the peninsula has dramatically increased in the past few years. These outlaw Chinese fishing crews are also sometimes aggressive. In several cases they have rammed South Korean Coast Guard vessels. In 2008 and twice in 2011, Chinese fishing crews resisting arrest killed or injured ROK Coast Guardsmen.

Bilateral economic cooperation will continue and deepen. It is possible South Korea could move toward greater accommodation of China, trading freedom of action for the improved relations that would facilitate greater economic access. As China rises, however, several factors point to the expectation that bilateral tensions and South Korean suspicions of PRC intentions will continue as well. Tensions between Seoul and Beijing will probably intensify because of three main issues. First, as China grows relatively stronger, the PRC government will expect greater deference from the ROK. From the ROK's point of view, this will look like PRC attempts to constrain Seoul's foreign and security policies. South Koreans will remain highly sensitive and resistant to perceived Chinese domination. Second, Seoul will see China's growing economic integration with North Korea as an intrusion into Korean affairs and an obstacle to South Korea's vision for the peninsula. Third, China's desire eventually to push U.S. military bases and alliances out of the region will clash with Seoul's desire to keep the alliance as an insurance policy. The stronger China grows and the harder it pushes the ROK, the more the ROK will value its security cooperation with the United States.

Burma (Myanmar)

China's rise is potentially advantageous to Burma in two ways. First, the increase of Chinese influence relative to that of the United States and other liberal democracies would seem to offer the Burmese government the prospect of a more hospitable international environment for authoritarian political systems. Second, a wealthier China is better able to assist Burma's economic development. But these advantages are offset and perhaps negated by the increased danger that a stronger China will dominate Burma. Therefore, the rise of China does not necessarily increase Burma's national security.

China has strong interests in maintaining a controlling grip on Burma. First, large parts of Burma are not under the control of the central government. Beijing is very keen to keep problems such as ethnic-based insurgency, drug trafficking, human trafficking, and other crimes from crossing the border into China. Second, the mutual economic relationship is deep and growing. Burma is important to China as a source of raw materials and agricultural products, and Chinese manufactured and mechanical goods are prevalent in Burma's markets. PRC firms are investing heavily to develop mines and infrastructure in Burma. Finally, Burma is strategically important to China. A Burmese government friendly to China anchors Chinese influence in mainland Southeast Asia and balances Vietnam, which has a more ambivalent relationship with China. Gas and oil pipelines through Burma can allow supplies offloaded at Indian Ocean ports to travel overland to southern China, bypassing the Strait of Malacca.

The Burmese junta is notorious for egregiously poor governance. Intolerant of dissent and dominated by the military, it has largely lost legitimacy with the Burmese people and remains in power through armed force and periodic brutal crackdowns against organized opposition. It overturned the results of democratic elections won by the party of Nobel Prize laureate Aung San Suu Kyi in 1990 and kept her under house arrest in most of the years since then. Nevertheless, Beijing supports the junta because the Chinese need a stable government in Burma. China is Burma's largest supplier of arms and military training. High-level PRC leaders frequently signal friendship with Burma. The Chinese have also often protected Burma from Western pressure, which the Chinese believe is aimed at bringing about political liberalization and an overthrow of the government. In 2007, for example, China employed its rarely used veto power in the UN Security Council to defeat a U.S.-sponsored resolution calling on Burma's government to protect its people's civil and political human rights.

This Chinese protection does not remove Burmese fears of Chinese domination. Built on a long history of national and ethnic tensions, anti-Chinese sentiment is prevalent in Burma. It is found among both the military and the democratic opposition to the junta, although in public statements both are discrete about displaying this sentiment. Burma's people are not completely pleased with the China-Burma economic relationship. Chinese companies are busily harvesting Burma's resources. Largely illegal Chinese logging has left large parts of northern Burma deforested, leading to flooding and landslides. Chinese workers and merchants have poured into Burmese cities. There may be as many as two million PRC nationals illegally residing in Burma. Many Burmese believe China is looting the country's natural wealth and corrupting its leaders while offering nothing in return but shoddy consumer goods. In political discourse within Burma, opponents of the government decry the military leadership as sellouts to the Chinese because of their reliance on China for weapons and diplomatic support and because many of them personally profit handsomely from business deals with the PRC. The military itself implicitly uses the threat from China to help justify the junta's rule over Burma, arguing that the military is the only national institution capable of holding the country together against the twin challenges of strong and avaricious neighbors and well-armed separatist movements by ethnic minorities, most of which have strong links to China and are regarded by other Burmese as Chinese.

The Burmese government has reportedly reached a consensus that the country has become too dependent upon China and strayed too far from its traditional foreign policy of neutrality and equidistance.[26] Recently, Burmese authorities have demonstrated that they are not patsies of the PRC. In 2009 Burmese government troops ostensibly carrying out an anti-drug-trafficking mission converged on an ethnic Chinese enclave in Kokang, Shan State. The fighting that resulted drove up to thirty thousand ethnic Chinese to flee across the border into the PRC's Yunnan province. At minimum, the episode showed that Burma's rulers were willing to place their own domestic agenda (in this case, weakening armed rebel groups) ahead of pleasing the PRC. Beijing angrily warned the Burmese government but took no further action. Another example involves the proposed Myitsone Dam. China wants to build a dam by 2017 at the confluence of two other rivers that join to form the Ayeyarwady (Irrawaddy) River. The project is highly controversial even within Burma's government. The electricity generated by the dam would mostly serve southern China. The building site is close to a major earthquake fault. The idea of damming the Ayeyarwady, which has great cultural significance, is offensive to many Burmese. The dam would also threaten nearby wildlife habitats and submerge villages inhabited by ten thousand people. Burmese President Thein Sein announced in 2011 that work on the project would stop while he was in office, apparently in response to public opinion.

One school of thought among outside observers has been that the main international security issue involving China and Burma is a rising China using Burma as an appendage through which to extend China's influence over Asia, in this case by gaining greater access to the Indian Ocean. This thinking relied heavily on reports of a large Chinese signals intelligence station (a listening post) on Burma's Great Coco Island, taken as a fact by the Western and Indian media for over a decade, despite denials from both Burma and China, until the Indian military announced in 2005 that there was no Chinese facility in the Coco Islands and probably never had been.[27]

Another school of thought, however, emphasizes that the Burmese are not submissive pawns in China's strategy. Rather, they highly value their independence, are suspicious of China's intentions, and have been successful in pushing back against what they consider excessive Chinese influence and in ensuring that the PRC's relationship with Burma is not exploitative. From this standpoint, Burma has been dependent on the PRC by default, willing to build a relationship with an alternative great-power sponsor but unable to find one because of the junta's pariah status. This suggests there is scope for strategic cooperation between Burma and the United States despite the political issues dividing them. Burma's military government has been highly fearful of a U.S. invasion, possibly assisted by Burmese nemesis and U.S. ally Thailand, that would aim to replace the regime. Despite this fear, in late 2011 the Burmese government took steps toward political liberalization that opened the way for improved relations with Washington. This move demonstrated the junta's desire to end international economic sanctions against Burma, but it also underscored a desire to avoid becoming a political satellite of China. The driving U.S. interest in Burma is not necessarily rolling back China's sphere of influence. Promoting civil and political human rights and halting Burma's development of weapons of mass destruction through cooperation with North Korea are also high on the U.S. agenda. Predictably, however, the Chinese leadership reacted to the signs of improvement in U.S.-Burma relations with suspicion that Washington was trying to tighten the noose of anti-China containment. Other Chinese elites are more broad minded, recognizing Burma's discomfort with overreliance on China and desire to get the West to lift economic sanctions. Some Chinese businesspeople see potential Burmese reforms as a positive development that could make Burma a more profitable economic partner.

China naturally sees Burma, a weaker state on its border, as part of a Chinese sphere of influence. The rise in China's relative power will likely intensify this Chinese expectation. With its growing economic, military, and diplomatic strength, China's ability to shape and influence Burma is increasing, making control of Burma more attainable. At the same time, China's need to harness Burma's potential contributions to PRC economic and strategic goals is becoming more urgent. China's preference clashes with Burma's resistance to Chinese domination and desire to diversify its dependence on the PRC. Burma faces an unwelcome dilemma of friction with or capitulation to its great-power neighbor.

Chapter Seven

MITIGATING FACTORS

China's rise is likely to revive or intensify security worries among its neighbors, undermining peace in the region. Fortunately, certain features of the international environment may exert positive and countervailing effects that mitigate the chances of conflict. These features might act as levees that contain storm-driven waters from disastrously overflowing.

Hopes for a Peaceful Adjustment in U.S.-China Relations

Some elements of today's international environment may cushion the power transition between the United States and China. To be sure, the rise of China increases the friction in some areas of U.S.-China relations. Because the United States is a superpower and China is a potential superpower or at least the potential successor to the United States as the strongest power in the Asia-Pacific region, the U.S.-China relationship falls into the category of a hegemonic transition. This makes the situation even more worrisome because the historical track record of hegemonic transitions demonstrates they are especially conflict prone. There is, however, good news: the unique circumstances of current U.S.-China relations contain features that make this relationship less susceptible to war than some previous hegemonic transitions.

There are several reasons why a Sino-U.S. conflict should be avoidable. In cases of great-power competition, a key consideration is the degree to which the two contending powers perceive each other as a direct security threat. In the cases of Germany-Britain in the early 1900s, Germany-Britain prior to World War II, and the United States–Soviet Union during the Cold War, each country perceived a high risk of being militarily attacked by its rival. In the case of China and the United States early in the twenty-first century, however, the sense of threat is relatively low and distant. China does not base its military forces in foreign countries. Other than Taiwan, there is no visible issue that China and America would go to war over. Moreover, the Sino-U.S. relationship lacks the intense global ideological competition that characterized the U.S.-Soviet rivalry. China long ago gave up supporting insurgent groups as part of a campaign to transplant the Chinese political and economic model into other countries. Although China does not share many Western values, the PRC government now practices state capitalism and preaches tolerance for a diversity of domestic political systems.

In contrast with hegemonic transitions of the past, both China and the United States are armed with nuclear weapons. In theory, nuclear deterrence dramatically lowers the chances of war. Nuclear weapons should make conflict less likely because both sides fear the possibility of escalation to a mutually devastating nuclear war. War occurred in the two pre-nuclear-age rivalries between Britain and Germany, but nuclear weapons are credited with helping limit U.S.-Soviet tensions to proxy wars on the peripheries of the two superpower camps.

In some ways, U.S.-China relations appear fundamentally stable. Both governments have major domestic challenges on which they would prefer to focus. Beijing and Washington need each other's cooperation on increasingly important global issues such as climate change, proliferation of weapons of mass destruction, and managing the international economy. The U.S. and Chinese economies are highly interdependent. China supplies a large percentage of the consumer goods Americans buy; without this supply Americans would have to pay more or settle for lower quality. China is the country that holds the most U.S. Treasury Bills, which helps underwrite America's massive debt. Conversely, China needs the United States to continue absorbing Chinese exports to prop up employment and prosperity in China. A collapse of the U.S. economy would also depreciate the value of China's huge stock of U.S. currency reserves. This interdependence between the two economies gives Beijing and Washington a compelling reason to manage disputes and avoid conflict. The U.S. scholar Robert Sutter argues that although the bilateral relationship has seen serious downturns in the past, these are less likely in the future because the relationship has become more "multifaceted and often deeply rooted."[1]

At present, the most likely trigger for a U.S.-China war would seem to be the Taiwan issue. Polls of public opinion in the United States create doubts over whether Americans would support sending U.S. forces to help defend Taiwan from a PRC military attack.[2] This is not comforting for Taiwanese, but it reinforces the optimistic scenario of a hegemonic transition without a hegemonic war.

There is still a consensus among Chinese elites that the United States will remain the world's strongest country for at least several decades and that China's strategy should be to generally cooperate with America and avoid creating the impression that a rising China threatens important U.S. interests. Chinese paramount leaders strive to demonstrate that they can successfully manage U.S.-China relations, which means keeping the relationship stable and constructive without sacrificing Chinese dignity or important Chinese interests. Jiang Zemin, PRC president from 1993 to 2003, said his goal in his relations with the United States was to "enhance mutual trust, minimize problems, develop cooperation, and avoid confrontation."[3] Jiang followed these guidelines so well that he was frequently the target of public criticism that he was not tough enough with the Americans.

Chinese antagonism toward America's regional great-power position has not been closely linked with China's rise in relative power. In the 1990s Chinese leaders and commentators tried to rally the Asia-Pacific region in opposition to U.S. influence. They decried American "hegemonism" and the "Cold War thinking" represented by America's alliances in the Asia-Pacific. This Chinese effort, however, was unsuccessful. Most of the region either saw the U.S. presence as beneficial or too strong to oppose openly. As the PRC got stronger, however, Beijing changed to a more moderate course. By the late 1990s, Beijing had settled on a policy of promoting cooperation with the United States and deemphasizing disputes unless the United States threatened a vital Chinese interest. In the 2000s, official Chinese references to opposing "hegemonism" greatly decreased from 1990s levels. The Chinese took the position that they were not attempting to push the United States out of its defense cooperation activities in the Asia-Pacific or to supplant the United States as regional hegemon. Beijing continued to express general opposition to untrammeled American global power and specific opposition to certain U.S. security policies in the Asia-Pacific, such as arms sales to Taiwan. But the Chinese ceased calling on U.S. allies and other states in the region to reject the U.S. alliance system. For example, former Vice Premier Qian Qichen said in 2005, "China respects the American presence and interests in the Asia-Pacific region. We welcome the United States playing a positive and constructive role in the region."[4] If there has not been a close correlation so far between China's rise and China's opposition to U.S. influence in Asia, there is less support for the prediction that a showdown between the United States and the even stronger China of the future is inevitable.

Successful navigation through this turbulent period will be possible if China continues to be reasonably supportive of international norms and if Washington does not appear to be trying actively to inhibit China's growth in power. China's rise has been peaceful, and the United States has already begun making adjustments, painful though they might be, to account for a world and an Asia-Pacific region in which Chinese power must be respected.

The System Works—for China, Too

The international system that most countries uphold is strong and highly successful, and Beijing presently does not appear either desirous or capable of hijacking and transforming it. The political world is "anarchic," meaning there is no overarching authority to which national governments must answer. Nevertheless, international activity is not completely without order. Today's world features an international system that is unique to our era of history. An international system is the collection of rules and institutions accepted and supported by most of the international community of nations. The current system includes, for example, institutions such as the United Nations, the World Trade Organization, the International Court of Justice, and the International Atomic Energy Agency. It also includes norms and rules such as diplomatic immunity, the Geneva Conventions for the humane treatment of victims of war, the Law of the Sea, commitment in principle to global free trade and to the nonviolent resolution of disputes among governments, and the idea that people are universally entitled to democracy and human rights (although the definitions and applications of those terms are highly contested).

Debate among Chinese elites over how to deal with the international system reveals three general schools of thought. According to the first, the current international system remains much like the world of the Opium War period: it largely serves a Western agenda of subjugating and exploiting weaker countries. If China engages with this system, it can only do so on the West's terms and thus risks being caught in a new form of unequal treaties. The second view is far more moderate: now that China is an influential great power, it benefits from and can shape the international system. Therefore the system is worth keeping and China should work to stabilize it. The third school of thought is that China should try to institute a new and more benevolent system based on the principles arising from China's experience. This debate leaves ample room for the Chinese leadership to decide to work within the current international system rather than working against it. Compared to the Cold War years, the center of gravity of Chinese thinking has clearly moved toward viewing international relations as a game in which everyone rather than only one great power can win and toward seeing China as a member of the international system rather than as a victim of it. For two decades one of the Chinese leadership's fundamental slogans in the area of foreign affairs was the call for "a new international economic and political order," first promulgated in 1988 by Deng Xiaoping. In 2007, however, the CCP quietly adjusted this slogan to "assume our due international obligations, play a constructive role, and work to make the international order fairer and more equitable." The change suggests reforming the current system from within rather than overthrowing it.[5]

China clearly favors changes to the current international system: more emphasis on the sovereignty of states (i.e., the right to handle their "domestic" affairs as they see fit without foreign interference) and on raising living standards and less emphasis on democratization, protecting human rights, punishing "rogue" regimes, and deregulating international financial markets. But while the Chinese can articulate specific complaints about the current system, beyond a few vague generalities Beijing has not spelled out a new, alternative system of rules and institutions. China appears in no hurry to junk the present international system, as much of it has been conducive to increased Chinese wealth, influence, and prestige. It is possible that a rising China could accept modifications in the current system that would not threaten systemic overthrow and could be peacefully negotiated. To the extent that this is true, the ascendance of China would not destroy the rules and institutions that other countries believe make the world more secure.

Previously suspicious of multilateral forums because of the potential for other states to gang up against China, Beijing in the 1990s came to view multilateralism as a useful vehicle for promulgating China's viewpoints and bringing Chinese influence to bear on the shaping of international opinion. The exchange of views between China and its foreign dialogue partners has been a two-way street. Some analysts maintain China has "learned" from years of interaction with the international community, particularly the Association of Southeast Asian Nations (ASEAN). The argument is that this interaction has given China not only a greater understanding of the international community's expectations of responsible behavior but also has increased Chinese acceptance of global values and attitudes. In some instances China is arguably becoming more supportive of the norms underpinning the current international system even as China's power to challenge those norms grows. Some Chinese elites say China accepts values such as democracy, the rule of law, and free trade. If the interpretation and practice of these concepts is different in China than in the West, the differences are gradually narrowing, despite setbacks such as the rollback of liberties in China under the rule of Hu Jintao. China's view of its own security might also be changing in ways that will reduce tensions with the West. Chinese opposition to U.S. military bases and activities in Asia is moderated somewhat by the recognition among some Chinese analysts that U.S. influence in the region is not all bad, as it can help prevent or contain crises in places such as Afghanistan, Kashmir, the South China Sea, and Taiwan.[6] During the Cold War, China saw the superpowers as its main security challenges. Since then, China has put increasing emphasis on nontraditional security threats such as damage to the environment, global financial instability, infectious disease, and food scarcity. These nontraditional threats tend to require cooperation rather than competition with the other major powers. Some analysts argue that in general, integration into the global economy has given Chinese leaders a more cosmopolitan outlook, increased the variety of groups and individuals within China that have influence over foreign policy decisions, and made Chinese policy making more transparent. These changes might help avert an aggressive or belligerent Chinese foreign policy.[7] The PRC international relations scholar Shen Dingli predicts that despite China's tradition of hiding weakness from a potential adversary, China will become more militarily transparent in the future and is already moving in that direction. This offers hope for reducing another point of friction with the United States and its allies.[8]

If foreign analysts worry that China may try to overthrow the current, U.S.-supported international system, they may take some comfort in the discovery that many Chinese analysts have the exact opposite fear. These Chinese analysts support the international system because they believe it is premised on the principles that all countries are sovereign and enjoy equality under international law regardless of size or level of economic development. Many Chinese perceive it is the United States, not China, that has been hostile to the international system because the United Nations and other institutions sometimes stand in the way of American attempts to act unilaterally in pursuit of narrow interests not shared by the global community. These Chinese do not see the international system as an obstacle to China's agenda; rather, they wish the international system will remain strong enough to impose limits on U.S. foreign policies that fail to win a consensus of international support. In recent years the PRC Foreign Ministry has said "China always disapproves of any action" by the United States, NATO, or a U.S.-led coalition "that goes beyond the authorization of the UN Security Council."[9] China has rarely used its veto power in the Security Council, often going along reluctantly with resolutions supported by the United States.

The political survival of China's top leaders and of the CCP itself requires that the government maintain the pace of national economic growth, which in turn depends on an international environment that allows for free-flowing trade and investment and gives China access to foreign capital and technology. China's prosperity under the status quo creates strong incentives both to keep the current system and to avoid an open confrontation with the major powers that sponsor the system. When the need for economic growth has clashed with Chinese strategic preferences, Beijing has made compromises. The PRC has maintained diplomatic relations with the United States and Japan despite deep Chinese opposition to many U.S. and Japanese policies, including U.S. support for Taiwan and Japan's gradual rearmament. The Chinese government decided to stay the course in its relationship with Washington even after the bombing of the Chinese embassy in Belgrade by U.S. aircraft in 1999, which most Chinese believed was intentional. Instead of openly shifting to a confrontational posture, the PRC has hedged by building up its military capabilities and increasing cooperation with other countries uncomfortable with U.S. unilateralism.

China an Uncertain No. 1

Up to now there is no consensus in Beijing that China should strive to replace the role now played globally by the United States. China does not want to be a superpower. The common sentiment among Chinese elites is that China should avoid taking a leading global leadership role for two reasons. First, the PRC still has many large, long-term domestic challenges to contend with, and these have top priority. China could not maintain an international leadership position without first consolidating its internal strength. Second, the lesson of history is that aggression does not pay.

China's recent experience with the G-7 and G-8, as well, evinces a willingness on the part of Beijing to forgo a preeminent global role even if an upgrade is available. In the 1970s the world's seven major industrialized democracies (the United States, the United Kingdom, Germany, Japan, France, Italy, and Canada) began to meet annually to discuss global issues and attempt to coordinate their national policies. China long disparaged this group, the G-7, as an exclusive club for wealthy Western countries. Russia joined the group in 1997 to make it the G-8. As China gained recognition as a major global economy, it received invitations to join G-8 meetings in 1996, 1998, and 2000, but it turned these invitations down. Beginning in 2003, however, China took the more pragmatic approach of attending G-8 meetings as an observer while continuing to advocate a more inclusive process for making global economic policy. Beijing also joined the G-20, a similar group with membership expanded to twenty. By engaging with the G-8, Beijing made its influence felt while continuing to champion the interests of the Third World. At the same time, the Chinese do not seem bent on seizing the opportunity to raise their status within the group. Many international observers believe global leadership is moving from the G-8 to a "G-2" composed of the United States and China. Not all Chinese elites like this idea. Having condemned the G-7 as a "rich countries' club" that disregards the interests of the developing world with which China identifies, Chinese worry that being part of a G-2 would make them a target for resentment by their excluded Asian neighbors, upsetting regional harmony.

The position of superpower carries global responsibilities. China, however, has not shown a willingness to take risky or costly actions in the service of broader international interests (as opposed to narrow Chinese interests). China is not among the world leaders in providing foreign aid or disaster assistance. Although its nonproliferation record has improved, China has been less than zealous in support of international norms against the spread of weapons of mass destruction. China's lenient approach toward "rogue" regimes with which the Chinese have important economic relationships (such as North Korea, Iran, and Sudan) has frustrated the major Western governments. In practice, Beijing has shown itself uninterested, at best, in expanding the protection of civil and political human rights internationally.

In the Asia-Pacific region, China does not provide the public goods[10] that regional states have come to expect from the United States. The United States absorbs a huge deficit in its trade with Asia and devotes a level of resources toward maintaining military forces in the region that no other country could match. Most Asia-Pacific states see these forces as reassuring rather than threatening. The United States makes commitments and absorbs burdens on behalf of regional stability that China has not.[11] The point here is not that Washington is altruistic. Rather, America has come to accept that it serves U.S. interests to make a heavy investment in providing public goods for the region. Beijing does not demonstrate nearly as strong a commitment to this idea.

Even if Beijing *did* aspire to global domination, the Chinese would encounter several serious obstacles. First, China is a long way from being strong enough to displace the reigning superpower. At present, China cannot openly challenge the United States for supremacy. The PRC is technologically behind the U.S. military and cannot match what the United States spends on defense or on defense-related research and development. Picking a fight with the United States would be to China's great disadvantage. Unless the United States became far more aggressive and threatening toward the international community than it now is, China would be unable to recruit strong allies to join in an open attack on U.S. interests. And as noted earlier, China's ability to exert power externally is also restricted by serious internal problems requiring attention and resources. These problems include the income gap between rich and poor and between eastern and western parts of the country, environmental degradation, water shortages, ethnic tensions, and outbreaks of large-scale social discontent over various perceived failures by the authorities.

Second, it would not be easy for China to sweep away the current international system. The U.S. scholar G. John Ikenberry argues that the system of rules and institutions built by the major Western democracies is extraordinarily robust: it is accessible and highly beneficial to countries that participate in it, yet it is difficult to overthrow because it has broad legitimacy and demands compliance with its rules. The system offers China unique opportunities, institutions, and protections. The World Trade Organization, for example, helps reduce protectionism against Chinese exports. China's influence within the IMF and the World Bank will grow as China grows. On the other hand, to change this order China would have to confront not only the United States but the entire capitalist-democratic bloc. Therefore, says

Ikenberry, China has more reasons to accept and integrate itself into the system than to oppose the system. The pacifying effects of the international system, he predicts, will overcome the tensions created by the hegemonic rivalry with the United States.[12]

Third, China's spectacular economic growth rate may not continue long enough to establish China as the anchor of the global economy and the unquestioned leader of the international system. As of 2008, China had achieved an average 9.7 percent annual real GDP growth rate over twenty-nine years. Some economists believe that around the year 2030 China's spectacular rate of growth will begin to level off and to approximate the slower growth rates of today's industrialized countries such as the United States and Japan. By that time, the flow of cheap laborers from rural areas into China's cities will slow down, China's working-age population will stop growing, and the large proportion of retirees will become a huge economic burden on Chinese society. If these projections are correct, absent a major economic slowdown, China will probably surpass the United States as the world's largest economy but will settle down soon thereafter. China will not build such a dominant economic imbalance that the United States is no longer a formidable competitor.

Finally, Asia-Pacific states do not accept China as the region's leader. Recent Chinese behavior has revived historical suspicions. In the eyes of many regional governments, China was a troublemaker during the Cold War, showing disdain for international norms and promoting insurrection in neighboring countries. Regional opposition to China was a major factor behind the formation of ASEAN in 1967. In the post–Cold War era, the Chinese have shown flashes of chauvinism and bullying on some issues. Although Asia-Pacific countries are eagerly seeking opportunities to trade with China, no U.S. friends or allies appear willing to trade in their security relationships with Washington for one with Beijing. In the eyes of most regional states, the United States remains uniquely qualified and desirable as a power that can provide strategic stability and, in particular, ensure that China does not force its will on the region.

Balancing Against China

A consistent feature of international politics is balancing behavior. Faced with the emergence of a new great power and potential hegemon that potentially impinges on their security, the lesser powers in the region may in theory react in one of two ways. The first is accommodation, which means joining with the rising power and avoiding any major policy decisions that would displease it. The second strategy is balancing: weaker states band together to form a coalition to protect their interests against the rising power. To pursue the strategy of accommodation, the weaker country not only takes care not to annoy the strong power, but may also try to prove itself useful by adding its voice in support of the strong power's agenda in multilateral organizations. By doing so, the weaker country hopes to avoid being attacked or coerced and to enjoy the benefits of a good relationship with the strong power, such as privileged economic access. Accommodation has two disadvantages. First, making sure it pursues no major policy that offends the strong power may require a substantial sacrifice of the weaker power's own interests. Second, if the strong power turns aggressive and aims to subdue or conquer all of its neighbors, the weaker partner may escape this fate only temporarily, and in the end, when its own turn comes, it has no potential allies left to call upon for help. For these reasons most medium and small states prefer the second avenue for dealing with a strong power: joining a countervailing coalition. By pooling their strength through strategic cooperation, several smaller states might be able to balance against the strength of a great power that poses a common threat to them. Their chances of matching the capabilities of the rising hegemon are greater if their coalition includes another great power, if one is available. The downside for small states of aligning themselves with a rival great power is that such an act will likely damage their relationship with the rising power.

States may employ *internal* balancing by increasing the proportion of national resources devoted to military strengthening. Alternatively, *external* balancing involves a state seeking increased security cooperation with another state to provide protection against a third state that both fear. Analysts also make a distinction between "hard" balancing and "soft" balancing. The former takes the form of formal military alliances aimed at a third party or an arms buildup that is clearly aimed at certain potential adversary. In soft balancing, defense cooperation or political coordination between states is informal and downplayed, and arms buildups are limited and not tied to the specific capabilities of a rival. Soft balancing is expected among states that perceive potential danger from a powerful neighbor but are desirous to avoid an open confrontation because they are much weaker than or economically dependent on the powerful state.

In principle, the natural inclination of states not to leave themselves vulnerable before a powerful potential adversary and the abundant historical record of balancing behavior in Asia give rise to the expectation that except for those countries in a hopeless strategic position (weak states that are on or near the Chinese border and have no defense partnership with another major power), Asian states will balance against a China perceived as domineering.

It may simply be impossible for China to impose its will on a reluctant world because the world would resist. Even as the strongest power in the world, China would not be able to dominate a coalition of major and middle powers that had decided to cooperate against China. As the lone superpower, the United States has been unable either to cow the other powers into full accommodation or fully to win their trust. During the George W. Bush administration, much of the international community reached the conclusion that U.S. policy had become dangerously unilateral, with Washington insisting on the pursuit of narrow U.S. interests regardless of the preferences of other governments. These other governments, including U.S. allies and friends, responded by resisting U.S. plans, sometimes jointly. The unipolar United States saw anti-American "soft" balancing by China, Russia, and even the European Union, plus many smaller states, beginning with the Iraq War.[13] The United States in the post–Cold War era reached an extraordinary apogee of power that America may not be able to sustain for much longer and that China may never attain. While superpowers face constant complaints for failing to satisfy onerous and contradictory expectations from the rest of the world, the United States enjoys a relatively high degree of international legitimacy. Since China is not a superpower, it can maintain a lower profile, dodge more responsibilities, and make fewer enemies than the United States. Already, however, China has accrued resentment from foreigners through such policies as aggressively extracting resources from poor countries, bringing Chinese laborers to overseas work sites rather than hiring local workers, turning a blind eye to the atrociously bad governance records of some business partners, and punishing small countries that have supported Taiwan's government. While the United States has been the "least distrusted power" in Asia,[14] China carries the historical baggage of attempts to establish a sphere of influence in Asia during the premodern era and support for regional insurgencies during the Cold War. Most recently Beijing has put the region on edge with sweeping claims to disputed territories and the rapid enhancement of the

PLA's power-projection capabilities. If we could compare the two countries in a way that equalized their power levels, the United States is arguably less disliked than China. If, then, the American superpower faced international opposition despite incomparable U.S. power and legitimacy, it follows that a Chinese superpower would meet a similar backlash if it misbehaved.

Most of the medium and smaller powers in the Asia-Pacific are following a middle way that combines elements of the accommodation and balancing strategies. Allies and other governments friendly to Washington have become more sensitive to Beijing's wishes. China has successfully persuaded some countries in the region not to form new alliances or make large increases in their military spending to counter China's enhanced power and influence. Regional countries want to trade with China and are doing it more. This might lead to greater Chinese influence over Asia-Pacific governments, as the Chinese could use business opportunities as an enticement to force these governments to make policy changes in conformity with Beijing's wishes. Through the first decade of the new century, however, there was little evidence that the Chinese were successfully using their economic leverage to force regional governments to reduce their strategic cooperation with the United States. The region is not interested in joining an open campaign to encircle China militarily or even to form a defensive alliance against China. Most regional leaders are careful to avoid irritating China if possible. At the same time, however, they are paying the premiums for insurance policies of their own.

The United States' strategy of hedging against possible hostile behavior by a stronger future China includes a commitment to strengthening security cooperation with its allies Japan, Australia, and South Korea as well as greater recent interest in deepening the U.S.-India relationship and in revitalizing U.S. relationships with Southeast Asian governments. These governments are grasping opportunities to balance with Washington. Far from being dismissed as a spent force that must step aside to make way for a new Chinese era, U.S. military and diplomatic power is more welcome than ever in the Asia-Pacific region. The more relatively powerful China becomes, the more the region wants U.S. engagement. Even an America weakened by economic crisis and domestic political underperformance is not necessarily less desirable as a strategic partner. From the standpoint of other Asia-Pacific states, an excessively strong America may be prone to unilateral, narrowly self-interested action and to disregarding the interests of allies and friends, while a humbled America might value its partnerships more highly and try harder to sustain the relationships that ensure cooperation.

When China tried to harness the 2005 East Asian Summit to its own purposes, Japan and some Southeast Asian countries countered by insisting that India, Australia, and New Zealand be included to balance Chinese influence. The region accepted the unstated principle that China will behave more gentlemanly if Japan and India are also seated at the table. Rising worries about China's growing military power and intentions led to the "Quadrilateral Initiative": upgraded defense cooperation between the United States, Japan, India, and Australia beginning in 2007. China called the arrangement an "Asian NATO" and filed formal protests with all four governments. Underlying this cooperation was Japanese Prime Minister Abe Shinzo's notion of an "Asian arc of freedom," a bloc of democratic states in a strategic and economic partnership along the borders of southern and eastern China.[15] The tensions with China in 2010 caused the Japanese government to move closer to the United States. Japan's latest National Defense Program Guidelines report registered "concern" about China's military modernization and "insufficient transparency" and reaffirmed the alliance with the United States as "indispensable" to Japanese security. Tokyo committed to cooperation with Washington in "new areas" as well as a plan to "enhance security cooperation" (i.e., balancing) with South Korea, India, Australia, and Southeast Asia.[16]

Southeast Asian Balancing

In general, Southeast Asian governments work to preclude the subregion being dominated by any single great power. Each of these governments, however, has a unique relationship with China based on its own circumstances. Burma, Cambodia, and Laos are highly deferential toward China because they are small, poor, within China's shadow, and lack close ties with another great power to offset China's influence. Thailand and Vietnam try to avoid antagonizing China while maintaining defense links with the United States. The Thais buy some military equipment from the PRC and have participated in joint military exercises with the Chinese, but Thailand's security links with the United States are much more extensive. Indonesia and Malaysia are relatively confident because of their distance from China, size, and prosperity. They are not openly fearful of China. Yet they also welcome, discretely rather than effusively, U.S. defense links with the region. The Philippines and Singapore, historically less resistant to partnering with the West, are the most supportive of a continued U.S. military role in the Asia-Pacific. During the first decade of the twenty-first century, the Philippines' leadership was focused on domestic insurgencies rather than a possible threat from China. The country's air force and navy fell into disrepair. By 2010, however, perceived Chinese aggressiveness had reemerged as Manila's no. 1 security concern. On the South China Sea territorial dispute, the sharpest strategic dispute in Sino-Philippine relations, Manila has not signaled an intent to back down. "What is ours is ours," Philippine President Benigno Aquino III recently said. "Setting foot on [the disputed South China Sea feature] Recto Bank is no different from setting foot on Recto Avenue [a street in Manila]." He promised that "we will be seeing capability upgrades and the modernization of the equipment of our armed forces."[17] Singapore is perhaps Southeast Asia's most vociferous proponent of a continued U.S. military presence to maintain stability in the region. The Singaporean government has built a large pier at its Changi Naval Base to encourage visits by U.S. Navy aircraft carriers. Even the Singaporeans, however, stop short of advocating formal alliances or "containment" of China.

After the 1995 Mischief Reef incident, Beijing sought to assuage Southeast Asian fears through a diplomatic campaign presenting China as a peace-loving, cooperative country overflowing with economic opportunities for its neighbors. This campaign was largely successful in muting open discussion by Southeast Asian leaders of China as a threat to the region. China's campaign of reassurance diplomacy combined with a sense throughout Southeast Asia that the rise of China is inevitable and that China's neighbors should make the best of it rather than aggravating Beijing.

Nevertheless, Southeast Asian governments privately suspect that China wants to turn their subregion into a Chinese dominion, and few if any are prepared to acquiesce. Chinese power and influence poses several potential threats to Southeast Asian states. An immediate concern is whether domestic industries in these countries can survive the immense challenge of Chinese economic competition, not only in the supply of low-cost goods but also in the contest to attract foreign investment. Although China offered many concessions to Southeast Asian governments to smooth the agreement on an ASEAN-China Free Trade Area in 2002 (with implementation in 2010), observers in Southeast Asia also worry that deeper economic integration with China will strengthen China's control of the subregion and reflects a strategic PRC master plan. The worries about Chinese domination are based on historical precedent. The issue that currently generates the greatest amount of tension is the dispute over which nations have sovereignty rights in various parts of the South China Sea. China's increasing capacity to project force into the area—and its apparent willingness to use that force—might require Southeast Asian claimant governments to choose between yielding to a foreign power on a nationalism-charged issue and fighting a losing military conflict against stronger PLA units. Southeast Asian countries would also suffer collateral damage in a U.S.-China conflict. If forced to take sides in such a war, they would suffer political, economic, or perhaps even military retaliation from the side they chose against.

Southeast Asia is balancing against China, albeit in subtle ways. Governments in the subregion have cooperated with each other more as they have perceived U.S. power in their subregion declining relative to Chinese power. Southeast Asian states try to steer a middle course between open opposition to China and acquiescence to Chinese regional domination. Part of their approach is trying to "socialize" China: welcoming Chinese representatives to join multilateral discussions of strategic, political, and economic issues in the hope of getting them to think and behave more like their regional neighbors. Another part of the strategy is soft balancing: encouraging the United States to reaffirm strongly its commitment to helping keep the peace in eastern Asia so that U.S. influence can counterbalance that of China; providing facilities and access to U.S. military forces as a way to deter China; and inviting other great powers to take up a stake in preserving regional peace and stability. Southeast Asian governments crave constant U.S. assurances that Washington will remain a strategic player and balancer in the subregion and not abandon them to Chinese domination. The arrangement that Southeast Asian states think will provide both regional stability and maximum autonomy for individual governments is a hierarchy of outside powers with the United States as the most powerful state, China a close second, followed by middle powers Japan and India, and finally lower-tier middle powers South Korea and Australia.

"Peaceful Rise" Means Beijing Gets It

Countries with fast-growing economic and military capabilities make their neighbors nervous. China is probably more sensitive to this phenomenon than any other rising power in history. In the 1990s several Chinese scholars published prominent analyses highlighting what Western theorists believed about the emergence of great powers. This Chinese analysis pointed out that Western historians linked the emergence of new great powers with the outbreak of major war, and that foreigners were likely to view the rise of China within this context.[18] The Chinese leadership appears acutely aware of the soft anti-China balancing already underway and is frightened that this balancing might attract more governments and take on a harder edge. To undercut the rationale for such a strategy, Beijing has carried out a package of policies under the rubric of "peaceful rise" or "peaceful development."

By the early 1990s, analysts outside China were discussing the implications of China's rapid and sustained economic growth for regional security. Many of these analysts saw dangers in the emergence of a great power with an authoritarian political system, a postwar record of frequent uses of force against other countries, and a demonstrated disregard for many international norms. Chinese officials dubbed this school of thought the "China threat theory" and devoted considerable effort to attacking it. Many of those who warned about the dangers of a stronger China were Americans. Chinese responded with the assertion that Americans harbor a hidden anti-China agenda designed to suppress China's growth and thereby maintain America's privileged position in Asia. Chinese allege that the U.S. government has interests in hyping the threat posed by a strong China, that the U.S. defense establishment needs China to fill the role of the former USSR as an archenemy in order to justify large military budgets, and that American armaments industries in partnership with Washington hope to continue their lucrative sales to Taiwan. A more charitable Chinese reaction is that the Americans are ignorant of the aspects of Chinese culture and history that support Beijing's claim that China is an inherently peace-loving country.

To counter the China threat theory, on countless occasions over the last two decades, Chinese officials, media, and state-affiliated scholars have repeated the mantra that a stronger China will be peaceful, will threaten no other country, will not strive for hegemony, and will not even aspire to superpower status. Chinese diplomats have offered standard pieces of evidence to back up this prediction. The historical record, they say, describes a premodern China that was strong but peaceful and nonaggressive. They cite the benevolent interpretation of Admiral Zheng He's voyages. They make the argument that Confucian culture imprints upon Chinese the importance of achieving social harmony, which results in a cooperative and compromise-seeking foreign policy. Chinese diplomats also assert that since the Chinese people have been victims of imperialism and hegemony, they would not allow their own government to carry out a similar kind of victimization. Finally, they argue that for the foreseeable future China will need a peaceful international environment to achieve economic development, which will preclude a strong China from being a troublemaker.

In 2002, Zheng Bijian, a former advisor to Hu Jintao, promoted the idea of "peaceful rise" (*heping jueqi*) to undercut the China threat theory. Zheng argued that China wants prosperity, not world domination or an ideological struggle with the West; that China wants international politics to be more democratic and less conflictual; and that as a globalized country benefitting from engagement with the international system, China will not be a disruptive great power along the lines of Nazi Germany, fascist Japan, or the Soviet Union. China is acquiring the resources, capital, and technology it needs for national development through peaceful relations and openness to trade with other countries. Therefore, said Zheng, the world can confidently expect that a stronger China would reinforce rather than threaten world peace.[19] In 2003 and 2004, senior Chinese leaders including President Hu Jintao and Premier Wen Jiabao used the term "peaceful rise" in their public statements. The idea was well received outside China. It evidently influenced U.S. Deputy Secretary of State Robert Zoellick's important September 2005 speech envisioning a U.S.-China partnership if China could behave as a "responsible stakeholder" in the international system, as Zoellick's speech made some of the same points that Zheng had been making about China. Within China, however, many officials and scholars questioned the utility of the slogan. Some argued that it was too peaceful and others that it was not peaceful enough. One objection was that the word "peaceful" might embolden Taiwan independence activists to conclude that China would not go to war over the permanent political separation of Taiwan from the mainland. Other critics said the word "rise" would alarm the global community and make an anti-China alliance more likely or that it was premature to talk about China "rising" in view of the country's many unsolved economic and social problems. The latter criticisms influenced the leadership, and by mid-2004 senior leaders had changed over to the slogan "peaceful development" (*heping fazhan*) to present a sugar-coated encapsulation of China's growing international impact.

Some of the PRC's policies reinforce the verbal assurances that China as a great power will be peaceful and cooperative. China establishes "partnerships" with neighbors and more distant important countries, keeps the Chinese economy reasonably open so foreign countries will also benefit as China grows, and participates in multilateral organizations to increase China's international influence and reiterate the message that China is benign. The "peaceful development" campaign also provides a strong incentive for China to stay quiet about the U.S. military presence in East Asia unless the Americans directly challenge a vital Chinese interest.

This remarkable effort on the part of Beijing to reassure the world about China's future intentions indicates the depth of the PRC's fear that the rise of China will bring forth balancing behavior and other defensive reactions from the international community. The prospect of other countries cooperating against a threatening China is indeed a strong disincentive against Chinese misbehavior—provided this disincentive is not superseded by other considerations.

Chapter Eight

PERSISTENT RISK OF CONFLICT

We have seen that some aspects of the current international political system should help reduce the chances of conflict resulting from the rise of China. Unfortunately, there is another set of countervailing factors that ensure a continuing risk of tensions that could lead to war. Four phenomena related to the rise of China will push the PRC toward conflictual relations with other Asia-Pacific countries. First, as China grows stronger, the Chinese tendency to see PRC security policies as defensive will worsen security dilemmas with its neighbors. Second, China's historically based expectation of a Chinese sphere of influence produces uncompromising Chinese positions and even bullying on international issues in China's neighborhood. When the relative growth of Chinese power combines with China's sense of entitlement to control parts of the region, the likely result is serious friction as Beijing moves to settle long-held grievances. Third, the characteristics of the PRC's domestic political system and environment might make China prone to external conflicts. Finally, with the rise of Chinese power and influence, the scope of the U.S.-China rivalry will expand from regional to global.

Aggression Is in the Eye of the Beholder

It seems either cynical or self-delusional for Beijing to promise that China will be a peaceful, cooperative, and nonhegemonic power while at the same time the Chinese pursue policies that its neighbors would characterize as domineering and in some cases aggressive. But this is nothing new in international politics. History shows that two characteristics are typical of modern great-power behavior, whether the example is fascist Japan, Nazi Germany, the USSR, or the United States: they carry out assertive or aggressive foreign policies that impose constraints on other states, and they describe their policies as justifiably self-defensive and even beneficial to the foreign peoples who are affected. Similarly, PRC behavior includes some actions that other governments in the region consider to be aggressive, belligerent, and destabilizing. The Chinese, however, see these policies as justifiable, "principled," and consistent with Beijing's stated commitments to support peaceful and just international relations. Indeed, the Chinese have difficulty viewing any of their actions as anything but defensive.

According to the PRC government, China "never engages in aggression," threatens no other country, opposes "the big bullying the small," and "does not impose its own will upon others."[1] China's is certainly not the only government that tries to present itself in a favorable light, even if Beijing's efforts often appear ham-fisted and propagandist because of the CCP's Leninist lineage. Yet there seems to be something else at work here. It surfaces in the commentary of PRC officials and analysts. Prime Minister Wen Jiaobao and other PRC authorities have repeated the statement that "over the past hundred years, China has always been bullied by others. China has never sent a single soldier to occupy even an inch of foreign land."[2] Given that governments sometimes believe their own propaganda, this is a disturbingly fallacious statement. First, it implies that if China didn't bother others during the last hundred years, it follows that China will not bother others during the next hundred years. This overlooks the important point that China as a powerful country will likely behave differently than it did during the period when it was a weak and poor country. Second, the statement implies that China cannot be accused of bullying if it does not have troops occupying foreign land. There are, of course, many other ways to bully, and Beijing has employed some of them. Finally, the statement completely dismisses the issue of disputed territory. The governments of India and the other South China Sea claimants would say the PRC *is* militarily occupying foreign territory. Yan Xuetong, dean of the Institute of Contemporary International Relations of Tsinghua University, is one of China's premier international affairs scholars. His interpretation of recent events in the region is hard to dispute: "China's neighbors have asked the U.S. to intervene in Asia and have wanted the U.S. to lead Asia to counter China's rise." Surprisingly, however, the policy Yan recommends is that "China must speed up its military development" because "without sufficient military power, China can't protect the other Asian countries." He seems to mean that a militarily strong China will convince other Asian states they don't need U.S. "protection."[3] This is the exact opposite of what we have seen in the region thus far, and which Yan himself pointed out, which is that growing Chinese military strength increases the region's desire to retain U.S. power as a balancer. Jian Junbo, a professor at the Institute of International Studies at Shanghai's Fudan University, recently observed that China "never claims other countries' territory."[4] This, however, is circular logic that does not account for the possibility that other countries might dispute China's claims. Well-known PRC strategist Peng Guangqian displayed a stunning insensitivity to the security fears of other Asia-Pacific countries when he said, "Only Taiwan separatists and those people who have ulterior motives regarding China would feel uncomfortable about China's advanced weapons."[5]

On the other hand, some Chinese thinkers demonstrate an admirable capacity for clear-minded analysis. Among them is Shi Yinhong, a scholar at Renmin University in Beijing, who observes, "If the Chinese government is clever, it would do well to think about the reason why the U.S. is suddenly so popular in the region. Is it because China has not been good enough when it comes to diplomacy with its neighboring countries?"[6] Mainstream and official Chinese thinking, however, often appears unable or unwilling to see PRC actions as anything but "defensive" and justified. It may not be oversimplifying too much to say that in mainstream Chinese thinking, all of China's security policies are defensive by definition. China's historical outlook has produced what the scholar Andrew Scobell calls a "cult of defense."[7] While China actually relies heavily on offensive military action, Chinese strategists are conditioned to interpret this action as defensive. Aggression is rationalized as self-defense. Chinese military writings emphasize the principle of not being the first to strike. They also make clear, however, that the first "shot" in a battle may be political rather than military. Thus a perceived *political* threat to China may justify a preemptive Chinese *military* attack. This is what happened in the 1950 Chinese intervention to preserve the shrinking North Korean state, in the 1962 Chinese incursion into border areas disputed with India, and in the 1979 Chinese attack on Vietnam to punish Hanoi for its invasion of Cambodia and overthrow of the pro-China Pol Pot regime. Starting a war in response to a politically tense bilateral dispute may not qualify as "defensive" to most observers, but to Chinese it does.

Distinguishing between self-defense and aggression is often a matter of interpretation. But by any reasonable criteria, China's policy has been a mixture of both. Even in the post-Mao era, when Beijing has pursued international reengagement, made peace with its neighbors to facilitate economic development, and promoted a favorable international image of China, the Chinese have occasionally exhibited sharp and seemingly incongruous departures such as the campaign of military intimidation aimed at Taiwan in 1995–1996 and the Mischief Reef affair of 1995. Some observers believe the PRC's rapid and determined military buildup clashes with the comparative lack of external threats to China and with Beijing's insistence that all the Chinese want is a peaceful environment for economic development. Most Chinese, however, see no contradiction here.

Another temptation for a great power is to establish military bases on foreign territory. At present, Beijing proudly declares that China has no foreign bases and neither should anyone else because they are imperialistic, not defensive. This is an issue that the Chinese believe favorably distinguishes them from the Americans. But not for long, perhaps. Small numbers of Chinese troops have reportedly guarded some Chinese facilities overseas. Chinese leaders have told the Pakistani government they want to establish PRC military bases in Pakistan to monitor and suppress activities that aid separatist and terrorist groups in Xinjiang. After an attack on the Mekong River near the Golden Triangle (where the borders of Burma, Thailand, and Laos meet, south of China's Yunnan province) killed thirteen Chinese sailors, the PRC began sending police boats armed with machine guns to patrol the Mekong in 2011. The CCP-affiliated newspaper *Global Times* seemed to be preparing its audience for a new era of "defensive" bases outside of China when it opined in 2011, "If China is going to play an important role in the Asia-Pacific region and on the international stage, as urged by the international community, it eventually will need to establish overseas military bases in cooperation with other countries."[8]

The Chinese tendency to consider all of its security policies as defensive makes Beijing undersensitive to the security concerns of its neighbors. As China grows relatively more powerful and therefore more capable of harming other states in the region, these states will naturally feel less secure unless China can convincingly assuage their worries. If, however, Beijing sees no need to take concrete steps toward assurance and confidence building because of the Chinese belief that PRC policies are clearly defensive and that the worries of other states are not legitimate, rising insecurity will cause at least some Asia-Pacific governments to take defensive countermeasures against China. This will contribute to a spiral of suspicion and rising tension. Ordinarily, the desire for international prestige and the fear of anti-China balancing steer the Chinese toward cautious and cooperative behavior. But these two forces have comparatively little restraining power where the Chinese believe they are acting defensively. Caution and restraint are more likely to give way to national pride and unvarnished territoriality.

A Chinese Sphere of Influence

A sphere of influence is an area of foreign territory over which a state has influence, control, or privileges not enjoyed by other states. Beijing's desire and intention is to make eastern Asia (Northeast Asia and Southeast Asia), Central Asia, and possibly parts of South Asia a Chinese sphere of influence. If this Chinese ambition is realized, China would sit at the top of a hierarchy of regional states, with the other governments required to obtain Beijing's approval for their major external policies. On many issues geographically located on China's periphery, the Chinese take a proprietary position and defend this position stridently and sometimes belligerently. The Chinese have a strong capacity to see this behavior as part of the PRC's morally "principled" foreign policy and as consistent with promises that a stronger China will be a force for peace and global justice. This explains why the Chinese government has often adjusted its policies on global issues under international pressure, but Beijing is less responsive to foreign opinion when it comes to issues close to China's borders. Chinese aggressiveness in the areas Beijing deems to be rightfully part of China's sphere of influence is relatively immune to fears of encouraging anti-Chinese activity among foreign governments.

There are two strong motivations for China to aspire to be the preeminent power and rule maker within the region. The first is security. For the foreseeable future, the Chinese will suspect that the bottom line of America's strategy in Asia is containing China. Gaining a dominant position in the region will allow China to clear out U.S. strategic influence and to suppress other possible rivals.

The second motivation for a Chinese sphere of influence is the compulsion to fulfill China's historical sense of its own destiny. Although the Chinese argue that history backs up their assurances that "China will never seek hegemony," there is plenty in premodern Chinese history that indicates the opposite. During the Warring States Period of 475 to 221 b.c.e., seven (some historians add an eighth) Chinese kingdoms fought for supremacy over the core of the Chinese empire. Qin eventually prevailed, uniting China and establishing a long period of Chinese regional supremacy. Analysts of contemporary China argue that this period is particularly important. Deng Xiaoping and PLA leaders have particularly urged Chinese to study the Warring States Period. The key features of this period were a struggle for power among roughly equal sovereign states and the emergence of a preeminent state that went on to dominate the region. The main lesson seems to be that a stable international order is not based on states seeing each other as equals. Rather, peace and stability stem from a recognized hierarchy. The interest of Chinese officialdom in the Warring States Period and its aftermath increases the possibility that these interpretations of China's past will find their way into the roadmap for the new era in which China returns to its historical position as East Asia's strongest power.

Another part of that roadmap may be inspired by the tribute system that prevailed in premodern East Asia. According to one theory, centuries of following the tribute system shaped regional thinking about the relationship between China and its neighbors so deeply that with the reemergence of a strong China the region will fall back into the old pattern. The countries of Northeast and Southeast Asia will again recognize China as the region's supreme power, and order will be based on adherence to China's preferences regarding regional issues.

In 1823, the U.S. government under President James Monroe announced the Monroe Doctrine, which stated that Washington would not tolerate colonization or attempted recolonization by the European countries in the Western Hemisphere. It signaled that the period of European control of parts of Central and South America was over and that from then on the United States would be the unquestioned dominant power in the New World. The scholar John Mearsheimer argues that Japan attempted to implement its own version of the Monroe Doctrine for Asia in the 1930s and 1940s and that a strong China will try to do the same. Specifically, Mearsheimer predicts that China's Asian Monroe Doctrine will include the following elements: China will try to increase its lead in national power over potential regional rivals Japan, Russia, and India; China will attempt "to dictate the boundaries of acceptable behavior to neighboring countries, much the way the United States makes it clear to other states in the Americas that it is the boss"; and Beijing will seek "to push the United States out of the

Pacific-Asia region, much the way the United States pushed the European great powers out of the Western Hemisphere in the nineteenth century."[9]

Chinese plans for a sphere of influence on the PRC's periphery obviously conflict with U.S. plans to remain a major strategic player in the Western Pacific. Some scholars argue that peace in East Asia is stable because China and the United States already have distinct spheres of influence: China dominates the continental areas of eastern Asia; the United States dominates the maritime areas. China should feel reasonably secure because the United States is not mounting a serious challenge to Chinese influence on the Asian landmass.[10] The problem with this assessment, however, is that China is seeking to expand its influence into the maritime areas—from the Chinese coast to the first island chain and even beyond.

A dominant power might provide protection and public goods, but the dark side of a sphere of influence is the bullying of countries that do not conform to the dominant power's wishes. Far from transcending this typical inclination of great powers, Beijing has not been shy about using China's economic, political, and military power to impose China's will on other governments, either because they are in China's neighborhood or because they have tread on what Beijing considers to be an "internal" matter.

In September 2010 Japanese authorities detained the captain of a Chinese fishing boat for ramming two Japanese Coast Guard vessels that tried to shoo his boat away from the disputed Senkaku/Diaoyutai Islands. Videotapes of the incident appeared to corroborate the Japanese side of the story. One reason why Beijing's reaction was excessive and disturbing was that the Chinese retaliated against Japan in aspects of their bilateral relationship that are not related to the territorial dispute. Beijing cancelled a planned visit of one thousand Japanese youth to the Shanghai Expo. A day *after* Tokyo relented to Chinese pressure and set the Chinese captain free, a move for which the Japanese government suffered much domestic criticism, Chinese authorities arrested four Japanese employees of the Fujitsu Corporation on what appeared to be groundless "espionage" charges. The Chinese government instructed Chinese travel agents to stop promoting tours to Japan. Japanese officials and businessmen reported that the Chinese cut the supply of rare-earth minerals to Japan over the boat incident. Rare-earth minerals are necessary for making many high-tech products, and China happens to control over 90 percent of worldwide production.

When Southeast Asian countries banned or complained about imports of food and personal care products from China that turned out to be tainted with poisons and carcinogens, the Chinese government responded with noncooperation, threats, and retaliatory trade barriers. In the South China Sea, where sovereignty is disputed between Beijing and five other governments, China has demanded that the other claimant states not discuss the issue among themselves or coordinate a shared position before negotiating with the PRC. China reportedly pressured Southeast Asian governments not to raise the South China Sea issue during the July 2010 ASEAN Regional Forum meeting in Hanoi. This failed, as the foreign ministers of several Southeast Asian states voiced their concerns. During a closed-door meeting, Chinese Foreign Minister Yang Jiechi angrily threatened to punish these states through China's economic power.[11]

China has also bullied small countries outside the region over the Taiwan issue. As the deployment period for UN peacekeepers in Haiti drew to a close in 1996, Haitians feared a return of crime and violence. Haiti's government asked for an extension of the peacekeeping mission. China threatened to veto the extension because Haiti, which has diplomatic relations with Taiwan, had invited Taiwan's vice president to attend the Haitian president's inauguration ceremony. After regional states (including Cuba) criticized Chinese obstructionism, China agreed to the proposal only after insisting that the size and time period of the UN deployment be reduced. In 1997, China vetoed a proposal before the UN Security Council to send peacekeepers to Guatemala to supervise the peace settlement ending that country's civil war. Chinese officials said the veto was the result of Guatemala's diplomatic relations with Taiwan. Beijing eventually withdrew its veto rather than suffer a diplomatic defeat when the United Nations prepared to move the decision to the UN General Assembly, where it was certain to pass. When Macedonia, newly independent from Yugoslavia, switched diplomatic recognition from China to Taiwan in 1999, Beijing quickly retaliated by vetoing a Security Council plan to extend a much-needed UN peacekeeping deployment.

Insecurity Within, Strife Without

The PRC's domestic political circumstances may make China conflict prone. Many analysts argue that Chinese foreign policy is inherently quarrelsome because of the nature of the PRC political system. The characteristics of CCP governance inside China include intolerance of criticism, limited respect for civil and political human rights and the rule of law, little accountability of the state to society, and nontransparency in decision making. Reflected in China's international relations, these characteristics generate friction with other countries, especially the liberal democracies in the Asia-Pacific region. An example of how PRC foreign policy can be an extension of PRC domestic policy is found in Beijing's clear pattern of supporting foreign dictators, even those considered international pariahs. The list of cases includes Robert Mugabe of Zimbabwe and Hugo Chavez of Venezuela. During the Arab Spring of 2011, the official PRC media characterized the anti-Mubarak protestors in Egypt as troublemakers. The Chinese supplied arms to the regime of the Libyan tyrant Muammar Gaddafi and continued to plan for new sales even after it became clear the discredited regime was losing its fight against the rebels.

In November 2011, China awarded its "Confucius Peace Prize" to Vladimir Putin, who is perhaps most infamous for his dismantling of democracy in Russia as well as his brutal military campaign against the Russian province of Chechnya in 1999–2000. The Chinese award committee specifically praised Putin's "iron hand and toughness." One commentator observed, "Apparently Muammar Gaddafi, since deposed and now dead, wasn't eligible" for the Confucius Prize.[12] This impulse to bond with fellow authoritarians has arguably worked against Chinese interests because many authoritarian governments have defied Chinese wishes (North Korea is a good example), and their countries are often excessively risky places for Chinese investment. Beijing persists in this policy, however, because it sees Western liberalism as its main enemy and considers these dictators as natural allies in the struggle to resist foreign ideological pressure. Chinese leaders want to undercut "people power" in other countries because they fear it happening in China. The CCP government worried that the "Arab Spring" of popular uprisings in Middle East countries that began in late 2010 might inspire crowds of disgruntled Chinese citizens to take to the streets and that Washington would try to exploit another opportunity to push for peaceful evolution. The Chinese took note when U.S. Senator John McCain warned that "the Arab Spring is coming to China."[13]

Beijing emphasizes that China's Confucian culture makes China inherently harmony seeking, which will have a positive effect on international affairs as China grows relatively stronger. The Confucian tradition, however, is not necessarily conducive to cooperation. In social relations, it establishes a hierarchy that breeds arrogant behavior by those who perceive themselves as superiors toward their perceived inferiors. Carried over into international relations, this thinking would lead the statesmen of a powerful country to expect deference from smaller countries.

The CCP regime is insecure to a degree that borders on paranoia. The government fears the growing power of Chinese society relative to the state and worries that discontent could erupt into a threat to overthrow the political order. According to a 2011 report by the U.S.-China Economic and Security Review Commission, the Chinese government spent $83.5 billion on internal security measures in 2010, an amount that exceeded China's official military budget. Domestic policing measures included a project to saturate the Chinese city of Chongqing with half a million security cameras. Since the CCP is not an elected government, the basis of its legitimacy is narrow and fragile. Therefore the CCP must lean on other pillars for its legitimacy: providing economic prosperity and defending China's honor. If there is an economic downturn, the Beijing leadership might need to rely more heavily on a chauvinistic, contentious foreign policy to maintain the support of the Chinese public. The scholar Fei-Ling Wang observes that despite the PRC's growing power and impressive accomplishments, the leadership maintains a "peculiar sense of insecurity in a secure world" and a strong sense of "vulnerability." The result is that even criticism from foreigners "is often met with defensive and ultra sensitive counterattacks."[14] How well the leadership stands up for China's international status and dignity is one of the most important variables in the CCP's legitimacy. Thus, the CCP regime's sense of domestic insecurity could lead to confrontational foreign policies and excessive responses. The fear of appearing in the eyes of the domestic audience as weak before foreigners impels the Chinese leadership to speak and act with bravado. This increases the chances that crises involving China will escalate rather than dissipate. On certain issues involving either the legitimacy of the CCP or intense nationalism, China is liable to disregard international norms and sensibilities. For example, Beijing's official reaction to its jailed dissident Liu Xiaobo winning the 2010 Nobel Peace Prize highlighted the regime's insecurity. The award, said the PRC Ministry of Foreign Affairs, was part of an ideologically motivated Western effort to impede China's development. In its various confrontations with other Asia-Pacific countries over use of the international waters near China's coast, the PRC's rough and reckless treatment of foreign vessels has caused friction and brought Beijing much condemnation from abroad. Evidently, however,

Beijing saw these costs as preferable to the domestic anger that would have resulted from perceived PRC passivity in the face of foreign intrusion.

Policy making by the PRC central government has gradually become more decentralized. The process now involves input from many different groups, including regional governments, the PLA, other government agencies, research institutes, and even the mass public. Sometimes there is a "least common denominator" effect: a tough or nationalistic response to a foreign policy issue by one major actor compels the others to fall in line. In the areas where it has influence, the military consistently presses for an assertive Chinese stance. If the PLA made the PRC's foreign policy, overall tensions between China and its neighbors would be considerably higher. The Chinese scholar Huang Jing compares today's young PLA officers to the angry young Japanese officers who drove Japan toward an expansionist policy in the 1930s. PLA thinking, says Huang, is "on a collision course with a U.S.-dominated system."[15]

China is in a transitional period during which many Chinese simultaneously feel *both* greater entitlement to international deference because of their rising power *and* sensitivity to what they see as continued victimization. This is a flammable combination. Anxious to bolster its mandate to rule, the CCP takes every opportunity to reinforce its message to China's people that the PRC continues to make gains in its drive to become a powerful, influential, and prestigious player in international politics. The message increases the Chinese public's expectations that the time has arrived for China to rectify past injustices and for other countries to submit to China's will rather than the reverse.

There is a disconnect between an increasingly pushy and impatient public and a cautious leadership. An authoritative 2012 survey showed that most of the Chinese public expects their country to be the world's strongest power within twenty years, while most Chinese elites do not.[16] In recent years the Chinese public as well as the PLA leadership has more forcefully called for the Chinese government to defend Chinese interests even at the risk of causing friction with the United States. These demands may continue to rise as China itself rises.

Beijing attempts to manage public opinion through such means as censoring the Internet and issuing content guidelines to Chinese media outlets. These efforts are only partly successful. Beijing can mobilize the public by playing up certain issues, but the government cannot always channel the mass public's energy in the direction Beijing desires. The public is also able to self-mobilize even against the government's will. When an event or incident touches on nationalistic Chinese sensitivities, Beijing may feel compelled to take an injudiciously tough position toward a foreign government in anticipation of a strong public reaction that first targets foreigners and then quickly pivots to a critical assessment of whether the leadership of China is showing enough valor in defense of China's dignity. Wang Yuzhu, an analyst at the Chinese Academy of Social Sciences, says "It was different 10–15 years ago; we made many compromises, for instance, to gain access to the World Trade Organization." Now, however, "Our government can't easily give in to other countries even a little" because "people in China follow international relations issues more and more. So any compromise we make, people know about" and immediately criticize.[17] This dynamic will contribute to tougher PRC posturing on international disputes and less space for Beijing to compromise with other states. Domestic political forces may trump China's desire to build good foreign relations and a positive international image, even against the wishes of Chinese elites.

Chinese leaders have argued that China will be a peaceful great power because their main interest is only to raise their people's living standards. A twist on this argument, however, is that in order to meet the demands for prosperity at home, Beijing will feel compelled to prosecute an aggressive foreign policy aimed at securing Chinese access to vital resources and a privileged position for China in foreign markets.

While in some cases the mass public pushes the government, the reverse also occurs. The government benefits from a "circle the wagons" effect when the public perceives that China is under diplomatic attack. Stoking nationalism by playing up foreign hostility might be the leadership's most reliable way of mobilizing public support and the only basis for winning the loyalty of Chinese citizens who are otherwise unhappy with the CCP regime. In these cases, the CCP government may realize short-term domestic political gain, but only at the risk of an unnecessary increase in international tensions.

A Democratic China?

If China's political system contributes to conflict between the PRC and other countries, perhaps a change in that system would make the region more peaceful. Two big questions here are whether China will become a democracy and how this might affect China's relations with the other Asia-Pacific governments. In principle, Chinese elites, including CCP members, say China should move toward democracy. What they have in mind, however, is not necessarily Western-style democracy. While Americans tend to see democracy and liberties as ends in themselves, the Chinese view them as possible means for achieving the goals of prosperity, fairness, and national prominence. The Chinese attitude toward democracy is shaped by deep cultural preferences for a strong state, stability, and hierarchical social relations. Chinese elites have a range of views about democratization. They generally are not enamored of Western liberal democracy. Some see it as inappropriate for China. Western institutions per se will not solve China's problems, they say, and Westerners are arrogant to try to fit China into their model. Many Chinese think Westerners are intentionally trying to weaken China by introducing chaos through democratization. Chinese often associate democracy with instability: the mob rule of the Cultural Revolution, the collapse of the Soviet Union, the danger of unfettered civil liberties interrupting China's economic development. Says Liu Qing of the Chinese think tank China Institute of International Studies, "People [in China] like political stability. People have a vivid memory of what chaos means. The prevailing attitude is: Don't rock the boat."[18] The CCP does its best to play on fears of the Chinese public that putting another party in charge would result in chaos, a decline in prosperity, and increased vulnerability to foreign enemies. China's increasing prosperity is not necessarily creating a corresponding pressure for political liberalization. In contrast to past CCP practice, the party tries not to alienate the rich, but instead it strives to take care of the elite and middle classes. The great majority of China's millionaires are CCP members or close relatives of party members, a fact that should temper any expectations that China's newly affluent middle class will lead a movement to challenge the CCP's monopoly over political power. Many of the newly rich are joining the party, seeing membership as an advantage in an economy where opportunities and access often depend on personal connections.

Movement toward democratization in China seemed to backslide under President Hu Jintao. Communist Party officials are not interested in legalizing rival parties that could present them with a serious challenge. Many of them want to liberalize the political system to create greater accountability of leaders to the public and to decrease corruption and abuses of power, but they plan to keep these changes within the framework of continued one-party domination by the CCP.

China, then, is not on the verge of becoming a liberal democracy. Still, China is changing rapidly. The frequency of "mass incidents," in which anywhere from a dozen to thousands of people clash with police, is apparently increasing in China, which some observers see as a sign of the end of the CCP dynasty. The openness of political discourse and the strength of civil society (private, volunteer organizations not under the direct control of the state) have clearly and steadily increased in China over the last few decades. So has prosperity. These have been the precursors of democratization in other countries. Some form of democratization might be necessary for China's economic and social development to continue. The (probably irreversible) growth in the strength of Chinese society, the likely need for political reform to maintain rapid economic development, and the rapid pace of change within the country combine to raise the possibility that a dramatically transformed political system might emerge within two or three decades. A system that includes fair elections, a choice of parties, and expanded civil and political liberties is one of the possible outcomes. There is a fair chance that China will evolve into some form of democracy at about the same time it becomes powerful enough to challenge the United States for regional supremacy.

What effect would democratization in China have on regional security? The "democratic peace theory" holds that democracies rarely if ever go to war against each other. It raises hopes that the expansion of democracy throughout the world should reduce the incidence of war. Global democratization would make war virtually obsolete. According to this theory, if China converted to a democracy, the relations between China and Asia-Pacific democracies such as the United States, Japan, Taiwan, India, South Korea, and the Philippines would dramatically improve because the threat of war between them would disappear.

In China's case, however, peace through democratization is a false hope. One of the arguments supporting the democratic peace theory is that authoritarian governments can drag their people into unpopular wars that benefit the elite class but that democratic leaders are deterred from going to war without public approval out of fear they will be voted out of office. Although Chinese leaders are not popularly elected, they are as sensitive to public opinion as the national leaders of many democratic countries. Some of China's most confrontational foreign policies—such as the refusal to accept postwar Japan as a fully rehabilitated country, the assertion of Chinese rights over the international waters east and southeast of China, and the PRC's claim to sovereignty over Taiwan—clearly have the support of the Chinese public. In effect, on these issues China is already "democratic" because policy reflects the will of the majority of the PRC citizenry. Chinese foreign policy in these areas would not change because of a democratization of China's system of government.

Another argument supporting the expectation that a democratic China would be peaceful is that brainwashing by a government-controlled media and education system makes the Chinese people support Chinese foreign policies that cause international tension. If democracy allowed for a "marketplace of ideas," the Chinese people could consider a variety of viewpoints and might choose compromise and conciliation instead of conflict with their Asia-Pacific neighbors. This argument, however, is invalid. The mass nationalism that underpins support of assertive foreign policies is chosen by the Chinese people, not forced upon them. The Chinese do not uncritically accept the rhetoric of their own government. They also have access to other sides of the story, including commentary from the countries with which China has disputes. About sixty million Chinese traveled abroad in 2011, and an estimated five hundred million Chinese use the Internet. Many Chinese who study in the West return home with reinforced feelings of Chinese nationalism. Furthermore, loosening the government's control over the media does not exclusively promote peaceful international relations. A free media can also spread inflammatory commentary. If China had fewer controls on its press, Chinese leaders could not prevent the media from reporting concessions and compromises made by Beijing to defuse crises with foreign governments. The Chinese domestic media did not report, for example, that Beijing agreed to pay the United States $2.87 million in compensation for damage to U.S. diplomatic buildings in China caused by anti-U.S. rioting after the bombing of the Chinese embassy in Belgrade in 1999. Many Chinese would have severely criticized their leaders for this payoff. In a China with a free press and democratic elections, some peacemaking efforts by the Chinese government would be more constrained.

Some research suggests that even where authoritarian states convert to a democratic system, the reputed pacifying effects on the state's foreign policy do not appear right away. On the contrary, new democracies with political institutions that are not yet well established are even more likely to go to war than authoritarian states. This is because unrestrained nationalist impulses are translated directly into national policy.[19] It is not difficult to imagine that a newly democratic China would be war prone. Bureaucrats and national leaders tend to be calculating and cold blooded, while the mass public is comparatively emotional, strategically short sighted, and concerned with moral principles. Democratization would not extinguish Chinese nationalism. It would, however, weaken the government's ability to act as a moderating buffer between an agitated populace and external policy. An elected and fully accountable government would be forced to pander to raw popular impulses. In some cases the Chinese public has proved more belligerent than the government, forcing the authorities to play a delicate game of indulging domestic anger while trying to limit the damage to China's foreign relationships.

The democratization of the PRC would not by itself solve the issues disputed between China and its democratic neighbors, nor would it necessarily reduce the tensions caused by those issues.

From Regional Rivalry to Global Rivalry: The Case of Iran

Beijing's views on global issues have often differed from the views of the industrialized democracies. When the PRC was weaker, this did not necessarily matter because on many of these issues China had little or no influence. But the ascension of an authoritarian China with a strong sense of history and a peculiar worldview diversifies the club of major global players and complicates the management of global affairs. Increasingly, China's cooperation is essential to the solution of global problems. It is clear that a reasonable amount of agreement between China and the other major powers is necessary and desirable. It is not so clear, however, that China can work together with the United States and other governments to solve difficult security issues.

Iran tests the idea that China and the United States have sufficient common interests in a peaceful and orderly world to enable them to coordinate their policies aimed at meeting global security challenges. U.S.-China cooperation on Iran should not be impossible. Iran is outside of China's immediate neighborhood, so the intense Chinese feelings of nationalism and historical entitlement that complicate issues within China's intended sphere of influence do not apply. China is against nuclear proliferation in principle. Like Washington, China wants to avoid a Middle East conflict that might interrupt the outflow of oil supplies. Unfortunately, however, as with the North Korea case, Iran turns out to be an illustration of the fundamental difficulty of achieving Sino-U.S. comanagement of the international system.

For many observers, including Americans, Iran is a "rogue" state. Iran has been on the U.S. government's list of state sponsors of terrorism for over twenty-five years. Human rights monitoring groups say the Iranian government routinely incarcerates and tortures peaceful dissenters. The government of Iranian President Mahmoud Ahmadinejad has called for the destruction of the state of Israel and alleged that the U.S. government perpetrated the 9/11 terror attacks. Washington and Western European governments strongly oppose the current regime in Tehran developing nuclear weapons. Iran is a signatory of the Nuclear Non-Proliferation Treaty (NPT) as a non-nuclear weapons state. Iran is allowed to build a nuclear energy program but is obligated to observe safeguards designed to ensure its commitment not to develop nuclear weapons. Since 2003 the International Atomic Energy Agency (IAEA) has reported that Iran is in violation of its safeguard agreements because it has secretly carried out activities consistent with an intention to make nuclear weapons. Tehran says it has a nuclear energy program but not a weapons program and accuses the United States and other governments of a campaign to slander Iran through "fabrications."

UN sanctions are a major component of American and Western European efforts to force a closure of Iran's nuclear weapons program. China is caught in the middle. Beijing can ill afford to antagonize Europe and the United States unless faced with a life-or-death issue involving Chinese national territory or sovereignty. China also hopes to avoid opening itself to international criticism for failing to support nuclear nonproliferation. Yet the PRC also has strong economic and strategic interests in maintaining its bilateral relationship with Tehran. China tries to balance these conflicting interests. Beijing cooperates minimally and superficially with the sanctions program while at the same time protecting Iran and deepening the bilateral partnership. This inevitably undermines the effectiveness of Western pressure on Iran, possibly thwarting a peaceful solution.

The Chinese leadership may indeed share some of the West's fear that an Iranian nuclear capability will make the world more dangerous. Iran's acquisition of nuclear weapons would add stress to a region that is already a political tinderbox. It would also weaken the international nonproliferation regime. But there are other considerations for the Chinese that make them reluctant to join the United States in pressuring Tehran to stop its alleged nuclear proliferation. Iran and China have a strong business partnership. China became Iran's largest trading partner in 2009. The PRC was the second-largest source of imported weapons for Iran during the decade of the 2000s. The most important aspect of the economic relationship is energy. As a newly emerging great power in a world of long-established and politically liberal great powers, China's search for energy supplies has led it to fill a market niche by buying from countries (such as Iran) that much of the international community shuns because they are considered outlaw states. The Western sanctions against Iran provided China with opportunities to gain new business in Iran by filling the void left when other partners of Iran departed. China is the largest foreign investor in Iran's energy industry—by a large margin. The PRC has signed a $40 billion deal to refine Iran's oil. Iran is a major oil supplier to China, providing up to 15 percent of China's oil and 11 percent of China's total energy imports. These percentages are expected to rise.[20]

Friendship with Iran offers China several strategic benefits. Iran is a rising, major player in the Middle East, arguably the region's most powerful state. The relationship with Iran helps maintain Chinese influence in a strategically important area and counters U.S. influence with Israel, Saudi Arabia, and Iraq. Friendship with Iran increases China's credibility as a champion of the Third World as well as a friend of the Muslim world. China's "new energy silk road" to Iran lessens Chinese dependence on the sea lanes through the Indian Ocean, which are vulnerable to interdiction by the U.S. or Indian navies. If a conflict with the United States led to a U.S. attempt to cut off the flow of seaborne oil shipments to China, Iran might be the only one of the Persian Gulf states willing to supply oil to China through an overland pipeline. A nuclear weapons capability would strengthen Iran's ability to defy U.S. pressure. A strong, anti-U.S. Iran diverts American resources and effort away from China. Fewer U.S. forces in East Asia and greater U.S. dependency on China's cooperation to solve global problems are both to Beijing's advantage. Iran has observer status in the Shanghai Cooperation Organization (SCO), which China cofounded and which many observers believe is primarily intended to block the expansion of U.S. influence into Central Asia. Iran has applied for full membership status, but the process is stalled because the SCO's rules prevent any country under UN sanctions from becoming a full member.

Below the surface of UN Security Council unity, the fundamentally divergent interests and worldviews of China and the United States cause to the two countries to view Iran differently. China and Iran share a sense of being anciently great civilizations that suffered humiliation at the hands of the Western powers in modern times. Chinese believe U.S. involvement in the Middle East in general, and particularly the sanctions and threats to use force against Iran, are greater dangers to regional stability (and the continued flow of oil supplies) than a nuclear-armed Iran. Chinese commentators also decry what they call the hypocrisy of the United States, which can accept nuclear proliferation in Israel and India but not in Iran. The Chinese argue that American accusations lack credibility because a principal American rationale for invading Iraq in 2003, Saddam Hussein's alleged possession of or interest in developing weapons of mass destruction sufficiently strong to threaten other countries, proved unfounded. Compared to China, which has a constructive and valued relationship with the Iranians, it is relatively easy for Washington to play hardball with Iran because U.S.-Iran relations were ruined long ago. The cost of punishing Iran is much higher for China than for America, a fact the Chinese feel escapes the Americans. Similar to the North Korea case, the prospect of a nuclear-armed Iran is far less threatening to China than to the United States. Iran's nuclear weapons pose no direct threat to China or to any close Chinese ally. Most Chinese analysts see U.S. policy toward Iran in the context of what they believe is the larger U.S. agenda: to democratize authoritarian states and to gain control of Persian Gulf oil to ensure continued U.S. global domination. They see this alleged U.S. agenda dictating the American push for sanctions against Iran. Given the Chinese self-image cultivated by the CCP, siding with the United States against a smaller, poorer Third World country would put the Chinese leadership in a difficult position in the eyes of the Chinese public.

Chinese assistance to the Iranian missile and nuclear programs, and U.S. efforts to stop that Chinese assistance, both date back to the 1980s. China was a major supplier of arms to Iran during the 1980–1988 Iran-Iraq war. Iran's use of Chinese-supplied Silkworm missiles fanned U.S. anger against both Iran and China. Between 1997 and 2003, under heavy U.S. pressure, Beijing promised to stop helping Iran's nuclear program, committed to obeying the Missile Technology Control Regime (an international agreement to restrict the transfer of missile-building knowhow), and released an official policy paper detailing the measures the PRC would take to support the nonproliferation of weapons of mass destruction. Some Chinese companies continued to supply Iran with nuclear and missile-related technology. The U.S. government has frequently sanctioned the Chinese companies caught doing this. It is not clear whether these Chinese firms selling proscribed arms and technology to Iran did so with the knowledge or approval of China's central government. Nevertheless, the extent and persistence of continued Chinese nuclear assistance to Iran suggests that at least part of the PRC government believes a nuclear or virtually nuclear Iran would be a strategic asset to China by counterencircling the United States.

Given this complex combination of interests, Beijing tries to have it both ways with Iran. In 2006 Beijing appeared to fall in line with Western powers against Iran. The PRC ended its opposition to reporting Iranian noncompliance with IAEA guidelines to the UN Security Council and began supporting UN resolutions and limited sanctions against Iran because of the nuclear issue. Beijing's wish to avoid an Israeli airstrike against Iran's nuclear facilities was likely a factor in the decision to relax Chinese opposition to punishing Iran.[21] At the same time, however, China has tried to use its influence at the United Nations to ensure that sanctions would be ineffective by stalling the process and by weakening the punishments prescribed if Iran failed to meet the demands of the Security Council's resolutions. China's support for sanctions has been highly qualified: they must not hurt "the Iranian people" or interfere with normal trade activities, including those with Chinese companies. As UN and U.S. sanctions drove many foreign firms to leave Iran, China invested more heavily in Iran. European refining companies stopped selling gasoline to Iran in compliance with sanctions. China compensated by increasing its sales (for which Iran pays a premium above the world market price) to become the source of one-third of Iran's gasoline imports. When restrictions on Iran's ability to use the international financial system made it difficult for China to pay the Iranians for oil purchases, Beijing and Tehran began discussing payment through a barter system. Beijing champions Iran's right to nuclear energy and China's right to assist. Chinese officials have diplomatically supported Tehran by maintaining high-level visits to the otherwise largely isolated country and characterizing the nuclear weapons controversy as a problem between Iran and the United States rather than Iran violating its commitments under the NPT.

Whether China is revolutionary or status quo oriented, liberal democratic or Leninist, China and the United States will never have identical interests or preferences. With China growing in power, there will be more issues on which China has different preferences from the United States *and* sufficient influence to sabotage any U.S. policy with which the Chinese disagree. As the Iran nuclear issue demonstrates, the rise of China means an expansion of the potential areas of U.S.-China contention outside of East Asia.

Stress on the Safety Net

China is undersensitive to the security concerns of the countries on the Chinese periphery but hypersensitive to perceived containment of China. This contributes to a cycle of actions and counteractions between China and its neighbors in which each side sees its own behavior as defensive and the other side's as aggressive. The PRC's aspirations to regional domination will either restrict the policy options of other Asia-Pacific states or create friction with them. The prospects of democratization in the PRC are uncertain, and in any case the hope that democracy would suddenly make the PRC more accommodating toward its democratic neighbors' interests is misplaced. The competitive aspects of U.S.-China relations will continue to overshadow their common interests in cooperating to maintain global peace. These aspects of the rise of China increase tensions that could lead to international conflict. Such tendencies to being prone to war will threaten to break through the safety net created by the forces that deter what other countries see as aggressive Chinese behavior.

Chapter Nine

NORTH KOREA

Bothersome Client State

China generally supports the current international system. Beijing wants to present itself as a peace-loving and responsible country to undercut anti-China balancing. There is some convergence between Chinese and U.S. views on managing international affairs. But despite all this, China and the United States have found themselves in serious disagreement over nuclear proliferation by the Democratic People's Republic of Korea (DPRK), more commonly known as North Korea.

China and the United States continue to have fundamental strategic disputes; great powers always do. As we know, the Chinese must choose their battles carefully, lest they press too hard in too sensitive an area and cause a backlash that decreases their overall security. But the deterrent effect of anti-China balancing behavior has little relevance to, and therefore little effect on, China's policies toward North Korea. In this case, China's behavior is not aggressive but passive-aggressive. China refuses to join with the United States and other governments in the disciplining of a state that threatens international stability. China's actions are not *directly* threatening to the system or to other states. Indeed, China ostensibly takes the role of moderator and peacemaker. As Beijing realizes, this is not sufficient cause for states to increase their balancing against China.

Nevertheless, the net effect of China's North Korea policy on international security is negative. Outlaw states threaten peace if they can defy international pressure to conform to globally accepted rules and norms. A stronger China is more capable of shielding such states if the Chinese choose to do so, as they have in the nuclear weapons crises involving Iran and North Korea. Insistent on pursuing its own narrow national interests, Beijing indirectly degrades the security environment for others—and possibly for itself as well—through shortsightedness and unintended consequences.

An optimistic view of the rise of China is that a stronger China will indeed be "a force for peace." In declaring its opposition to North Korea's nuclear weapons program, China seemed to share common ground in the early 2000s with the United States, South Korea, and Japan on a major regional strategic challenge. It seemed that Washington and Beijing could work together, building trust and compensating for their disagreements on other issues. Unfortunately, by the end of the decade North Korea became yet another major strategic dispute between China and the United States, exposing irreconcilable agendas and deepening mutual suspicions.

The latest North Korean nuclear crisis has shaken confidence in the hope that a great-power partnership between China and the United States can amicably manage Asia-Pacific strategic affairs. The rise of China to a level of wealth and power closer to that of the United States will neither eliminate bilateral strategic conflicts nor ensure successful comanagement of regional affairs by the United States and the PRC.

The Long Crisis

Beijing largely stood on the sidelines during the first North Korean nuclear crisis in the 1990s. According to the deal that seemingly ended the crisis, South Korea, Japan, and the United States would supply North Korea with heavy oil and two new nuclear reactors, suitable for energy but not weapons production, in exchange for Pyongyang shutting down its plutonium-based nuclear bomb program. In 2002, however, the U.S. government announced that North Korea had admitted to the existence of a clandestine uranium-based nuclear bomb program and ceased shipments of oil to North Korea. North Korea responded by restarting its plutonium bomb project and withdrawing from the Nuclear Nonproliferation Treaty. This marked the collapse of the deal and the beginning of a second nuclear crisis. Seeing a deteriorating situation with a growing risk of military conflict between North Korea and the United States, China overcame its reticence to take the lead in international affairs and sponsored the Six Party Talks, which included North and South Korea, the United States, China, Russia, and Japan. China had a huge stake in the success of the Six Party Talks. Their failure would be a major loss of face for China and for its president, Hu Jintao. To prod

Pyongyang to attend the first round of the talks in August 2003, Beijing provided a bribe of extra oil and food supplies. In 2005, the talks yielded a joint statement in which all six parties endorsed denuclearization of the Korean Peninsula in exchange for South Korea supplying electric power to North Korea and the United States promising not to attack. China gained considerable international prestige and praise from Washington for brokering the apparent settlement. Soon thereafter, however, the talks broke down, and North Korea renounced its willingness to give up its nuclear program.

Pyongyang embarked on a campaign of provocative acts that included practice ballistic missile launches, nuclear tests, and military incidents that killed South Koreans. The DPRK wanted to resume talks with the United States to press demands for recognition as a nuclear power and a new round of economic aid. Seoul and Washington insisted that negotiations must be about North Korean denuclearization. Following a familiar pattern, Pyongyang used belligerent acts in an attempt to break the diplomatic stalemate by intimidating its opponents into returning to negotiations ready to make concessions. These provocations defied Beijing and severely tested China's loyalty to Pyongyang. Prior to each of North Korea's nuclear tests in 2006 and 2009, the Chinese warned the DPRK regime not to proceed. Afterward, Beijing publicly condemned Pyongyang's behavior. In 2009, the North Koreans proclaimed they would never return to the Six Party Talks, an insult to China. The campaign culminated in 2010. In November, the regime revealed that its clandestine uranium-based nuclear program was well advanced. Two violent acts occurred in the coastal area to the west of the demarcation between North and South Korea. The South Korean Navy warship *Cheonan* exploded and sank in March, with the loss of forty-six lives. An international investigative team concluded that a North Korean torpedo sank the ship. In November, North Korean artillery struck ROK-occupied Yeonpyeong Island, killing two marines and two civilians. Although many Americans and other observers saw these acts as unvarnished aggression, Pyongyang might have seen both incidents as attempts to even the score with the ROK in a long-running feud. The boundary establishing jurisdiction over the sea and islands in this area is disputed between Seoul and Pyongyang. North Korean sailors died in skirmishes with the ROK Navy in 2009 and 1999. The shelling of Yeonpyeong Island closely followed a South Korean military exercise in the area. The North Korean acts, however, can be considered provocations because they were disproportionate and served the larger purpose of contributing to a posture of belligerence that North Korea wanted to present before pushing for a new round of talks in 2011.

PRC Interests in North Korea

Officially, the PRC has always supported Korean reunification. Itself a "divided country," China could hardly do otherwise. But the status quo of two Koreas has been strategically favorable to China. North Korea has been an ideologically compatible buffer state between the PRC and U.S. military bases in South Korea. A united Korea would be larger, more powerful, and no longer distracted by inter-Korean rivalry. Koreans might more strongly press their case that some territory on the Chinese side of the border should belong to Korea. The united Korea would likely remain a liberal democracy with close ties to the West. It might also continue to be a U.S. ally. The strategic rationale for favoring a divided Korea has diminished. Beijing now has a constructive relationship with the Seoul government. The disadvantages of a united Korea might be outweighed by the problems the North Korean government creates, including reinvigorating U.S. influence in the region. Many Chinese analysts, particularly the younger ones, believe China would be better off with a united Korea and are amenable to a tougher Chinese policy toward Pyongyang. While some Chinese officials and analysts still believe China needs North Korea as a buffer state, others could accept a united Korea controlled by Seoul and still allied with the United States. The consensus among the Chinese leadership, however, is to stay the course: try to manage the nuclear issue, avoid a collapse of the regime, and continue to encourage gradual reform in North Korea.

The overriding Chinese interest is stability on the Korean Peninsula. Beijing wants to buy North Korean resources but does not covet North Korean territory. Chinese occupation of northern Korea in the event of a collapse of the DPRK central government is an often discussed scenario. The Chinese, however, are not interested in absorbing a desperately poor, backward, and ethnically Korean region that would not passively accept Chinese overlordship.

Beijing hopes for a continuation of the Kim dynasty in the DPRK because regime change would create several messy problems for China. The Chinese border provinces would face a massive influx of North Korean refugees. China would be under international pressure to help pay the costs of relief and reconstruction in northern Korea. Unemployed North Korean soldiers might resort to brigandry on the Chinese side of the border. Control over the DPRK's nuclear weapons and material would become uncertain. South Korea would likely divert its investment capital away from China and into northern Korea. A collapse of the DPRK regime might include increased military tensions and possibly a confrontation between Chinese forces and ROK or U.S. forces approaching the Chinese border from the south in a replay of the early stage of the Korean War. When it became clear that Kim Jong Il had selected his unaccomplished youngest son to succeed him as paramount leader, Beijing held its nose and accepted Kim Jong Un as the best bet to avert political turmoil on the peninsula. After the death of Kim Jong Il in December 2011, the government-controlled PRC media emphasized that stability in North Korea is the paramount concern and that the planned accession of Kim's son Kim Jong Un to the paramount leadership was succeeding.

Another important consideration for the PRC is its economic relationship with North Korea, which is independent of the bilateral strategic relationship. The Chinese government seeks to integrate North Korea economically with northeastern China. Most Chinese trade with and investment in North Korea is organized by the provincial governments of China's Liaoning and Jilin Provinces, which are interested in local economic development, not larger geopolitical goals. North Korea is a source of coal and minerals with relatively low transportation costs because of its proximity. Jilin, which lacks access to the sea, hopes a rail link and use of the North Korean port of Rajin will provide a gateway to international markets. China has poured money into building transborder infrastructure and is promoting joint economic development in areas near the border. A collapse of DPRK central government authority might result in the theft or destruction of Chinese property in North Korea. Chinese officials and businessmen also worry that deals they have struck with Pyongyang might not be honored if the South Korean government became the new authority over northern Korea. For this reason, South Korea is reportedly willing to reduce PRC resistance to reunification by promising that Seoul would continue to offer the Chinese favorable terms for extracting minerals from northern Korea.[1]

The Chinese are relatively confident the North Korean government can endure. While Western analysts have repeatedly predicted the regime's imminent demise, Chinese analysts have consistently said it would survive through various crises, including famines and the leadership transitions from Kim Il Sung to Kim Jong Il and from Kim Jong Il to Kim Jong Un. The Chinese want not just survival but also reform of the regime, which should result in more constructive internal and external policies. Beijing has persistently urged the Pyongyang government to follow the example of post-Mao China: market-oriented reforms to invigorate the economy, seeking peace with neighboring countries, and retaining an authoritarian one-party political system to uphold domestic order. If Pyongyang evolved in this direction, China could look forward to a stable, more prosperous, and less crisis-prone country on its border. Yet the Chinese are careful not to push Pyongyang too hard. They believe excessive pressure alienates the North Koreans, squandering China's limited influence and increasing Pyongyang's interest in seeking a relationship with the United States to reduce the DPRK's reliance on China.

China is widely suspected of having helped North Korea develop nuclear weapons—mostly via Pakistan through the infamous scientist A. Q. Khan. As a weaker country during the Cold War, China acted as a spoiler to an international system perceived as U.S.-dominated and anti-China. As a great power with global interests, however, China will have a greater stake in maintaining international peace and stability. If there was previously a Chinese rationale in support of North Korea obtaining nuclear weapons, the problems of such a policy now clearly outweigh the benefits. By the time of the second North Korean nuclear crisis, which began in late 2002, Beijing's official position of opposition to North Korea getting nuclear weapons was credible. This objective, however, is not China's highest priority. Furthermore, some Chinese analysts now believe, like most foreign experts, that Pyongyang is no longer willing to give up its nuclear weapons but wants talks to persuade the United States to accept officially North Korea as a nuclear weapons state.

China Tries to Manage a Prickly Comradeship

Despite the fraternal rhetoric about being "as close as lips and teeth," the relationship between the PRC and North Korea has often been testy. Behind the veneer of comradeship, North Korean and Chinese elites generally dislike each other. As for wider Chinese society, older generations and those who live outside the cities tend to hold to the Korean War–era view of North Korea as blood brother and ideological soulmate. Younger and city-dwelling Chinese, however, are put off by the DPRK's poverty and troublesome policies and identify more closely with modern, wealthy South Korea. China's only formal military alliance is with Pyongyang and dates back to 1961. Chinese leaders have made it clear in recent years, however, that the alliance is a dead letter; China will not automatically rush to assist if the North Koreans get into a war.

During the Cold War, Pyongyang played China and the Soviet Union against each other, taking advantage of Beijing's willingness to provide aid to counter Soviet influence. The breakup of the USSR and the loss of Soviet support left the DPRK with nowhere else to turn but China. This gave China the leeway to end its "one Korea" policy. Beijing normalized its relations with Seoul in 1992 and supported South Korean admission into the United Nations. Beijing also began shifting its economic relationship with the DPRK from handouts (subsidized sales or outright donations) to normal commercial transactions.

Beijing has supported denuclearization, but only within the following conditions. First, Beijing holds that the United States should make concessions to assuage North Korea's legitimate security worries. Second, the Chinese say the issue should be settled through peaceful dialogue and negotiation, not through military force or coercion. Third, China argues that trying to solve the crisis by using sanctions against North Korea will increase the likelihood of either belligerent behavior or regime collapse. Beijing argues for decoupling the nuclear issue from China's normal course of trade with the DPRK or provision of humanitarian assistance. This approach has the effect of neutralizing much of the international community's leverage over North Korea. The PRC has struggled to balance competing interests: on one hand, protecting North Korea from pressure that might lead to regime collapse; on the other hand, avoiding the perception that China was again playing the role of spoiler, swimming against the tide of international opinion. Throughout the crisis, Beijing has tried to position itself as a mediator, calling on both Washington and Pyongyang to make compromises. As North Korea implemented a series of belligerent actions in disregard of Chinese counsel, Beijing's displeasure with Pyongyang became more apparent, gradually producing public criticism by Chinese officials and Chinese acquiescence to limited sanctions. But the bottom line for China has been sheltering the DPRK regime.

After North Korean missile launches in July 2006, China lobbied for a gentler UN Security Council response. China agreed on a compromise resolution, which Washington considered a small victory. With the North Korean nuclear test in October 2006, however, Chinese policy visibly hardened. One Chinese analyst said it was this event that made the Chinese realize North Korea was not just America's problem but also China's problem.[2] Beijing issued a very strong condemnation, using wording similar to what the Chinese government said in reaction to the NATO bombing of the Chinese embassy in Belgrade in 1999. China acquiesced to Security Council Resolution 1718, which demanded that the DPRK suspend its missile program as well as abandon its nuclear program; called for voluntary inspections of suspect North Korean ships and aircraft; embargoed the sale to North Korea or the purchase from North Korea of weapons other than small arms; and froze the funds of North Korean individuals or companies connected with the missile or nuclear programs. But at China's insistence, enforcement of the arms embargo was made voluntary. China also said it would continue to provide economic assistance to North Korea, as the "humanitarian" issue was separate from the nuclear issue. After the second DPRK nuclear test in May 2009, Beijing was reportedly "furious" with Pyongyang. The Chinese withheld the usual ceremonial official statements of praise and appreciation for North Korea. Official Chinese commentary on North Korea and its actions grew colder and less sympathetic. Beijing was less resistant toward UN resolutions and sanctions and tolerated unofficial commentary that criticized Pyongyang for being obstinate and provocative. China voted in favor of Resolution 1874, which strengthened the arms embargo and imposed specific financial sanctions. Nevertheless, China did not appear to make a serious effort to enforce the sanctions. An airliner intercepted in Thailand in December 2009, which presumably overflew Chinese airspace, was carrying banned weapons exports from North Korea. China also continued with business as usual, increasing its trade with the DPRK. The two countries reached additional deals for North Korea to supply minerals and for China to build infrastructure, deepening their economic interdependence. South Korean observers argued that China was taking advantage of DPRK weakness and dependency to establish permanent, strategically useful connections with North Korea.

Debate about North Korea in the Chinese media after the second nuclear test was unusually broad and open. The conservative position saw the DPRK as a bulwark or a balancer against the U.S.-Japan alliance and U.S.-led attempts to "contain" China. But an emergent revisionist position held that China should not continue to countenance provocative behavior by

Pyongyang because China has a vital interest in regional stability and in gaining world recognition as a responsible major power. Some analysts argued that Beijing should join with Seoul and Washington in taking a harder line with the North Koreans because Pyongyang's actions were making the status quo worse than the hypothetical dangers of regime collapse. Other Chinese analysts argued that the PRC's error was in letting the PRC-DPRK alliance die: if China would have assured Pyongyang and warned its adversaries that China would retaliate against any attack on North Korea, the Pyongyang government would not have concluded that it needed nuclear weapons in the first place. No consensus, however, emerged in favor of a policy change.[3] Ultimately, the Beijing leadership decided to continue backing rather than abandon Kim Jong Il's regime because the North Korean state appeared more vulnerable than ever.

In contrast to the strong denunciations of Pyongyang from Seoul, Washington, and Tokyo, China publicly took a self-described "impartial" position on the *Cheonan* incident, refused to condemn Pyongyang, and as usual called for restraint by all parties. China's weak reaction and hosting of Kim Jong Il in Beijing less than a month after the attack angered South Koreans and helped pave the way for a stronger ROK defense policy and new military exercises with the United States. In Japan, Prime Minister Hatoyama Yukio specifically mentioned the *Cheonan* attack as a reason for giving up on his previous commitment to move a major U.S. military base off Okinawa. U.S. President Barack Obama challenged Beijing. "There's a difference between restraint and willful blindness to consistent problems," he said. The Chinese Foreign Ministry spokesman Qin Gang responded, "China is a neighbor of the Korean Peninsula, and on this issue our feelings differ from a country that lies 8,000 kilometers distant."[4] The contrast between U.S. and Chinese interests over North Korea had become plainly visible.

When North Korean artillery shelled Yeonpyeong Island, Chinese officials and media took the accustomed approach. They avoided strong condemnation of North Korea, emphasizing Pyongyang's claim that the South Koreans fired first into North Korean territory and the DPRK forces then returned fire, and called for restraint and an immediate "emergency" session of the long-stalled Six Party Talks. This Chinese proposal suited Chinese and North Korean interests but was completely unacceptable to Seoul and Washington. Pyongyang's apparent strategy was to unnerve the democracies with destructive acts as a means of forcing them back to the negotiating table. Both Seoul and Washington had previously not only emphasized the necessity of breaking out of the past pattern of rewarding Pyongyang for belligerent behavior but also demanded that before resuming the Six Party Talks the North Koreans had to recommit to their 2005 denuclearization pledge and accept responsibility for the sinking of the *Cheonan*. Beijing was calling for the abandonment of these two preconditions and capitulation to Pyongyang's tactic of extortion. Even after toughening their treatment of Pyongyang, Chinese officials continued to oppose the use of force in implementing inspections and to insist that sanctions should not impede the development of economic relations between China and the DPRK. In fact, Beijing's economic relationship with North Korea made the sanctions ineffective.

In 2012, the new Kim Jong Un regime reaffirmed the established pattern. Pyongyang announced a plan to launch a "peaceful" three-stage rocket in violation of a UN Security Council prohibition on DPRK missile testing. Beijing joined other countries in warning Pyongyang not to proceed with the test. Kim defied Chinese warnings. Most governments strongly condemned the North Korean launch (which failed), while Beijing called for "restraint" from "all parties."[5]

The question that arises here is why Beijing kept to its basic policy of supporting the continuation of the Kim government even when Pyongyang spurned China's advice and caused the Chinese huge difficulties. There are two reasons. First, despite its frustration with Pyongyang, the PRC remained trapped by its fears. Second, the thinking of China's top leaders remains heavily influenced by decades-old assumptions. Recent high-level meetings between Chinese and North Koreans still emphasize the old theme of battle-tested ideological comradeship. With senior Chinese leaders continuing to view the relationship within the context of the Korean War alliance and remaining sympathetic to North Korea's plight as an isolated and weak country threatened by the powerful United States, it has been difficult for Beijing to accept a cold-blooded reassessment of how the Pyongyang regime fits into the PRC's security interests. Consequently, inertia is strong in China's North Korea policy.

China has shown some willingness to implement its own sanctions against North Korea. The Chinese reportedly suspended oil and diesel fuel deliveries to North Korea briefly for political reasons. After North Korea's 2006 nuclear test, Chinese banks in the Chinese border city of Dandong reportedly restricted financial transactions with North Koreans, which may have decisively influenced Pyongyang's decision to return to multilateral talks quickly. After Pyongyang disregarded Chinese warnings not to launch its controversial rocket in 2012, Beijing temporarily suspended its usual policy of sending North Koreans caught in China without authorization back to the DPRK. It is the sanctions pushed through the United Nations by Washington that Beijing resists. Chinese analysts believe it was a mistake for China to go along with U.S. sanctions in the past because the result was a loss of Chinese influence over North Korea. The consensus view on international sanctions, however, is that they are most likely to be effective when they are multilateral. This makes China's reluctance to fully support international sanction efforts a problem.

North Korea as an Irritant in Sino-U.S. Relations

The Chinese and Americans have conflicting interests wrapped up in the North Korea problem. Superficially, U.S. and Chinese interests appear identical because both governments oppose North Korea having nuclear weapons. But while denuclearization is the top priority for the Americans, Chinese support is highly conditional, as we have seen. Washington sees the North Korean crisis primarily as a nuclear proliferation problem. North Korean nuclear weapons are a compelling danger to the United States. When mounted on missiles now under development, they could strike U.S. bases in the region, threaten American allies, and eventually target the U.S. homeland. Perhaps an even greater danger is the possibility that Pyongyang might transfer nuclear material or technology to a terrorist group planning an attack against an American city. From a U.S. standpoint, these risks strengthen the case for an overthrow of the Kim regime. Americans are already amenable to the idea of regime change because of deep disdain for Pyongyang's authoritarianism, massive human abuses, animosity toward the United States, and long record of violent acts since the Korean War armistice. At the same time, the Chinese are correct to point out that because the United States is situated an ocean away from North Korea, Americans are less fearful of the consequences of regime change than the frontline countries of China and South Korea. Conversely, North Korea's nuclear weapons do not directly threaten China or Chinese quasi-allies. Unlike the United States, China is not a major target of the international terrorist groups most likely to contemplate a nuclear attack. China is not a fount of modern Western culture nor a major supporter of the state of Israel, and it does not base troops in the Middle East. For China, the dangers of a collapse of the North Korean government far outweigh the dangers of a nuclear North Korea. China wants denuclearization, but not at the cost of regime change. The Chinese prefer to live with a nuclear North Korea rather than put the regime under serious pressure. Thus, in practice, the U.S. and Chinese approaches to dealing with the problem of North Korea's nuclear weapons program turn out to be nearly opposite.

After the DPRK's second nuclear weapons test, Washington feared that China was committed to protecting the regime even if that meant letting it keep its nuclear weapons and that China's strategy was to persuade the Americans and South Koreans to accommodate Pyongyang. Beijing feared the United States and South Korea had given up on diplomacy and were working toward regime change. The mutual disappointment resulted from Chinese and American expectations of each other that proved unrealistic and, when unmet, further strained bilateral relations. Based on the Chinese government's public stance in favor of denuclearizing the Korean Peninsula, most Americans assumed the Chinese would use the full measure of their (presumably decisive) influence over North Korea to accomplish this goal. Admiral Mike Mullen, chairman of the U.S. joint chiefs of staff, expressed a widely held American view amid high tensions in 2010: "China has enormous influence over the North, and therefore they have a unique responsibility. Now is the time for Beijing to step up to that responsibility and guide the North, and indeed the whole region, to a better future." PRC Ministry of Foreign Affairs spokeswoman Jiang Yu responded, "I want to ask those people who bring accusations against China what they have done to contribute to the regional peace. Military threats won't solve the problem, but to increase tension."[6] U.S. observers gradually discovered that China's relationship with North Korea is too complicated for such a straightforward Chinese approach. This not only disappointed Americans but caused many to see Beijing as duplicitous. Many Americans concluded that what they saw as Beijing's refusal to exercise its decisive influence over North Korea at best demonstrated that China was not a responsible member of the international community and at worst indicated that China secretly wanted to use a nuclear-armed North Korea to help undercut U.S. leadership in the region.

For their part, most Chinese analysts blame the United States for the crisis and place the onus for solving it on Washington. This notion has no traction in the United States, where the mainstream view is that Pyongyang is the offender and must agree to denuclearize *before* any bargaining can take place. But in China's view, it was the decades of ideologically motivated U.S. antagonism that compelled the North Koreans to seek security through a nuclear deterrent. The root problem, according to the Chinese, is strategic mistrust. Therefore, Washington should seek to build trust by making large compromises that address North Korean concerns. Instead, the Chinese see the Americans expecting other parties to meet U.S. demands: Pyongyang must give in despite unmet security concerns, and China must risk its own relationship with Pyongyang by pressuring the North Koreans to submit. The Chinese also do not accept the American idea that China is the key player, uniquely empowered to resolve the crisis. Chinese contend that China's influence over North Korea is limited and fragile; it is the United States that holds the key to resolving the crisis; China can do no more than apply a little oil to loosen the lock.[7] When Americans talk about China having unique and powerful influence over North Korea, they refer to Pyongyang's reliance on the PRC for not only economic assistance and diplomatic support but even more fundamentally for supplies of most of North Korea's food and energy needs. Many Americans expect China to cut off these supplies to force the DPRK to change its policies. The Chinese argue that the more likely result of such a cutoff would be even more hostile North Korean behavior and possibly a collapse of the Pyongyang regime. While Washington and Seoul have said China has a responsibility to punish Pyongyang, the Chinese have maintained that the responsible policy on their part is to defuse rather than escalate tensions and to mediate a negotiated settlement. The possibility of an unintended clash among Chinese, South Korean, and U.S. forces trying to stabilize North Korea in the wake of a regime collapse is frightening. The need for discussions between Beijing, Washington, and Seoul on coordinating military actions during such a crisis is obvious and compelling. When U.S. officials have raised this issue, however, their Chinese counterparts have declined to engage in serious discussions.

The evolution of the North Korea issue from a point of common interest to a source of strategic friction between the United States and China culminated in the dispute about a U.S. aircraft carrier training in the Yellow Sea. In response to the attack on the *Cheonan*, Seoul and Washington announced that they would conduct joint naval exercises in the Yellow Sea as a show of force. Premature media reports said these drills might include the U.S. aircraft carrier *George Washington*. This drew a strongly nationalistic reaction from China. Goaded by public opinion and the PLA, the

Chinese government demanded that the U.S. aircraft carrier stay out of the Yellow Sea, which is up to four hundred miles wide and bounded on one side by U.S. ally South Korea. Chinese commentary said an American aircraft carrier in neighboring waters was a threat to China, even though the planned naval exercise was clearly aimed at North Korea. Ironically, the Chinese themselves helped create this so-called threat. Had Beijing joined in strong condemnation of Pyongyang, Seoul and Washington could have scaled back their own military response. The sinking of the *Cheonan* was an act of war. Seoul's response, even if it included exercises with a U.S. carrier, was remarkably restrained. The Chinese should have expressed appreciation rather than pique. The preemptive Chinese demand that the *George Washington* stay out of the Yellow Sea had the opposite of its intended effect. Whether or not it had planned to do so previously, the U.S. government pointedly sent the *George Washington* into the Yellow Sea in November 2010, seeing this as necessary to demonstrate that the Chinese did not have the right nor the power to preclude the United States from defense cooperation with one of its allies in international waters. An issue that once seemingly united Washington and Beijing had become a cause of deteriorating bilateral relations. Many Chinese analysts lamented that China was the "loser" while the United States emerged as the "winner" from the North Korean provocations of 2010 because the heightened sense of crisis made U.S. allies more supportive of a strong American military presence in the region.

The North Korea issue in U.S.-China relations has connections with the tensions over Taiwan. First, a natural association stems from the fact that Taiwan is the strategic quandary where Beijing most wants something from Washington (a cessation of arms sales) and North Korea is the strategic quandary where Washington most wants something from Beijing (pressure to force Pyongyang to change its policies). For Chinese, says the PRC academic Jia Qingguo, "Sub-consciously, these two issues are linked."[8] The logic of a trade or bargain involving these two issues is irresistible. Observers in Taiwan continually worry that this might occur, despite constant denials by U.S. officials. A second connection is the PRC's possible use of North Korea to complicate American efforts to protect Taiwan. The Chinese analyst Shen Dingli has argued that a North Korean regime hostile to the United States serves "to pin down U.S. forces in a Taiwan Strait contingency [and] deters America's consideration of possible military intervention" in defense of a Taiwan threatened by the PLA. North Korea's ability to act as "a guard post for China" is even greater if Pyongyang is armed with nuclear weapons, he says. Thus, for Shen, the Americans should stop selling arms to Taiwan if they want to denuclearize North Korea. Shen's analysis seems to assume that Beijing could turn off Pyongyang's nuclear program at will, which other Chinese analysts say is not true.[9]

Not Such a "Force for Peace" in This Case

China has concluded that, in the case of North Korea, the evils of the status quo are preferable to the evils of regime change. This has led to a Chinese policy of shielding Pyongyang from serious pressure to change its policies while Beijing tries by other means to work toward a peaceful settlement. In principle, it is difficult to fault Beijing's consistent calls for calm and negotiations. By offering to host the Six Party Talks, Beijing opened a peaceful avenue for the governments involved to try to get the outcomes they want. Protecting North Korea from the consequences of its actions, however, has negative effects on regional security and even on PRC security. Stronger Chinese pressure on North Korea to cease provocative actions and begin the process of denuclearization would probably result in a period of severely damaged Sino–North Korean relations but might eventually succeed in moderating North Korean behavior by leaving North Korea completely isolated and desperately in need of foreign assistance. On the other hand, Chinese support for a nuclear-armed North Korea that routinely employs limited military action to intimidate its intended negotiating partners is a poor policy for attaining the Chinese goal of stability. Beijing's policy helps ensure continuous tensions and a high risk of another Korean War. In that event, the Chinese would get all the disasters they fear from a collapse of the North Korean government (an almost certain outcome of such a war) plus the additional problems of a military conflict between nuclear-armed opponents fought on China's doorstep. The Chinese are already paying a cost for their policy in the strategic adjustments that the United States, South Korea, and Japan are making, adjustments contrary to Chinese interests. These three countries have increased their security cooperation amid disappointment with China's lukewarm reaction to belligerent North Korean actions, solidifying the U.S. bloc while reducing their trust and confidence in China as a strategic partner. North Korea's nuclear weapons program is also an incentive for South Korea and Japan to deploy nuclear weapons of their own, an outcome China strongly opposes. As North Korea continues to develop its nuclear weapons and missiles, it moves closer to becoming a direct threat to the United States, increasing the possibility that China's nightmare of another military conflict on the Korean Peninsula might be realized. Thus, by acquiescing to Pyongyang's nuclear status out of fear of hastening regime collapse, China may be unintentionally bringing upon itself even more serious longer-term security problems.

Thus far the rise of China has not had a decisively constructive effect on the North Korea conundrum. On the positive side, Beijing's preference has turned against North Korea possessing nuclear weapons, and the Chinese felt confident enough in China's new strength and prestige to take the risk of sponsoring the Six Party Talks. As China aspires to global and regional leadership, Beijing is more aware of the harm done to China's international prestige by not reining in North Korean actions that challenge international norms. At the same time, however, the Chinese have more prestige to lose than before and know they would lose face if they pushed Pyongyang hard but failed to moderate North Korean policy. Contrary to Chinese expectations, China's increased economic leverage over North Korea has not increased China's influence over Pyongyang's security policies. A stronger and more far-sighted China has shown little responsiveness to U.S. and South Korean objectives, which does not bode well for joint Sino-U.S. management of regional strategic affairs in the future. Nor has Beijing demonstrated enthusiasm toward implementing international norms at the expense of very narrow Chinese national interests. Despite China's desire for a positive international image, the Chinese government has sheltered Pyongyang even in the face of indefensible North Korean policies. The chief driver of China's North Korea policy is the desire to avoid regime collapse at nearly all costs. There is no apparent reason why this basic Chinese calculation would change as China continues to increase in economic and military might. A stronger and richer China will still be highly averse to the expected problems of a sudden power vacuum in North Korea. The passage of time might allow for a revolutionary policy reassessment within the PRC government or for a political transformation inside the DPRK that could lead to a change in North Korean policies. But the rise of China per se will not solve the problem of Pyongyang alienating itself from post–Cold War Asia.

Chapter Ten

TAIWAN IN THE PRC'S LENGTHENING SHADOW

If the security of Taiwan is understood as its people's ability to choose their own political destiny without the threat of a military attack from the PRC, then the rise of China directly and seriously threatens Taiwan's security. While Chinese leaders are insisting to the rest of the world that a stronger China will be peaceful and nonaggressive, Beijing maintains a standing threat to use military force against Taiwan if the island's inhabitants move from de facto independence to formal independence by amending key national titles and documents to cut the symbolic ties with the Chinese mainland. As China becomes stronger, it is able to bring greater pressure on the international community to cease supporting Taipei, it gains more economic leverage over Taiwan that might translate into political influence, it becomes more capable of carrying out a military conquest of Taiwan, and it can impose a greater cost on any nation that tries to help defend Taiwan in the event of a cross-strait war.

The Origin of the Taiwan "Problem"

Taiwan is a proud, self-made democracy of twenty-three million people and one of the world's top twenty-five economies. Yet in the eyes of all but a handful of small states, Taiwan is officially not a country. Taiwan is represented in international settings under strange names such as "Chinese Taipei" (the Olympic Games) and "Separate Customs Territory of Taiwan, Penghu, Kinmen, and Matsu" (World Trade Organization). This requires some explanation.

Ironic from today's standpoint, premodern Chinese governments considered the island a nuisance, a haven for pirates and rebels. For much of China's history, Beijing made it illegal for Chinese to live on Taiwan. Chinese who migrated there did so to get away from China, not to claim the island for China. A sizable Chinese community developed on Taiwan during the 1600s under a thirty-eight-year stretch of Dutch control over part of the island. Beijing (under the Qing dynasty) annexed Taiwan in 1683, relatively late, and did not make it a province of China until 1885. Control of Taiwan passed from the last Chinese dynasty to upstart great power Japan in 1895: the island was one of the spoils of Japan's victory in the Sino-Japanese War. Many of the Chinese residents felt the mainland China government had sold them out. While the Japanese occupation authorities harnessed Taiwan and its people to the needs of the Japanese empire, they also built economic infrastructure and helped some ethnic Chinese get education and technical training. Taiwan's ethnic Chinese community developed politically through a growing sense of Taiwan nationalism and a decades-long struggle to wrest democratic rights from the Japanese colonial government. By the time World War II ended, Taiwan was more wealthy and politically progressive than any province in mainland China. Meanwhile, while Taiwan was under Japanese occupation, mainland China saw the 1911 revolution, which overthrew the monarchy and established the Republic of China (ROC) and the onset of a long civil war between the forces of the ruling Kuomintang (Nationalist Party) and the Chinese Communist Party (CCP).

With the defeat of Japan and the reestablishment of rule from mainland China, Taiwan became caught up in two long-term political conflicts. The first is the conflict between Chinese nationalism and Taiwanese nationalism. The long-established ethnic Chinese communities on Taiwan, which had formed a distinct identity as "Taiwanese," were profoundly disappointed by the rough treatment they received at the hands of the new mainland Chinese ROC administration beginning in 1945. Contemptuous and rapacious, the mainlanders saw Taiwan as a place of questionable patriotism (because of Japanese efforts to make Taiwanese think of themselves as Japanese imperial subjects) and a treasure house of resources to be stripped off and sent to China, where the war against the communist rebels was reaching a climax. ROC officials also managed Taiwan's economy poorly. Taiwanese resentment against the ROC government exploded in an islandwide insurrection in 1947. The Nationalist government retaliated by dispatching troops, who conducted wholesale massacres. Common estimates of the number of Taiwanese killed range from ten to twenty thousand. The divide between Taiwanese and "Mainlanders" deepened just as a massive additional influx of Mainlander officials and troops was beginning. Defeated in China, the ROC Kuomintang government relocated to Taiwan in 1949 with the promise of reconquering the mainland in the future. Most members of the long-established Taiwanese community saw Taiwan as a separate country from China, while the post-1945 Mainlander residents and their progeny saw Taiwan as part of China (the ROC, not the PRC). The KMT authorities, however, proscribed debate both over whether Taiwan was part of China and whether the KMT was China's rightful government. As Taiwan grew more prosperous, an authoritarian Kuomintang regime eventually yielded to demands for democratization. The free political discussion allowed by multiparty democracy has exposed Taiwan's contested identity, and proindependence candidates and activists have broadened the political spectrum.

The second conflict involving Taiwan is the dispute about sovereignty over the island. The governments in Beijing and Taipei both claim it. Taipei argues that the CCP regime never ruled Taiwan and that Taiwan's links to China are through the ROC rather than the PRC. The PRC aims to restore Taiwan's former status as a dominion of the Beijing government, now in the CCP's hands. To the CCP regime, an autonomous Taiwan has been a symbol of the Century of Shame, a political rival, and a challenge to the CCP regime's claim that it has restored China to greatness. Japan took Taiwan at a time when China was weak and prostrate before predatory great powers. The United States intervened in 1950 to thwart Beijing's imminent plans to invade Taiwan and finish off Chiang Kai-shek's KMT government. The ROC on Taiwan held the "China" seat in the United Nations until other member countries (over U.S. objection) moved to give the China seat to Beijing in 1971. Taiwan was a base for U.S. military forces until the United States severed its alliance with the ROC in 1980 as part of the shift of U.S. diplomatic recognition from the ROC to the PRC. Beijing argues that the Americans have continued a surreptitious defense relationship with Taiwan since then through arms sales and contacts between U.S. and Taiwan military officers. Taipei has competed with the PRC for diplomatic allies around the world and has embarrassed the CCP government by pointing out Chinese bullying and pettiness toward Taiwan.

Although the Chinese leadership seems steadfastly committed to getting Taiwan, they have shown a willingness to be patient until unification becomes feasible. Mao Zedong said "Let it come after one hundred years," and the "hundred years" was figurative, meaning it could take even longer. His successor Deng Xiaoping said China could wait one thousand years.[1] Until then, the PRC continues to assert its claim, urge closer relations between Taiwan and the PRC, and insist that Taiwan must not close off the possibility of political unification by declaring independence. Despite being de facto independent, Taiwan retains certain formal and legal ties to the "China" of the Republic of China era. Taiwan's constitution, for example, still contains passages indicating that its jurisdiction includes the Chinese mainland. Beijing insists that if Taiwan's government cuts the ties to the mainland and thereby officially and permanently separates itself from China, the PLA will use force to overturn that separation. There is little doubt the threat is serious. Many Chinese elites argue, and many ordinary Chinese believe, that China cannot be a full-fledged, respected great power without recovering Taiwan. The CCP government has made recovering Taiwan a litmus test of its own legitimacy. Since the PRC public would see Taiwan's independence as a failure of historic proportions by China's national leaders, and since China currently faces no significant military threat, Taiwan can be considered the PRC's number one security challenge. Absent this PRC threat to use force, the people of Taiwan would likely vote to declare themselves a formally independent nation.

Based on the PRC's claim that Taiwan is part of China, the Chinese insist that the rest of the world must not treat Taiwan as a separate country. Governments that wish to have normal diplomatic relations with Beijing cannot have them with Taiwan. International organizations that want China's support or cooperation cannot imply that Taiwan has statehood. Hence the odd names instead of "Taiwan" or "Republic of China."

The conflicts within Taiwan and across the strait over Taiwan's relationship to China are represented in Taiwan's two major political parties. While neither is pro-PRC, the Kuomintang has reflected Mainlander sentiment while the newer Democratic Progressive Party (DPP) reflects the Taiwanese view. In the past, the KMT supported eventual unification with China (on the condition that Taiwan's liberties and prosperity could be protected), while the DPP supported leaving open the possibility of formal independence from China. More recently, both parties have moderated their positions and moved toward the middle. The Kuomintang favors maintaining the symbolic links with the mainland by keeping the Republic of China nomenclature. It accepts the principle that in some sense both Taiwan and the

PRC are part of "China," even if they have different interpretations of what "China" means. This has allowed the KMT government of President Ma Ying-jeou to lower cross-strait tensions and to implement agreements that have greatly increased economic and social interaction. While the DPP says a formal declaration of independence is not necessary, its supporters generally want to distance Taiwan from China. The DPP resists the notion that Taiwan is part of "China" in any sense, arguing that this would constrain Taiwan's future choices.

Democratization on Taiwan has sharpened the cross-strait dispute. Although the KMT regime under Chiang Kai-shek and his son Chiang Ching-kuo and the CCP regime under Mao Zedong clashed bitterly over which government had the right to rule Taiwan, both sides accepted the "one China principle" that Taiwan was part of China. Observers on the PRC side would eventually take a more nostalgic view of their former foes the Chiangs. Chiang Ching-kuo's successor as president, Lee Teng-hui, campaigned to secure for Taiwan more of the benefits usually associated with statehood. Taiwan's president from 2000 to 2008, DPP member Chen Shui-bian, carried out a policy of distancing Taiwan from China in accordance with the proindependence sentiment of his core supporters. Beijing felt compelled to send a variety of belligerent signals to Taiwan, clashing with concurrent Chinese efforts to project an international image of peaceful cooperation and good global citizenship.

While the DPP government had rejected the "one China principle," after the election of KMT candidate Ma as president in 2008 Taipei returned to the position that Taiwan and the mainland are both part of the Republic of China. This satisfied Beijing that Taiwan's government professed at least a version of the "one China principle." Cross-strait tensions greatly decreased, and Taiwan signed several important bilateral agreements with China.

Taiwan's people object to the issue being characterized, as it often is, as the "Taiwan problem." They note that Taiwan has done nothing but become a prosperous democracy whose people wanted to be treated internationally with the same dignity accorded to citizens of other nations. It is the PRC, rather, that has been the "problem" by threatening to use force against Taiwan.

Regrettably, the CCP regime has chosen to take the position that unification with Taiwan is essential to modern China's security and prosperity and that Taiwan's political independence would signal a failure by the PRC government. This makes it impossible for the leaders in Beijing to acquiesce to

Taiwan independence, even if the only recourse is war. The root of the dispute lies in seeing the issue in different ways. From the PRC point of view, the island of Taiwan is "Chinese" territory, and, as the ruler of "China," the CCP government has sovereignty over this territory. This cannot be altered by the wishes of the people who happen to inhabit the territory. From the point of view of Taiwan's people (and most Americans), however, the wishes of the people inhabiting the territory are decisively important.

In deference to Beijing, few countries now have formal diplomatic relations with Taiwan. Few if any more would establish formal relations if Taipei declared itself independent against China's wishes. Thus, Taiwan claiming formal independence would not necessarily be a very consequential change. This makes Beijing's threat to resort to war even less justifiable.

The situation is a collection of compromises. Beijing has tolerated de facto independence as long as Taiwan leaves intact the few remaining threads that connect Taiwan to China and keep alive the hope of eventual unification. Taiwan's people put up with an awkward status quo rather than provoke an attack by the PRC. Most of Taiwan's trade partners find unofficial ways to carry out business so as not to ruin their relations with the PRC.

China's Strategy Toward Taiwan

China's rise potentially makes the PRC strategy more effective. The strategy has a coercion component and an enticement component. The first coercive feature is deterring Taiwan independence through an intimidating military posture. This includes both threats and capabilities. The PRC government has announced and repeatedly reaffirmed that it would use military force if necessary in response to Taiwan declaring independence. China's 2005 Anti-Secession Law reinforced this commitment, saying that in the event of "incidents entailing Taiwan's secession from China" or if "possibilities for a peaceful unification should be completely exhausted," the PRC will resort to "nonpeaceful means" to restore China's "territorial integrity." In the summer of 1950 Beijing contemplated invading Taiwan, the last stronghold of the KMT forces and the ROC government, by ferrying PLA troops across the Taiwan Strait in armed junks. The United States put an end to these plans by announcing that as part of the U.S. reaction to the outbreak of the Korean War, the U.S. Seventh Fleet would "neutralize" the Taiwan Strait by preventing a PRC assault against Taiwan. Through the 1990s, strategic analysts laughed off the threat of a PRC invasion of Taiwan as the "million-man swim." China simply lacked the means to transport a large number of soldiers across the Taiwan Strait in a rapid, organized, and survivable fashion. During the past decade, however, the PLA has deployed modern amphibious assault ships and vehicles. Growing numbers of advanced PLA warships, submarines, and aircraft challenge Taiwan's ability to stop PLA troops before they could reach the island's shores. Perhaps even more frightening to Taiwan's people are the missiles the PRC has aimed at Taiwan, the number of which was approaching two thousand at the end of 2011. The PLA's military buildup has made Beijing's threats against Taiwan independence credible. Where possible, Beijing tries to enlist U.S. help in deterring Taiwan independence. The Chinese succeeded in pulling Washington into an awkward position of publicly chiding the Taipei government when Taiwan had a DPP president in 2000–2008. Washington told President Chen Shui-bian not to change the status quo (which, as Washington defined it, meant no formal independence) and warned that U.S. forces would not necessarily intervene if a cross-strait war was provoked by Taipei. This followed Washington's conclusion that Chen was following a dangerous course of dismantling Taiwan's ties with the Chinese mainland in spite of U.S. appeals for him to act more cautiously. Washington felt Chen was disregarding the U.S. interest in preventing a cross-strait conflict.

The second coercive feature of China's Taiwan strategy is to isolate Taiwan internationally. Beijing brings heavy pressure to bear against countries the Chinese perceive as supporting Taiwan independence. Such support may include selling weapons to Taiwan, hosting high-ranking Taiwan government officials, or welcoming Taiwan's participation in international organizations without Beijing's assent. The PRC government is extremely diligent in searching out and punishing what it sees as violations of the promise to maintain nonrecognition of Taiwan. (One example: I watched an international women's volleyball tournament in Canberra, Australia, in 1996. When the Taiwan team was playing, supporters in the crowd waved small Taiwan flags they had brought into the arena. A Chinese sports official at the scene demanded that the arena's administrators ban the flags, threatening that otherwise he would use his influence to keep international sports events out of Australia in the future.) The PRC has used its UN Security Council veto only six times. Two of these occasions involved punishing small countries for their relations with Taiwan: withholding peacekeepers from Guatemala in 1997 and Macedonia in 1999.

This Chinese pressure is designed not only to dissuade foreigners from assisting Taipei but also to make continued autonomy costly, humiliating, and inconvenient for Taiwan's people, as a constant inducement for them to seek a settlement with Beijing that would allow them full international privileges as PRC nationals.

The enticement features of the PRC's Taiwan policy involve promoting cross-strait linkages and offering concessions. The PRC has consistently tried to increase economic interdependence and social interaction across the Taiwan Strait to reduce Taiwan's resistance to unification. The PRC's premise is that encouraging more Taiwanese to visit and do business with China will stimulate their sense of Chinese identity and raise their understanding of the benefits Taiwan could gain from a closer association with China. The Chinese are eager for Taiwanese to see and be proud of the progress China has made, exemplified by the gleaming skyscrapers of Beijing and Shanghai. As a sweetener, the PRC is willing to offer economic agreements in which Taiwan benefits more than China. Taiwan has enjoyed a steady trade surplus with China. Nevertheless, Taiwan has opened itself up to trade with China only gradually over the last two decades, partly because Taipei is wary that excessive dependence on the economic ties with China will give Beijing leverage to influence the political aspects of Taiwan's cross-strait policy. To China's approval, the floodgates have now opened. China is the top destination for Taiwan's exports (44 percent). Cross-strait trade is over $100 billion per year. Taiwanese have invested between $100 billion and $300 billion in China. Direct airline flights between Taiwan and mainland Chinese cities began in 2008 and grew to over five hundred weekly by 2011.

The second enticement feature of China's strategy to promote unification with Taiwan is offering the Taiwanese (what Beijing thinks is) an attractive deal. The idea of "one country, two systems" became famous as the basis for Hong Kong's return to PRC control in 1997, but Beijing originally offered it as a model for a merger with Taiwan. Through several decades and several major speeches, PRC leaders said that even after unification Taiwan could keep its capitalist economic system, appoint its own local leaders, and retain its armed forces. Taipei would have to recognize the regime in Beijing as the central government and give the PRC jurisdiction over Taiwan's foreign affairs.

The success of the enticement component of the PRC's Taiwan strategy is questionable. Attempting simultaneously to coerce Taiwan's people and win their hearts and minds is self-contradictory, to say the least. China is a suitor who approaches the fair maiden Taiwan with a bouquet of flowers in one hand and a gun in the other. Beijing has had difficulty understanding Taiwan's society and political system. Until recently, the Chinese leadership was unwilling or unable to recognize Taiwanese nationalism. In an important speech about Taiwan in 1995, PRC President Jiang Zemin said, "Our not undertaking to give up the use of force is not directed against our compatriots in Taiwan but against the schemes of foreign forces to interfere with China's unification," as if the Taiwan people's resistance to absorption by the PRC was solely because of meddling by foreigners. In more recent statements, Chinese leaders have revised their position to say the threat to use force "is not targeted at our Taiwan compatriots but a handful of Taiwan separatists."[2] This is still out of touch with the fact that the majority of the Taiwan "compatriots" not only eschew political unification with Beijing but see themselves as a distinct people from PRC nationals. Based on annual surveys conducted by Taiwan's National Chengchi University, the percentage of people on Taiwan who consider themselves "Chinese" has steadily fallen over the last two decades. Over 50 percent of Taiwan's people now consider themselves "Taiwanese," and another 40 percent "both Chinese and Taiwanese," while only about 5 percent self-identify as "Chinese."[3] In March 1996, Taiwan held its first direct presidential election. Prior to the vote, PRC armed forces held exercises intended to intimidate the Taiwan from voting for the reelection of incumbent President Lee Teng-hui, whom Beijing had branded as a Taiwan separatist. Lee particularly angered Beijing by visiting the United States in 1995 to give a speech at his alma mater, Cornell University. China saw the granting of a visa to a high-level Taiwan official as a breach of the U.S. commitment to follow a "one China" policy. A few days before the election, the PLA fired missiles into the waters near Taiwan's two main ports of Keelung and Kaohsiung, disrupting shipping and airliner traffic. Lee condemned the missile exercises as "state terrorism." The PRC tactic completely backfired. Lee was running against two other candidates, and preelection polls had indicated he would win the election with a plurality. Aided by popular anger against China's ham-fisted attempt to influence the election, Lee received a majority vote of 54 percent and a strong national mandate for his second term. PRC Premier Zhu Rongji similarly tried to influence Taiwan's 2000 presidential election. A few days before the voting, Zhu publicly warned Taiwan voters against choosing a proindependence candidate over a candidate who supported the "one China" principle, a clear attempt to reduce votes for the DPP's candidate, Chen Shui-bian. Chen went on to achieve what many considered a surprising victory in a close race, with Zhu's statement possibly supplying the boost Chen needed to win.

Beijing has also found it difficult to make significant concessions. To be fair, the Chinese have adjusted their "one China" position. During most of the period of the cross-strait standoff, the PRC insisted that Taiwan is part of China and that China is equal to the PRC. This implied that Taiwan's is a lesser government that cannot interact with Beijing, the central government, on equal terms. In the 2000s, Beijing moderated its position. The new characterization was that "the mainland and Taiwan belong to one and the same China." This accommodated Taipei's demand for "dignity" by implying that in principle both governments are equal in status. Beijing also quietly accepted the Ma government's idea of declaring a "diplomatic truce," meaning the two governments ceased the practice of trying to bribe each other's diplomatic partners to switch their recognition. This "truce" benefitted Taiwan, which had been losing the competition.

PRC concessions, however, do not go far enough to impress Taiwan. While it entails significant (promised) concessions on the part of Beijing, the "one country, two systems" offer has not proved attractive to Taiwan's people. They do not want to be ruled, even if indirectly, by Beijing, they do not trust the CCP government to keep its commitments, they are unwilling to renounce sovereignty over their own country, and they are wary of entering into a trap from which they cannot escape. Handing the control of their foreign affairs over to Beijing, for example, would make it impossible for Taiwan's people to obtain arms or military training from the United States. Neither KMT nor DPP supporters are interested in the "one country, two systems" offer.

Beijing effectively wields unofficial veto power over Taiwan's participation in important international organizations. The PRC is powerful and important enough that it can block Taiwan's prospective membership by threatening the other members of the organization with economic or political retaliation if they admit Taiwan. Taiwan also wants to sign free trade agreements with other governments but has found few takers because of PRC opposition. Beijing has acquiesced in a few cases to Taiwan's participation in international activities under a name that does not imply statehood. These instances could be seen as concessions, but they had as much to do with China's desire to stave off international criticism as with China's concern for the welfare of Taiwan. What matters most to Taiwan's people is that China continues to oppose Taiwan's international participation in principle and to make exceptions only on a case-by-case basis. During the SARS crisis of 2002–2003, China likely caused unnecessary additional deaths on Taiwan by insisting that Beijing represent Taiwan in the World Health Organization (WHO), preventing Taiwan's government from directly working with the WHO. (In 2009, international pressure finally shamed China into acquiescing to Taiwan gaining observer status in the WHO.) This systematic exclusion of Taiwan from international activities probably hurts more than it helps PRC interests. Keeping Taiwan out of organizations that promote international health, coordinate efforts to control climate change, or manage international air traffic makes Beijing appear an unreasonable, vindictive bully. On the other hand, allowing Taiwan to join issue-specific international organizations would garner a positive response from Taiwan and the rest of the world—without forfeiting Beijing's claim to sovereignty over Taiwan.

Another important Chinese concession would be to address Taiwan's security concerns by reducing the PLA forces arrayed against the island. The most prominent of these forces are the missiles. After the KMT's recapture of the Taiwan's presidency in 2008 assured Beijing that Taiwan was no longer drifting toward independence, some observers speculated that Beijing would announce a "withdrawal" of the ballistic missiles on the Chinese coast opposite Taiwan. This would have been an easy and strategically almost cost-free way for the PRC to improve its image in Taiwan. Withdrawal does not mean destruction or dismantling of the missiles. The PLA would merely move them from their firing positions into storage areas. Since these missiles are mounted on trucks and highly mobile, they can be quickly redeployed if necessary. Ma called on Beijing to remove the missiles, to no avail. The missiles not only stayed in place; their numbers continued to increase. The missiles are a testament to the extreme conservatism in Beijing's cross-strait policy. They undermine the stated Chinese goal of building cross-strait "trust," yet Beijing is apparently unwilling to move them without first obtaining a disproportionate concession. PRC officials have occasionally said they would consider withdrawing some of the missiles in exchange for a cutoff of U.S. arms sales to Taiwan. This would be a very poor bargain for Taiwan. For the price of adding a few days to the launch time of the missiles, the Chinese would eliminate Taiwan's only foreign supply of arms. China would be free to continue accelerating the growth of the cross-strait military imbalance by beefing up other weapons systems threatening Taiwan (aircraft, ships, submarines, etc.).

The rise of China strengthens elements of Chinese strategy. The acquisition of modern weapons systems makes the PLA more intimidating, both to Taiwan and to its potential rescuer, the United States. The steady expansion of the PRC's military budget discourages any hopes that Taiwan could keep up in an arms race with China. China's increased weight among the community of nations makes it more costly for other governments to offend China by conducting business with Taiwan of which Beijing disapproves. The achievements of Chinese economic development are increasingly apparent and impressive. China's economy has always been a draw to Taiwanese business, but the growing PRC market is an irresistible vacuum. Taiwanese now find parts of China livable and full of opportunity. A million Taiwan nationals live in and near Shanghai. The expectation that China's relative strength will continue to grow rapidly suggests that China's confidence will increase while Taiwan's leverage will diminish. It is easy for supporters of Taiwan's continued autonomy to conclude that Taiwan is gradually and inexorably losing the game. Some observers argue that Taiwan should negotiate a cross-strait political settlement now to get its best possible deal because in the future China will feel less need to offer concessions.

PRC Patience Is Pivotal

Perhaps the most important variable in cross-strait relations is Beijing's perception of whether the trend in Taiwan is toward unification or independence. If there is no proindependence momentum and the economic and social connections are increasing, Beijing can be relatively relaxed and patient. If, however, the island seems to be drifting toward independence, the military coercion component of PRC policy comes to the fore. Belligerent statements by Chinese leaders become sharper and more frequent, accompanied by visible PLA activities with obvious application to a cross-strait war scenario. Consequently, the atmosphere changed dramatically when the Chen administration gave way to the return of KMT rule under Ma's presidency. Beijing saw Chen as a national traitor but has confidence that KMT leaders oppose Taiwan independence. After Ma's government took office, PRC officials and scholars said China would not rush unification but was prepared to spend many years, even two decades or more, focusing on deepening economic and cultural exchange while giving Taiwan's people time to accept the notion of political association with the PRC. That suited Ma, who pledged to the Taiwan public that Taipei would not negotiate unification while he was president. Some Mainland Chinese quickly began to complain that Taiwan was taking advantage of Beijing, grasping the economic benefits of associating with China without any intention of making progress toward the political outcome the PRC wants.

Underlying Chinese assessments about the progress of cross-strait relations (with "progress" defined as movement toward unification) is a debate within China. The "patient" school of thought, dominant among the top civilian leadership, the Ministry of Foreign Affairs, and most think tanks, holds that time is on the side of unification. The growing Taiwanese identity on Taiwan is not necessarily an obstacle because it can be reversed if Beijing continues to work on economic integration and building cross-strait trust. The tougher issue of political integration will be easier to solve in the future, according to this viewpoint. By contrast, the "impatient" school of thought, common among the PLA leadership, sees the diminishing Chinese identity among Taiwan's people as a serious problem that indicates movement toward independence. Chinese with this view believe Taiwan is getting away with "peaceful separation" while enjoying the largesse of China's cross-strait economic policy. They think Beijing should push Taiwan to start making political concessions. They also fear that all the recent progress could be lost if the DPP returns to power.

The premise of the "patient" school of thought might turn out to be wrong. Economic integration and social contact will not necessarily result in Taiwan's people desiring to unify politically with China. In international politics, a pair of countries may have a close economic relationship and abundant social connections while remaining politically separated. The U.S.-Canada relationship and the Australia–New Zealand relationship are examples. The most common sentiment expressed by younger Taiwanese, including those who reside in mainland China, is that they welcome the opportunity to do business with China and to move freely across the strait, but they have no wish for Taiwan to become part of the PRC. Taiwan recently relaxed the restrictions on mainland Chinese tourists visiting Taiwan, and the number soon ballooned to over a million annually, with a long waiting list. One of the effects of Taiwanese rubbing shoulders with PRC visitors has been a stronger realization among Taiwan's people that their political and civic culture is different from that of mainland China. The result is a greater appreciation of Taiwan's distinctiveness, potentially strengthening the Taiwan people's commitment to maintaining their autonomy.

The USA and Taiwan

Taiwan is the greatest single source of tension in U.S.-China relations. It is the issue over which a war between China and America is most easily imaginable.

The U.S. government strives to maintain a delicate balance between its support for its small, democratic friend Taiwan and its massive authoritarian partner/competitor China. This has not been easy. Taiwan needs U.S. political and military assistance, while China demands that such assistance must stop or the Sino-U.S. relationship is in jeopardy. In practice, U.S. policy aims to assure and deter both the PRC and Taiwan. The assurance to the PRC is the commitment to the "one China" principle, while the deterrence is the insistence that China pursue its preferred settlement of the Taiwan issue by peaceful means agreeable to Taiwan's people. Washington assures Taiwan through arms sales and selective diplomatic support while deterring Taiwan from provoking the PRC by reiterating that the United States does not endorse Taiwan independence.

Under its "one China" policy, the U.S. government recognizes the regime in Beijing as the sole legal government of mainland China. This was a necessary condition for Washington and the PRC government to establish normal diplomatic relations in 1979. As part of the deal, Washington does not recognize Taiwan as an independent country. Consequently, business between the U.S. and Taiwan governments is conducted through "unofficial" channels and organizations. In practice, this largely means name changes. The U.S. office that performs the usual function of an embassy in Taiwan is called the American Institute in Taiwan; Taiwan's counterpart office in Washington is called the Taipei Economic and Cultural Representative Office. More concretely, the U.S. government also restricts high-level contacts between U.S. and Taipei government figures. Taiwan's President Chen Shui-bian (in office 2000–2008) perturbed the balance Washington strives to maintain. Chen took steps to weaken Taiwan's nominal ties to "China," which raised cross-strait tensions. This led a frustrated U.S. government to state repeatedly that Washington opposes "unilateral changes of the status quo by either side," meaning either an attempt by Beijing to force its will on the Taiwanese or an attempt by Taipei to move from de facto to formal independence.

Despite its diplomatic nonrecognition of the government on Taiwan, Washington takes the position that sovereignty over the island of Taiwan is unsettled. This is to be worked out peacefully and voluntarily between the people on both sides of the Taiwan Strait. Washington has tried to maintain its neutrality on the question of Taiwan's ultimate destiny by saying the United States "does not support Taiwan independence." This phraseology is significantly different than saying the United States "opposes" Taiwan independence, which is the formulation Beijing would much prefer (and which U.S. officials have occasionally misspoken). To compensate Taiwan for the withdrawal of U.S. diplomatic recognition and the end of the U.S.-ROC defense treaty, Congress passed the Taiwan Relations Act (TRA), a law that obligates the U.S. government to provide arms and training "necessary to enable Taiwan to maintain a sufficient self-defense capability." Contrary to common misunderstanding, while the TRA says the United States has an interest in resisting "any resort to force or other forms of coercion that would jeopardize the security, or the social or economic system, of the people on Taiwan," it does not commit America to military intervention if the PRC attacks Taiwan. Although the U.S. government committed in a joint statement with China in 1982 to phase out arms sales to Taiwan, Washington argues that this promise is made under the condition that Beijing commits itself to a peaceful resolution of the cross-strait issue. Based on this interpretation, Washington holds that arms sales are justified as long as China maintains a threatening posture toward Taiwan. Beijing does not accept this reasoning and accuses the United States of continually breaking its pledge to halt arms sales.

PRC analysts accuse Washington of using Taiwan to contain China and to maintain America's strategic leverage in the region. Many observers in China (and in Taiwan, as well) believe Washington would not accept unification even if the people of Taiwan agreed to it. These observers are wrong; U.S. officials have neither the desire nor the ability to thwart voluntary unification. It is true, nonetheless, that Taiwan has strategic as well as political importance to the United States as well as to China. General Douglas MacArthur famously described Taiwan as an "unsinkable aircraft carrier." The "first island chain" bordering the South and East China Seas forms a partial barrier between the east coast of China and the Pacific Ocean. (There is also a "second island chain" made up of Japan's Nanpo Islands and the Mariana

Islands, including the U.S. military stronghold of Guam.) The first island chain consists of territories controlled by countries friendly to the United States: from north to south, Kyushu, the Ryukyu Islands, Taiwan, the Luzon Strait islands, and Luzon. Taiwan is the anchor of this chain. At 240 miles in length, it is a large landmass. It lies opposite the center of China's east coast. It is also the part of the chain that is closest to the mainland Chinese coast. In non-PRC hands, Taiwan and the other parts of the chain are potential chokepoints that could restrict the movement of PLA ships and aircraft by covering the available sea lanes with military bases and surveillance facilities. Conversely, controlling Taiwan would provide the PRC with a massive platform for air and naval bases, an extension of the Chinese coastline two hundred to 250 miles eastward, and unfettered access to the Pacific Ocean from Taiwan's east coast. This would offer PLA forces a commanding position from which to control the western Pacific and to threaten U.S. bases on Okinawa or a U.S. Navy task force sailing in from the east. Many Chinese analysts see Taiwan this way, arguing that "if Taiwan maintained *de facto* independence. . . . China will forever be locked to the west side of the first chain of islands in the West Pacific," and thus "the essential strategic space for China's rejuvenation will be lost."[4] The PLA's emphasis on the strategic importance of physically occupying Taiwan suggests the Chinese military leadership would not be satisfied with a symbolic unification with Taiwan and would not favor honoring Beijing's promise to keep the PLA out of Taiwan as part of a negotiated settlement.

Chinese debating the Taiwan issue with Americans often invoke the analogy of the American Civil War. If the U.S. government went to war to reclaim Southern states that seceded from the union, Chinese ask, on what basis can Americans oppose the idea of China going to war to prevent the secession of Taiwan from China? The analogy, however, is faulty. The South rebelled against its own central government and left a political arrangement it had voluntarily entered into. The prewar association between the American South and the U.S. federal government was stronger than the association between Taiwan and the PRC. The CCP regime was never the central government of Taiwan or its people. Furthermore, the world has changed in the last century and a half. A secession question in the United States would be handled differently today. Rather than resolving the issue through war, the U.S. government would likely organize a referendum, similar to the way Canada has managed demands for Quebecois independence. Similarly, Beijing's use of armed force to put down a rebellion in the 1860s might be understandable, but such an approach today would be considered barbaric in light of modern norms.

Continued U.S. support for an autonomous Taiwan is uncertain, partly because of the rise of China. Americans have supported the ROC for sentimental, economic, and strategic reasons. During the Pacific War, Americans admired the Chinese for their resistance against their common enemy Japan. Although of dubious accuracy, the common American view was that the Chinese leader Generalissimo Chiang Kai-shek was a Christian and democratic reformer. After the shock of the CCP takeover of the mainland, Chiang's ROC on Taiwan inherited American hopes as "free China." The Taiwan government's authoritarian and sometimes brutal behavior undermined American support. With Taiwan's democratization in the late 1980s, however, American support for Taiwan surged. Americans praised Taiwan as not only an economic success story but as a model pupil of liberal democracy and a consistent friend to the United States. The specter of a large "communist" country bullying a small and admirable democracy tugs at American heartstrings. But sentimental support for Taiwan is likely to wane over time. It is stronger among older Americans who were adults during the Cold War. Younger Americans can more easily make a dispassionate and pragmatic assessment of the relative importance of China and Taiwan to U.S. interests.

There is no longer an economic rationale for supporting Taiwan's autonomy from mainland China. During part of the Cold War, the PRC promoted an alternative international economic system to the system sponsored by the United States and Western Europe. If a country joined the Communist bloc, it might withdraw from the global economy. This rationale for supporting Taiwan's autonomy has disappeared. The provinces of the PRC are now open to international trade and investment. If it became part of China, Taiwan would presumably remain accessible to foreign trade (except, of course, for buying weapons to defend itself against China).

The strongest remaining basis of U.S. support for Taiwan is strategic, resting on several arguments. First, China is a potential adversary. If Taiwan becomes part of the PRC, China can add Taiwan's physical and human resources to the pool of China's national strength, making China a more formidable opponent. Second, an autonomous Taiwan pins down Chinese forces. Chinese occupation of Taiwan, on the other hand, would extend China's strategic reach into the Pacific and release PLA ships and submarines from the confines of the first island chain. Third, Taiwan serves to restrict Chinese geopolitical aspirations. A postunification China could turn its attention from the cross-strait issue to projecting its power farther from the Chinese coast and challenging the United States or its allies over other strategic issues. The final and strongest strategic argument is that a U.S. "abandonment" of Taiwan to absorption by Beijing would cause other countries in the region to conclude that the United States has become a paper tiger. Countries friendly to the United States would lose confidence in Washington's willingness or ability to protect them, and governments hostile to the United States would be less fearful of the consequences of getting on Washington's bad side. All would see China as the new regional great power. This perceptual shift would be strongest in the case of a forcible Chinese takeover of Taiwan. A PLA attack without apparent provocation by Taipei is the circumstance the region thinks is most likely to draw U.S. intervention. If Washington stood by idly in that event or failed to win after intervening, U.S. value as an ally would fall precipitously. A smaller number of analysts have argued that the American reputation would suffer even if Washington declined to block voluntary and peaceful Taiwan unification with China.

Although support for Taiwan is still strong in the U.S. Congress, there is a considerable segment of American opinion that favors discontinuing U.S. protection of Taiwan. Arguments backing this view start with the observation that China is much more important to the United States than Taiwan is, so it is unwise to spoil the relationship with the more important country for the sake of the less important. Economically, politically, and strategically, China has more to offer the United States than Taiwan does. Some observers have argued that if Washington washed its hands of Taiwan, U.S.-China relations would dramatically improve. A second argument is that the costs of American intervention in the cross-strait issue have risen and continue to rise as China becomes more powerful. This effect is not limited to a war scenario, in which China's ability to launch a punishing strike on a U.S. fleet steaming to Taiwan's rescue is increasing. In peacetime as well, Beijing's unhappiness with U.S. support for Taipei is a constant impediment to achieving the full cooperation with China that could benefit other U.S. interests. Critics of U.S. support for Taiwan go on to argue that Taiwan is a security liability to the United States, not an asset. Taiwan does not help defend the United States but may draw America into a war with China. The argument that America should protect Taiwan because it is a fellow democracy, these critics add, is invalid. Washington does not have the resources to protect all threatened democracies. The costs and dangers would be overwhelming.

The willingness of the U.S. public to fight on Taiwan's behalf is doubtful. According to a 2008 survey by the Chicago Council on Global Affairs, only 32 percent of Americans favor the intervention of U.S. forces if China invades Taiwan, and only 19 percent of Americans view a cross-strait war as a threat to vital U.S. interests.[5]

U.S. Arms Sales to Taiwan

To protect itself against its massive and covetous neighbor, Taipei has sought international support. Taiwan's government has sponsored technical assistance programs to Third World countries, emphasized Taiwan's fraternal political bonds with other democracies, and tried to gain membership in international organizations to earn international goodwill and respect. Taiwan hopes its foreign friendships will help deter PRC bullying through the expectation of an international outcry. Most importantly, Taiwan has appealed for U.S. protection. It was Washington's decision, not Taiwan's, to abrogate the U.S.-Taiwan alliance in 1980. Many Taiwanese bitterly recall this episode as a betrayal by the United States. Three decades later, however, the United States is the only government still willing to sell Taiwan arms.

U.S. arms sales are based on the premise that excessive PRC military superiority might lead to Beijing bullying or attempting to conquer Taiwan militarily. Taiwan's President Ma makes the additional argument, with the concurrence of Washington, that the arms sales make cross-strait peace and progress possible. Taiwan will not negotiate with the Chinese from a position of weakness and vulnerability, he says. A strong defense capacity is necessary for Taiwan to maintain this confidence, and arms purchases from abroad are necessary for Taiwan to keep its defenses strong. Thus, the arms sales contribute to peace and stability across the strait. Beijing makes opposite arguments: that U.S. arms sales to Taiwan justify and require a buildup of Chinese forces; that arms sales to Taiwan make war more likely by emboldening Taiwan separatism; and that without the arms sales, cross-strait relations would stabilize because Taiwan would stop dabbling in independence and reach an agreement with Beijing. Thus, the PRC's opposition to U.S. arms sales to Taiwan is inveterate. We should not expect China to relax this opposition in the future.

The rise of China endangers the U.S. policy of selling arms to Taiwan. Increased economic and political weight give the Chinese more leverage, and they have a demonstrated a willingness to employ this leverage. China typically reacts to announcements of a major U.S. arms sale to Taiwan with condemnatory statements and cancellation of some planned U.S.-China diplomatic activities. After the Obama administration announced a sale in January 2010, Beijing made an unprecedented threat to impose economic sanctions against the U.S. companies involved in manufacturing the weapons included in the sale. One of these companies was Boeing, which had supplied half of China's commercial airliners and was counting heavily on China as a future customer. The threat suggested Beijing had decided to increase the pressure on Washington to stop arms sales. At around the same time, some Chinese delegates to unofficial strategic dialogues told their American counterparts that Beijing was determined the arms sales should cease completely within a decade.

While China opposes all U.S. arms sales to Taiwan, Beijing has signaled that its reaction will vary depending on the content of each particular sale. This suggests the Chinese want to establish an understanding with Washington that prospective arms sales will fall into two categories. The sale of some items will bring the usual perfunctory protests from Beijing but will do no serious lasting damage to bilateral relations. The sale of certain other weapons and equipment, however, will trigger much stronger retaliation from Beijing. In effect, the Chinese are offering a compromise in which the Americans can, for the time being, keep up appearances as long as China's military superiority is not seriously threatened.

The United States assures Taiwan that the Americans will not "hold prior consultations" with China over the arms Washington offers to Taiwan. This was one of the "six assurances" that the Reagan administration offered Taipei in 1982. It is nevertheless clear that Washington discusses arms sales in meetings with Chinese officials, and Taipei worries that discussion might slip into negotiation. U.S. officials have described the task as achieving a balance between Taiwan's needs and China's objections. U.S. Defense Secretary Robert Gates compared it to threading a needle, and former National Security Council official Dennis Wilder called it working to "achieve a golden mean."[6] As China grows more powerful, it will naturally tend to demand greater consideration relative to Taiwan's. It is very likely in the near future that a "golden mean" will no longer be possible: Washington will not be able to claim credibly that it still follows the TRA unless it offers to supply Taiwan with a very potent arms package, and Beijing will make clear that such a sale would lead to a crisis in U.S.-China relations.

U.S. support for arms sales to Taiwan may already be weakening. The combination of Taiwan's defense efforts and U.S. arms sales to Taiwan is not keeping pace with China's military buildup and modernization. Washington acknowledges this. The U.S. Department of Defense annual reports on the PLA have concluded since 2004 that the balance of military power across the Taiwan Strait "is shifting in China's favor." Admiral Robert Willard, the commander of U.S. forces in the Asia-Pacific region, said in 2011 that "the disparity between combat power on either side of the strait is profound" and represents a "tremendous gap in capability."[7] Recent U.S. policy, however, has not tried to redress this imbalance. Then national intelligence director and retired admiral Dennis Blair, a former commander of U.S. forces in the Pacific, explained, "Taiwan should not be so defenseless that it feels it has to do everything that China says. On the other hand, China cannot be so overwhelming that it can bully Taiwan."[8] If the goal is keeping Taiwan from being "defenseless" and the PLA from being "overwhelming," this is a lower standard than is required by the TRA, which mandates providing enough arms for Taiwan to have a "sufficient self-defense capability." This raises two questions: how the U.S. government reckons that Taiwan remains able to defend itself despite a steadily worsening cross-strait military imbalance, and whether the American commitment to abiding by its own TRA law is quietly fading.

The Obama administration's September 2011 announcement regarding U.S. assistance to Taiwan's air force illustrated the difficulty of Washington's efforts to balance a complex set of competing considerations. Taiwan's warplanes include obsolete 1960s-era U.S. F-5 fighters as well as F-16 fighters the U.S. supplied to Taiwan in the 1990s. Fighter aircraft could potentially play a crucial role in repelling an attempted PLA invasion. Taipei wanted to buy more F-16s and requested a more advanced variant than the aircraft the ROC's air force currently flies. New F-16s would allow Taiwan to retire its decrepit F-5s. PRC officials, however, warned Washington that selling Taiwan the new F-16s would bring an unusually strong Chinese reaction. The Obama White House decided to upgrade the F-16s Taiwan already has with new equipment, making them better but not as good as the newer F-16 model Taiwan wanted. Beijing's response was relatively mild: boilerplate public statements of protest, but without the usual cutoff of military-to-military relations. U.S. Secretary of Defense Leon Panetta even said of the Chinese, "I would commend them for the way they've handled the news."[9] Some praised Washington's decision as a wise compromise that signaled continued U.S. support for Taiwan while limiting the damage to U.S.-China relations. Supporters of the decision added that the difference between an upgraded F-16 and a newer model F-16 is minor and that the upgraded F-16s would have capabilities comparable to those of the most modern fighters in the PLA's inventory. Critics of the decision said it failed to address Taiwan's need to replace its old aircraft without suffering a large drop in the size of the fighter force, that it indicated Washington had succumbed to Chinese pressure, and that it was improperly based on China's reaction rather than on Taiwan's defense needs. Still another view was that F-16 sales could serve as a political symbol of U.S. commitment but would do little to safeguard Taiwan. Because of increases in the number and accuracy of PLA missiles, a Chinese attack could quickly destroy Taiwan's military airstrips, rendering fighter jets useless.

What would happen if the United States stopped selling arms to Taiwan? One argument holds that the arms sales are unnecessary because Washington can deter a Chinese attack on Taiwan without either building up Taiwan's arsenal or preparing to send U.S. forces into the waters near Taiwan. Instead, the U.S. Navy can rely on its capability to cut off the supplies of energy traveling by ship from the Middle East to Chinese ports if a Taiwan Strait war breaks out. Therefore the U.S. government could have it both ways: it could cut back on arms sales to Taiwan and enjoy the benefits of improved U.S.-China relations without giving up the means to thwart a Chinese attempt to conquer Taiwan. This argument, however, does not account for the fact that the arms sales have two purposes in U.S.-Taiwan relations. The first and obvious purpose is to strengthen Taiwan's military forces against a possible PRC attack. An additional purpose is to signal continued U.S. political support for Taiwan. In the case of some weapons sales, the second purpose is sometimes more important than the first. In principle, Washington may conclude that selling a certain weapons system is not strategically justified but is necessary to prevent demoralization on Taiwan. Demoralization is exactly what Beijing hopes for, expecting it will bring Taiwan to the negotiating table. Past experience, however, suggests the opposite reaction is at least as likely. Taiwan's now-abandoned nuclear weapons program, opposed by both China and the United States, was active when Taipei felt a strong threat from China combined with a loss of confidence in continued American support.

The Rise of China and a Cross-Strait War

Does the rise of China make a Taiwan Strait war more likely? This question is difficult to answer because it depends on choices made by the three governments involved: Taipei, Beijing, and Washington. It is important to understand that the question of whether the PRC could "win" a conflict against Taiwan depends heavily on how "winning" is defined, how determined Taiwan is to resist, and whether or not the United States decided to intervene. For example, a hypothetical cross-strait conflict might consist of Beijing demanding that Taipei accept the "one country, two systems" model, Taipei refusing, the PLA imposing a blockade and launching a few missile attacks, and Taipei announcing that it had decided to give in to Beijing's demands. In this case, the PRC would win by forcing Taipei to change its cross-strait policy, and the win would come relatively easily because Taiwan wanted to avoid serious suffering and destruction and Washington stayed out of the conflict. If, on the other hand, Taiwan's government and people are willing to sacrifice their blood and treasure rather than submit to Beijing's demands—and the United States sends forces to back them up—a PRC win would be much more difficult and costly.

China has every reason to prefer settling the Taiwan issue through peaceful rather than military means. A cross-strait war would be immensely costly and highly risky for China. It would require partly destroying the territory the Chinese were fighting to gain, reducing its value and requiring more PRC expenditure for postconflict reconstruction. Worse would be the political damage. The Chinese would engender bitterness and hatred among Taiwan's people, rejuvenating the preexistent negative attitudes toward mainland Chinese for generations to come. Military occupation and CCP rule would face widespread dissent and perhaps armed insurgency.

Nevertheless, the Chinese government believes it must build and field the forces necessary to conquer Taiwan in order to persuade Taipei and the United States that a negotiated settlement on terms agreeable to Beijing is the only option open to Taiwan. From the PRC's point of view, the stronger and more credible the PLA forces facing Taiwan, the less likely they will be used. When the Chinese carried out their missile launches and other military exercises in 1995–1996 to intimidate Taiwan's voters and more generally to warn against independence, analysts understood that the Chinese gesture was largely symbolic, since the PLA did not have the means to capture Taiwan. The United States answered by dispatching two aircraft carrier battle groups to the waters near Taiwan. The episode highlighted the limits of China's military power. Afterward, Beijing undertook a focused buildup of the specific capabilities it would need to fight and win a cross-strait war, including amphibious transport for a large number of troops and their equipment. By the end of the first decade of the century, China reached a point where it might be able to conquer Taiwan if the United States did not intervene—and if the Chinese were willing to pay any price to achieve their objective.

The trends are toward China's chances of success gradually rising even under the assumption of U.S. intervention. To be sure, a military campaign to subdue Taiwan will always be a challenging and risky endeavor even for a strong PRC. Before the fighting started, China would face a dilemma between a surprise attack and the opposite approach of an intentionally unsurprising gradual escalation of force. A surprise attack would give the PLA a chance to achieve a quick victory before the United States could intervene with a naval task force. If PLA units occupied Taiwan's key government and military facilities before the main U.S. force arrived in nearby waters, Beijing would present the Americans with a fait accompli. Washington would be unlikely to try landing U.S. forces in Taiwan to fight a ground war in both forests and urban areas against an entrenched enemy.

Alternatively, Beijing could wage a long-term campaign that slowly increased the level of coercion against Taiwan until Taipei complied with the PRC demand (such as overturning a declaration of independence or agreeing to negotiate unification). China could proceed through stages of increasing intensity that utilized the full range of Chinese tools and weapons. A campaign might begin with nondestructive pressure such as threats, military maneuvers, and a virtual blockade of Taiwan's main ports, such as in 1996. It might include actions against Taiwan's economic interests on the mainland. The Chinese could confiscate Taiwanese-owned property or detain Taiwan nationals in China. Another means of nonmilitary pressure would be a cyberwar targeting the computer-controlled parts of Taiwan's economy. Beijing could then escalate to limited military action. This might include an actual blockade of Taiwan's ports carried out by the PLAN, an occasional missile strike on Taiwan territory, or seizure of one of Taiwan's smaller offshore islands by PLA troops. The next step might be a sustained missile bombardment of Taipei. Finally, if none of those steps succeeded, the PLA could attempt to invade and occupy Taipei and other key parts of the island. The advantage of this gradual ramp-up strategy is that it would give Taipei opportunities to capitulate short of an all-out invasion. The Chinese could thus hope to accomplish their goal using no more force and causing no more destruction than was necessary. The disadvantage is that the international opposition to the PRC would have a chance to mobilize fully. This might include economic sanctions against China, but the most important aspect would be the possible intervention of U.S. naval and air forces. Even in this case, however, the Chinese might be able to wear down an American commitment to opposing a PLAN blockade by avoiding direct combat with U.S. forces and dragging out the confrontation for months or years. It would be relatively expensive for the United States to keep forces on station in the Taiwan Strait compared to China's costs—not to mention that winning a conflict over Taiwan means more to the Chinese than it could ever mean to the Americans.

Observers on all sides agree that a declaration of formal independence by Taiwan is a "red line" that if crossed will trigger military action by the PLA, but it has never been precisely clear what specific action constitutes crossing the red line of independence. This has worked against the PRC's interests by creating space for a Taiwanese government to take small steps that by themselves did not justify war but that gradually distanced Taiwan from the mainland. China has lacked an effective response between verbal condemnation and war. This has emboldened independence-leaning activists on Taiwan to see Chinese threats as a bluff and to take additional steps. This occurred during the "de-Sinification" campaign of President Chen Shui-bian. Imagine the frustration in Beijing when Chen publicly declared that "Taiwan is an independent, sovereign state."[10] What looked like a building crisis subsided when Chen's agenda foundered. Referenda on Taiwan trying to rejoin the United Nations failed after insufficient voter turnout, partly because of open U.S. opposition. Chen's proposal to change the ROC constitution, which contains wording that links Taiwan to the mainland, failed to advance because of opposition by the KMT and like-minded allies in Taiwan's legislature.

While China faces challenges in a prospective cross-strait conflict, those facing Taiwan are greater. The rise of China makes it harder for Taiwan to maintain a formidable defense. Taiwan has the inherent military limitations of a small country plus some additional peculiarities. In the face of the PRC's buildup, Taiwan's government has ruled out attempting to arms race with China or to match increases in Chinese defense spending. Through the first decade of the twenty-first century, Taiwan spent 3 percent or less of its GDP on defense. In 2011, defense spending fell to 2.2 percent of GDP.[11] Taiwan plans to phase out compulsory military service and change to an all-volunteer force with a reduced size of about 215,000 (down from 275,000) by the end of 2014. The main political schism on Taiwan creates an obstacle to Taiwan's people achieving a unified approach to national defense. There is fundamental disagreement on the question of whether Taiwan or mainland China is the motherland. Opinions on dealing with the PRC range from capitulationism to advocacy of developing missiles that could strike Chinese cities as a way of deterring a Chinese attack. Many Taiwanese, especially those who want Taiwan to keep its distance from China, believe that despite what Ma says, his government is not serious about improving Taiwan's military defenses.

Nuclear weapons can be an equalizer for a small country, but for Taiwan this option is problematic. Taipei became interested in developing nuclear weapons after the PRC successfully tested its own bomb in 1964. Taiwan's work gained additional impetus as U.S.-China relations warmed in the 1970s and Taiwan feared abandonment by the Americans. Under U.S. pressure, however, Taiwan curtailed its activities and then dismantled its nuclear weapons program in 1988. A Taiwan nuclear capability has strategic downsides. Taiwan would attract criticism from the international community. China has warned that it would launch preemptive military strikes if Taiwan tried to deploy nuclear weapons. Taiwan's nuclear weapons might not deter a PRC conventional attack because the Chinese might not believe Taiwan is willing to take on China in a nuclear war that Taiwan could not win. Consequently, Taiwan remains a "virtual" nuclear weapons country: it has the technological skill to build the bomb, but its government has repeatedly promised that there is no active nuclear weapons development program.

A 2008 analysis by U.S. Naval War College professor William Murray highlighted some of Taiwan's difficulties. Murray argued that Taiwan's defense strategy was ill-conceived and would not stop a PLA attack. Control of the skies would be critically important in a cross-strait battle, as it would determine whether or not Chinese ships could safely ferry invasion troops or impose a blockade. Taiwan planned to rely on its fighter aircraft and well-trained pilots to achieve this goal. Murray argued, however, that Chinese missiles could quickly and without warning neutralize Taiwan's air and naval power by destroying airfields and docked warships. No matter how good the ROC Air Force's aircraft and pilots were, they would be unusable because PLA missiles could make craters in Taiwan's airfields faster than the Taiwanese military could repair them. Murray also criticized Taiwan's desire to buy diesel-powered submarines, saying these would be unsuitable as blockade busters. Murray recommended that Taiwan retrench into a "porcupine strategy": basing air defense on mobile antiaircraft missiles instead of fighter aircraft, putting more resources into hardening defense infrastructure to survive missile bombardment, and dealing with a Chinese blockade of the island not by trying to sink PLA Navy ships but by stockpiling supplies to enable the population to endure a cutoff of incoming cargo.[12] Responses to Murray's thorough critique pointed up other weaknesses. One counterargument was that if Taiwan implemented Murray's recommendations, Taiwan's people would interpret the change in strategy as a surrender to Beijing, undercutting public support for maintaining a strong defense. Another response was that Murray's strategy would leave Taiwan in a passive position and allow the PLA to dictate the time, place, nature, and objective of every battle to maximize Chinese advantages.

Taiwan's unofficial military strategy is to hold out for two weeks against a PRC attack to allow time for U.S. forces to arrive and turn the tide of battle against the Chinese. American intervention, however, has always been uncertain, and China's growing strengths make it even less so. At the time of the last Taiwan Strait crisis in 1995–1996, a U.S. aircraft carrier battle group could have helped defend Taiwan with miniscule risk of molestation by PLA forces. China's military improvements since then are raising the potential costs that American forces would pay if they attempted to help Taiwan fight off a PRC attack. The greatest danger to U.S. forces would come from Chinese missiles that could target U.S. bases on Okinawa and a U.S. aircraft carrier battle group. The Chinese DF-21 "carrier killer" ballistic antiship missile, for example, might force a U.S. task force to stay so far from Taiwan's waters that U.S. ships and carrier-based aircraft could not influence the battle. Again, the trend seems to be in China's favor. Large ships and air bases are increasingly vulnerable to accurate and powerful missiles; effective defenses against ballistic missiles lag behind.

If China's relative economic and military strength continues to rise, the demand within China for a win rather than a continuation of the status quo will grow stronger. The price Taiwan must pay to maintain autonomy from China is increasing.

China's "Security" Versus Taiwan's Security

The rise of China brings increased danger to the security of a democratic Taiwan. Until or unless Beijing reverses its Taiwan policy, a stronger China intensifies the pressure on Taiwan to give up its autonomy, thereby jeopardizing its hard-won liberal political system. If Taiwan chooses to stand up to this pressure, it faces the risk of military attack from the PRC. The potential destruction Taiwan could suffer from such an attack grows along with China's relative strength. The chances of a military conflict across the Taiwan Strait are greatest if Beijing perceives that, on one hand, peaceful inducements are not working because Taiwan's people continue to eschew political unification, while on the other hand the prospects of compelling unification by unleashing the PLA appear favorable to China. China's opposition to Taiwan independence is more likely to endure than America's commitment to protecting an autonomous Taiwan.

Cross-strait tensions could be posed as a conflict between China's security needs and Taiwan's security needs. If both sets of needs are equally legitimate, China getting its way on the Taiwan issue could be seen as an improvement in the overall regional security environment. A cold-blooded analyst might argue that increasing the security of 1.3 billion people at the expense of twenty-three million people is a positive development.

The respective security demands of the PRC and Taiwan, however, are not equally legitimate. Taiwan faces the real threats of national and physical destruction. A powerful country forcing its opinion on a smaller but autonomous and independently viable community under the threat of military attack is a step backward in the evolution of international politics. By contrast, the threats Beijing faces are manufactured. Contrary to the claims of PRC leaders, Beijing's sovereignty over Taiwan is not a fact but an argument based on a political decision. Taiwan independence is a political problem of Beijing's own making.

The autonomy of Taiwan does not threaten the safety or prosperity of the mainland Chinese. The PRC is becoming a powerful, important, and even a prestigious world power without Taiwan as one of its provinces. It is not Taiwan's autonomy that keeps the PRC's prestige from growing even more quickly. Rather it is the PRC mindset, exemplified by the threat to use force against Taiwan, that holds China back.

Chapter Eleven

THE SOUTH CHINA SEA DISPUTE

Ownership of the waters, seabed, and the "islands" (mostly reefs and rocks) of the South China Sea is disputed. What is collectively known in the West as the Spratly Islands group (Nansha, "Southern Sands," to the Chinese) is claimed in whole by China and Vietnam and in part by the Philippines, Malaysia, and Brunei. Taiwan makes the same claims as China, but on behalf of the Republic of China rather than the PRC. At stake are fishing rights, potentially large hydrocarbon deposits, valuable minerals in the seabed, and access to a strategically important waterway astride important shipping lanes. China has a particular interest in ensuring that no adversary could molest Chinese shipping in the South China Sea or use it to threaten China's southeastern flank.

The rise of China has emboldened Beijing to stick uncompromisingly to its expansive and unreasonable claims, to eschew compromise, and to rely increasingly on its growing comparative advantage in the capability to project military or quasi-military force into the South China Sea in defense of Chinese claims. Beijing intends to establish a maritime sphere of influence over the seas on China's periphery now that this objective is becoming feasible. This is exacerbating frictions with the United States as well as with China's Southeast Asian neighbors.

The "Nine-Dashed Line"

Beijing inherited from its predecessor government, the Republic of China, an official map produced in 1947 that included a broken line around most of the South China Sea, including the Spratly, Pratas, and Paracel Island groups and the Macclesfield Bank. The line hugs the coastlines of Vietnam, the Philippines, Malaysia, and Indonesia, apparently encompassing their EEZs. Official maps made by the CCP government have continued using this boundary, which became known as the "U-shaped line" or "nine-dashed line." Indeed, Chinese law forbids making a map of the region that does not include the nine-dashed line. In 2009 Beijing officially submitted its map with the nine-dashed line to the United Nations.

There are two problems with China's South China Sea claim using the nine-dashed line. First, it is unclear. Second, it has no basis in modern international law.

Pertinent international law is contained in the United Nations Convention on the Law of the Sea (UNCLOS or Law of the Sea), which 160 countries, including the PRC, have ratified. (While the United States has not ratified the convention, since the 1980s the U.S. government has instructed the U.S. Navy to abide by the principles in UNCLOS.) The nine-dashed-line claim is suggestive and alarming but imprecise. It does not connect with the specific guidelines in the Law of the Sea. A maritime area has distinct parts: the sea, the islands, and the seabed. There are also different degrees of ownership. If the Chinese intend to claim the area inside the nine-dashed line as territorial waters, this would mean foreign vessels (including U.S. Navy ships) would lose the right to sail through the entire South China Sea. If the Chinese claim rights to the resources in the area, they would deny to the Southeast Asian claimants rights to fish and explore for oil off their coasts. Beijing has refused to clear up these ambiguities despite constant appeals from foreign governments and analysts for China to clarify its claims on the basis of UNCLOS. Keeping the PRC's claim ambiguous is a deliberate Chinese strategy to reduce the chances of confrontation while at the same time maximizing what the Chinese might eventually gain. Instead of forcing an early showdown, Beijing would prefer to shelve the issue until the future when China is relatively more powerful, the United States is weaker, Chinese economic influence over Southeast Asia is more extensive, and the subregion is more likely to accommodate Chinese wishes. Beijing even denies that there is a problem: "China's position on the South China Sea . . . is in keeping with relevant regulations of international laws including the United Nations Convention on the Law of the Sea."[1] During the tensions of 2010 the PRC Ministry of Foreign Affairs offered no elaboration except to repeat the mantra that "China has indisputable sovereignty over the islands in the South China Sea and the adjacent waters," while the PLA's line was the even less clear statement that "China has indisputable sovereignty of the South Sea." The Foreign Ministry's position could have been an assurance that China doesn't claim all the area within the nine-dashed line, but it did not explain how much of the "adjacent waters" China claims, what level of "sovereignty" the Chinese think they are entitled to, and which of the features the Chinese consider "islands." The PLA's position seemed to leave open the possibility that China claims the entire South China Sea as PRC territorial waters. Finally, in April 2011 Beijing told the UNCLOS Secretariat that "the islands are entitled to a territorial sea, EEZ, and continental shelf." This moved China closer to basing its position in the Law of the Sea, but it raised as many questions as it answered about China's claims. For one thing, few of the features in the South China Sea (and none of the nine reefs and rocks that Chinese personnel occupy) qualify as islands under international law.

According to Chinese scholars, the South China Sea islands were *terra nullius* (land owned by no one) until Chinese sailors discovered them during the Western Han dynasty more than two thousand years ago. Afterward, the Chinese claim, China was the first country to name the islands, to carry out economic activities there, and to exercise jurisdiction over them. The Chinese government incorporated the islands into the Chinese empire during the Tang dynasty (618 to 907 c.e.) and even sent officials on inspection tours of the islands during the Ming Dynasty (1368–1644). Japan took the islands during the Pacific War, but there was no international objection when China reasserted its claim to the islands after the war. Even Vietnam accepted an official 1958 Chinese statement of ownership over the islands. (Hanoi, now a claimant, says it acquiesced at that time because it was dependent on China for aid in the war against the United States.) Other than a claim to some of the islands by the Philippines in the late 1940s, Beijing says there were no challenges to China's ownership of the South China Sea islands until a 1968 UN report said the seabed contains substantial oil deposits. The PRC's claim relies on the concept of "historical use." Under modern international law, however, discovery and intermittent contact are not enough to confer ownership. What counts is evidence of permanent settlement. In China's case, the evidence is weak. (In fairness to China, none of the other claimants makes a particularly strong case either.) The other possible bases in international law for China's claim are no better. Neither the principle of claiming an undersea continental shelf as an extension of the dry landmass nor the principle of islands generating an EEZ can justify China's nine-dashed-line claim. If the basis for China's U-shaped line is EEZs generated by the rocks and reefs China occupies, this is invalid under international law because only islands capable of sustaining human habitation (including a natural supply of fresh water) and economic activity can be the basis of an EEZ. Such a Chinese claim would also squeeze out the valid EEZ claims by the coastal states Vietnam and the Philippines. Under international law, overlapping EEZs must be divided through a negotiated compromise.

Although China's claim is unconvincing by the standards of modern international law, Chinese analysts argue that this body of law was written principally by Western countries and therefore does not reflect the traditional Asian way of conducting international affairs. The suggestion is that Asia should write its own rules. This line of argument bodes well for China, which may be on a course to dominating the region, but it is not so promising for the other claimants. The idea that Asia should maintain its historically unique form of international relations inescapably raises the prospect of a revival of the Chinese tributary system. Chinese scholars have specifically argued that China had already established sovereignty over the South China Sea over a thousand years before UNCLOS came along. The Chinese do not necessarily feel they must justify their claims within the guidelines of the Law of the Sea.

The Rising Power Is the Most Assertive

Many Chinese elites in think tanks and in the Ministry of Foreign Affairs take a moderate position on how China should handle its claims. They believe in avoiding the use of force, as this would be disadvantageous to China. They believe in emphasizing opportunities for cooperation and joint development.

Some argue for basing Chinese claims in the Law of the Sea. This moderate view, however, is clearly sidelined by a more jingoistic one. According to the latter, China has been tolerant and restrained despite being victimized by the other claimants. The problems over the South China Sea are attributable to U.S. collusion with the Southeast Asian claimant states, particularly Vietnam and the Philippines.

Washington, according to this view, is using "freedom of navigation" as an excuse to justify intervening on behalf of the objective of maintaining U.S. regional dominance. This school of thought holds that China should be assertive rather than reactive.

Reflective of this thinking, China has been the most aggressive of the South China Sea claimants. Beijing makes the most extensive claims. China is like Vietnam in saying that it owns all the South China Sea islands. China's nine-dashed line, however, goes far beyond the other claimants. The Southeast Asian claimants say the islandlike features in the South China Sea are not entitled to an EEZ, but China says they are. If other countries used the same logic China uses, half of the North Pacific Ocean between the U.S. western coast and Hawaii would be American territorial waters, and most of the Indian Ocean would be Indian territorial waters. China used military force to seize the Paracel Islands group (northwest of the Spratlys) from the South Vietnam government in 1974, killing over fifty Vietnamese in the process. Although Vietnam continues to challenge Chinese possession of the Paracels, the Chinese have refused to discuss the issue with Vietnam, saying the matter is settled. The PRC took several rocks and reefs in the Spratly Islands group from Vietnam in a battle in 1988 that killed over seventy Vietnamese. In 1994 China threatened to expel forcibly a Vietnamese offshore oil rig from an area both countries claim. The Association of Southeast Asian Nations (ASEAN) intervened to persuade Beijing and Hanoi to de-escalate tensions. The following year the Philippines discovered that the Chinese had built three makeshift structures on stilts, which the Chinese said were shelters for fishermen, on Mischief Reef, which was inside the Philippines' two-hundred-mile EEZ. In a rare show of unified opposition to China, the ASEAN members sent a protest to Beijing. This sobered the Chinese. Beijing reached a bilateral agreement with the Philippines to avoid further actions that might raise tensions in the South China Sea. PRC President Jiang Zemin committed during the APEC forum in November 1998 in Kuala Lumpur to use only peaceful means to resolve the dispute over the Spratlys. In 1999, however, with Southeast Asia weakened by a financial crisis, the Chinese resumed what observers in the Philippines decried as a "creeping invasion." A large Chinese construction force returned to Mischief Reef to erect a sturdy five-story building on a concrete foundation. This new fortified structure, which featured satellite communications, radar and gun emplacements, was clearly more than a shelter for fishermen.

China's unannounced dispatch of warships to the area, additional construction on a disputed island, and installation of a miniature military facility were also clear violations of China's agreement with Manila.

ASEAN wanted a regional Code of Conduct to restrict activities that might escalate tensions in the South China Sea. China and ASEAN could not reach an agreement, so they compromised with a weaker "Declaration on the Conduct of the Parties in the South China Sea" (DoC) in 2002. China and other signatories to the declaration promised to pursue their claims "without resorting to the threat or use of force" and "to exercise self-restraint in the conduct of activities that would complicate or escalate disputes and affect peace and stability." Peacemakers in the region hoped to shelve the issue of disputed territory so China and the Southeast Asian states could proceed with economic cooperation. Implementing the general commitments in the DoC required further negotiations, but China demonstrated it had no interest in making progress. Negotiations stalled partly because Beijing insisted they should be bilateral between the PRC and each individual Southeast Asian claimant, which would ensure a series of diplomatic mismatches in China's favor. The Southeast Asian claimants wanted to develop a group position before entering talks with China. (China was not the only country deserving blame for holding up the process; countries within ASEAN have disagreed over the urgency and method of moving toward a stronger and more formal Code of Conduct, which is specified by the DoC as an objective.) Tensions gradually increased beginning in 2007 because China and other claimants tried to strengthen their claims and to extract unilaterally oil and gas.

In March and July 2010, China sent ships into the South China Sea to conduct exercises of unprecedented size and complexity for the PLA Navy. The drills lasted several weeks and included firing seventy-one missiles of different types. This seemed to signal a PRC intention to fight to defend its claims if necessary. By any reasonable interpretation, the exercises violated the DoC.

Both China and the other claimants have arrested foreign fishermen in disputed areas on the charge of trespassing. The PRC, however, has gone beyond the others by declaring and attempting to enforce an annual summer ban on fishing in large parts of the South China Sea. Chinese patrol ships have detained hundreds of Vietnamese fishermen as part of this ban. Vietnam alleges that the ban is a political statement rather than a policy to prevent overfishing. China has threatened international oil companies working in the region on behalf of rival claimants. Harassment of U.S. Navy vessels in the South China Sea is unique to the PRC. While the ASEAN claimants (along with Indonesia, Japan, Australia, and the European Union) applauded U.S. Secretary of State Hillary Clinton's statement about the South China Sea in 2010, the Chinese objected forcefully to what they called "internationalizing" the issue.

China's improved naval capabilities have allowed the PRC to be especially assertive in defending and strengthening its claims. Neither Vietnam nor the chronically weak Philippine Navy can keep pace with a PLA Navy that is beefing up and operating in greater strength in the South China Sea. PLAN and Chinese maritime enforcement vessels have increased their presence around the disputed islands. In June 2011 the PRC sent one of its largest quasi-military patrol ships on a highly publicized reconnaissance cruise through the entire South China Sea, including a port call in Singapore. A few days later, the PRC media reported that because of "an increasing number of intrusions by foreign vessels and planes into Chinese waters and airspace in recent years," China's Maritime Surveillance force would increase from 260 vessels to 520 and from nine aircraft to sixteen by the year 2020.[2] The PLA's increasing aerial refueling capabilities, the launching of new classes of warships and submarines, and the eventual deployment of aircraft carriers will soon give China the means to seize and hold the disputed islands in a conflict with the other claimants.

A variety of Chinese entities have an influence on PRC policy, which tends to foster aggressive action. The Hainan, Guangdong, and Guangxi provincial governments each take a strong interest in the South China Sea. In addition to the PLA Navy, the Maritime Safety Administration, Coast Guard/Maritime Police, China Maritime Surveillance, and the Fisheries Law Enforcement Command all operate their own fleets of armed patrol vessels. Chinese describe the situation as *jiu long nao hai* (nine dragons make a clamor in the sea). Guidance from the central government has been minimal. Some of these agencies may be acting outside of the direct control of the civilian central government, which would help explain the disjuncture between some of the stronger PRC actions (such as damaging the equipment of foreign survey ships) and the reasonable-sounding rhetoric of the PRC Foreign Ministry. These various agencies compete against each other for government funding. This creates an incentive for each agency to try to distinguish itself through diligence and boldness in defending China's claims. That Beijing may not have ordered the most aggressive acts may be reassuring, but that Beijing allowed them is not.

A typical case of Chinese bullying occurred in June 2010. A small Indonesian coast guard vessel detained one of a group of Chinese fishing boats for illegally fishing in Indonesia's EEZ northwest of Natuna Island. Two much larger and better armed Chinese Fisheries Administration vessels trained their guns on the Indonesian ship and demanded release of the Chinese vessel, saying "These are our traditional waters. We do not recognize it as Indonesia's exclusive economic zone." From one of the Chinese ships came the threat, "If you do not release the fishing boat, we will open fire." Outgunned, the Indonesian ship complied.[3]

China, the United States, and the South China Sea

The South China Sea became a source of increased U.S.-China tensions beginning in 2009, mainly for two reasons. The first was the freedom-of-navigation issue, in which China's pushback against U.S. surveillance conflicts with what the United States sees as its right to operate in the South China Sea. The second was U.S. diplomatic intervention in 2010, with Secretary of State Hillary Clinton calling for a dispute settlement process that would give the Southeast Asian claimants a better chance of standing up to Chinese domination.

China's domestic environment in 2010 was conducive to an assertive stand on the South China Sea. The Chinese public believed their government should be more vocal in shaping international affairs in a world of growing Chinese strength and perceived diminishing American influence. Chinese elites were debating whether Deng's advice that China should keep a low profile still served the PRC's national interests. The top level of the central government was preparing for a leadership transition and could not leave itself vulnerable to charges of weakness in defending China's territorial claims. According to media reports, in early 2010 Chinese officials Cui Tiankai, assistant minister of foreign affairs, and State Councilor Dai Bingguo, President Hu's right-hand man on foreign affairs, told visiting U.S. officials Deputy Secretary of State James Steinberg and National Security Council Asia Director Jeff Bader that the South China Sea was a "core interest" for China. Previously, the Chinese government had only applied this term to PRC claims of sovereignty over Taiwan, Tibet, and Xinjiang. "Core interest" indicates unwillingness to compromise and a commitment to resort to force if necessary. Moving the South China Sea disputes into this category would have been a dramatic change in PRC policy. Subsequently, however, after an internal debate Beijing declined to make an authoritative public statement that would officially confirm such a change. But neither could the Chinese government authoritatively declare that the South China Sea was *not* a core interest of China, as this would rile Chinese nationalist anger against Chinese leaders. Nevertheless, some Chinese and Western commentators erroneously repeated the idea that the South China Sea had become a core Chinese interest, which added to an atmosphere of heightened tensions.

U.S. naval forces in the Pacific and Indian Oceans use bases from Bahrain to Guam. They must be prepared to concentrate forces quickly in either ocean when necessary. Unimpeded transit through the South China Sea, which connects the two oceans, is essential to this strategy. If the PRC cordoned off the South China Sea to passage by American vessels, U.S. Navy warships would be forced to take longer and slower routes through waters far to the south.

Chinese officials have repeatedly said their South China Sea claims will not affect the freedom of navigation of foreign shipping. Washington does not believe these assurances. In 2011, Admiral Robert Willard, commander of U.S. military forces in the Asia-Pacific region, told Congress he believes China aims to restrict peaceful activities by U.S. ships and aircraft in the waters between the Asian mainland and the first island chain: that is, the Yellow Sea, the East China Sea, and the South China Sea.[4] This stark dispute stems from different interpretations of the principle of freedom of navigation.

According to the Law of the Sea, foreign ships, including warships, have the right of unimpeded "innocent passage" through a coastal country's waters. Their passage is "innocent" unless they are engaging in certain specified forbidden activities. The prohibitions are stricter in the area classified as a state's territorial waters (within twelve nautical miles of the coast) than in a state's EEZ (between twelve and two hundred nautical miles from the shore). UNCLOS forbids spying from within territorial waters but not from the EEZ. The recent incidents in which the Chinese reacted aggressively to U.S. surveillance, from the EP-3 aircraft collision of 2001 to the 2009 harassment of the *Impeccable*, took place in or over China's EEZ, not PRC territorial waters.

In China's view, however, surveillance from inside the PRC's EEZ *should* be forbidden, even if international law allows it. Beijing's position reflects the notion that a strong China need not and should not tolerate unfriendly acts by foreign military forces in the oceans close to China—this is the sphere-of-influence mentality. The Chinese have tried to go beyond international law by extending Chinese domestic law across the near seas, implying a much stronger degree of Chinese ownership over the near seas than other governments would recognize. A PRC domestic law passed in 2007 requires that the activities of foreign ships in China's EEZ "not involve state secrets of China" and "not damage China's national security." A Chinese domestic law, of course, binds the United States no more than America's Taiwan Relations Act binds the PRC.

The clash between the Chinese and American views played out in the highly publicized Chinese harassment of the unarmed U.S. Navy surveillance vessel *USNS Impeccable* in March 2009. The *Impeccable* was likely gathering information on the activity of China's most advanced submarines and on the PLAN submarine base on Hainan Island. The U.S. vessel might also have been testing the PRC's defenses, monitoring how long it took the Chinese to detect and respond to an incursion by a foreign ship. According to the *Impeccable*'s crew, several Chinese ships gathered nearby and maneuvered in ways universally recognized by sailors as dangerous and unprofessional, including turning to block the *Impeccable*'s path. One of the Chinese crewmen attempted to snag the *Impeccable*'s towed sonar equipment with a grappling hook. Outsiders speculated about whether or not Beijing condoned the actions of the Chinese ships that harassed the *Impeccable*. Commenting on the incident, Ministry of Defense spokesman Huang Xueping expressed no regrets. "China conducts normal activities of law enforcement in its own exclusive economic zone to defend its rights and interests, and such activities are justified and lawful," he said.[5]

While it is understandable that the Chinese dislike the United States spying from short distances off their coast, U.S. surveillance from within the Chinese EEZ is in fact lawful; Chinese harassment of U.S. ships and aircraft is not.

Another way the South China Sea aggravated Sino-U.S. relations was that Beijing perceived that the United States was intervening to back the

Southeast Asian claimants against China, even though Washington does not officially support any claimant over another. At the urging of Southeast Asian governments but to the surprise of the PRC delegation, U.S. Secretary of State Hillary Clinton made a statement about the South China Sea disputes during the ASEAN Regional Forum Foreign Ministers' Meeting in Hanoi in July 2010. Clinton said the United States has "a national interest in freedom of navigation, open access to Asia's maritime commons, and respect for international law in the South China Sea"; "supports a collaborative diplomatic process by all claimants for resolving the various territorial disputes"; believes "legitimate claims to maritime space in the South China Sea should be derived solely from legitimate claims to land features"; and supports the 2002 DoC and "is prepared to facilitate initiatives and confidence building measures consistent with the declaration."[6] Clinton's statement challenged several aspects of PRC policy. It implied that the United States will not accept attempts by China to restrict U.S. military operability in the South China Sea, that Washington disapproves of bilateral negotiations that give China an unfair advantage, that China's nine-dashed line is an invalid claim, and that China should not use or threaten to use force in support of Chinese claims.

The Chinese reacted strongly to Clinton's statement. A response posted on the PRC Ministry of Foreign Affairs website said Clinton's comments "were in effect an attack on China" and part of "the scheme of some to internationalize the South China Sea issue." As for the Southeast Asian countries that welcomed U.S. intervention, Chinese Foreign Minister Yang Jiechi scolded them for failing to accord a rising China proper deference. "China is a big country and other countries are small countries and that is just a fact," he said. During this same period, Vietnam took several minor steps to upgrade its military cooperation with the United States, moving the Chinese media to warn that Vietnam risked becoming a "pawn" of the United States.[7]

After a rise in tensions up to mid-2010, by the end of the year some indications from Chinese officials and Chinese analysts participating in unofficial international conferences suggested Beijing realized that its anger diplomacy had backfired. Shi Yinhong, director of the Institute of American Studies at Renmin University in Beijing, reflected, "We always make some mistakes but perhaps last year we made a few more."[8] The PRC attempted to repair the damage by sending officials on "listening and assurance" visits to Southeast Asia. While in Singapore, presumptive future Chinese president

Xi Jinping pointedly said, "China sees all countries, big and small, as equals."[9] Many observers expected 2011 would be a year of Chinese conciliation, following the pattern set by previous Spratly Islands episodes. Instead, however, tensions intensified in 2011 with the reported cable-cutting incidents.

China's Near Seas Mentality

We can gain more insight into China's intentions toward the South China Sea by broadening the context to consider some of the PRC's behavior in the other near seas: the East China Sea and the Yellow Sea.

When Tokyo complained about PLA Navy helicopters buzzing Japanese ships that were observing Chinese Navy exercises near Japan, the Chinese ambassador to Japan responded with the question, "What would Japan think if PLA warships persistently followed Japanese military exercises?"[10] The ambassador's remark suggests the Chinese will insist that their forces cannot accept being "persistently" watched under *any* circumstances, even when they are far from China's EEZ.

Some of China's positions vary from one disputed maritime region to another. The driving factor seems to be whether it is China or some other country that would benefit. In the East China Sea, Beijing claims ownership over the entire continental shelf up to the Okinawa Trough based on the principle of natural prolongation (i.e., the seabed is considered a continuation of the mainland, albeit under the water). In the South China Sea, however, China opposes Malaysia and Vietnam making a similar claim.

China's latest position is that some or all of the South China Sea islands entitle the owner to claim the sea around them as territorial waters or an EEZ. Many of these "islands" are actually not islands but rather rocks and reefs incapable of sustaining human habitation or economic activity. China's view contradicts the position China takes on Japanese-owned Okinotorishima, a coral atoll about 1,700 kilometers south of Tokyo. Although tiny, Okinotorishima is no less an "island" than most of the South China Sea "islands." The Japanese hold that Okinotorishima entitles them to an EEZ in the surrounding waters. China does not dispute Japan's ownership but since 2004 has contended that Okinotorishima is not an island and therefore Japan cannot claim an EEZ around it. Thus, in similar circumstances, the Chinese argue they deserve an EEZ but Japan does not. This is a strategically important issue. Okinotorishima lies between Taiwan and important

U.S. military bases on Guam. Under the Law of the Sea, a Japanese EEZ in this area would outlaw the presence of Chinese warships engaged in hostilities with Taiwan or U.S. forces during a Taiwan Strait conflict. It would also prevent the Chinese from surveying the area to create accurate charts for the operation of Chinese submarines. Chinese scholars explaining PRC opposition to the Japanese claim have argued that attempting to give Okinotorishima an EEZ "has harmed other countries' navigation interests and marine survey [accessibility]"; that "If Japan's efforts succeed, other countries will not be allowed to fish or share other rich natural resources in a region that is currently regarded as international high seas"; and that the idea "is contrary to the principle of fairness."[11] Each of these arguments could be turned against China's own grandiose claims in the South China Sea.

China's protests against U.S. surveillance from within the PRC's EEZ are hypocritical, given that PLAN vessels routinely carry out intelligence gathering and survey activities in the EEZs of other countries in the region. The passage of a Chinese submarine through Japan's EEZ in the Osumi Strait south of Kyushu in 2003 caused alarm in Japan. The submarine was evidently in the area to spy on a joint U.S.-Japanese naval exercise near Kyushu. In response, the Chinese government pointed out that foreign military vessels have the right under UNCLOS to sail freely through an EEZ based on the concept of innocent passage. Official Chinese media said that since the submarine was sailing on the surface and was not trying to avoid detection, Japan should have understood that the submarine's activity posed "no hostility and is entirely normal training." By the same logic, the Chinese should accept that a U.S. Navy surveillance vessel in China's EEZ is "normal" and allowed by UNCLOS.[12]

The Yellow Sea is bounded by the Chinese and Korean coasts. In 2010, media reports said the U.S. aircraft carrier *George Washington* would participate in naval exercises in the Yellow Sea with South Korea as part of the U.S.-ROK reaction to North Korea's sinking of the South Korean warship *Cheonan* in March. Chinese officials and media stridently demanded that a U.S. carrier must not conduct war games in the Yellow Sea. From the U.S. standpoint, the Chinese demand implied that the PRC has the right to veto training activities by the United States and its ally off the Korean coast—in effect, that the Yellow Sea belongs to China but not to Korea. There was no principle of international law that supported the Chinese demand. Instead, Chinese commentators argued that the Yellow Sea is an area of "important Chinese interests" as well as "sensitivities" because a powerful foreign warship in the waters near the PRC invokes the Western "gunboat diplomacy" that victimized China during the Century of Shame. Therefore, the Americans "should show necessary respect to China," given "China's increasing national strength." The PRC scholar Shen Dingli argued that China would be justified in responding the same way the United States did to the Soviet attempt to build missile bases in Cuba in 1962. (In that case, the U.S. government invoked the Monroe Doctrine and, risking war, imposed a naval blockade to force the Soviets to back down.) Shen said that when China is stronger it might "forcibly prevent . . . such provocative actions in the future."[13]

The pattern of Chinese thinking and behavior toward issues involving the near seas reinforces two themes of PRC foreign policy. First, Beijing expects that as a great power it will enjoy a sphere of influence in its near seas that accords unique privileges to China. Second, Chinese interests take precedence over international law.

The Strong Need Not Compromise

Reasonable compromise solutions in the South China Sea are possible. A Chinese concession on a question of disputed territory would not be unprecedented. According to one analysis, in seventeen of twenty-three territorial disputes since 1949, China made "substantial" compromises with a foreign government, usually settling for less than half of the original Chinese claim.[14] China's infamous nine-dashed line originally had eleven dashes, but in 1953 the Chinese removed the two dashes indicating Chinese ownership of the entire Gulf of Tonkin in order to improve relations with Vietnam. After years of negotiation, Beijing agreed in 2000 to a division of the waters of the Gulf of Tonkin (bounded by the coast of Vietnam in the west and by China's Hainan Island in the east) that favored Vietnam, giving about eight thousand square kilometers more to Vietnam than to China.

The problem is that a rising China has no incentive to compromise on the South China Sea. Although China could get most of what it wants through negotiation and appeal to the Law of the Sea without appearing imperious and unreasonable, Beijing would prefer to maintain its maximum claim while waiting for China's advantages in size and power to grow so large that the other claimants have no choice but to capitulate. China rejects referring the dispute to a third party for adjudication. Beijing is interested in joint development only if the arrangement involves China plus one of the other claimants working jointly in a geographic area that both claim. Since China makes the largest claim, it will not agree to being treated as an equal with the other claimants in a possible group settlement. Up to now, none of the South China Sea island claimants has been militarily strong enough to force a resolution in its own favor. China, however, is moving toward acquiring sufficient strength to prevail in a test of arms anywhere in the South China Sea against an ASEAN state. China can outspend any of the other claimants in an arms race. A unified ASEAN position regarding the dispute might give Beijing pause, but this has been elusive. The Southeast Asian claimants see each other, along with China, as rivals. ASEAN's nonclaimant members are less willing than the claimants to support a strong ASEAN position on restricting China's agenda.

Allegations that the PRC has been aggressive should account for two mitigating circumstances. First, China is not the only country that has tried to strengthen its claims at the expense of its rivals; the Southeast Asian claimants have done the same. Second, the Chinese see their moves as largely defensive.

Indeed, one could characterize the Chinese as latecomers trying to keep up with the other claimants. During the Cold War, the Chinese were too distracted by the Soviet threat and other issues to press their South China Sea claims. The PRC lagged behind the Philippines and Vietnam in the occupation of specific islands, rocks, and reefs during the 1970s. During the 1980s, Chinese policy in Southeast Asia was mostly focused on the narrow goals of halting Soviet support of Vietnam and forcing the Vietnamese to withdraw from Cambodia. Nevertheless, the Chinese compensated for their slow start by using deadly force against Vietnamese personnel in 1988 while occupying six of the Spratlys.

The Chinese have said they are open to discussions about joint development of South China Sea resources. They have warned, however, that other claimants moving toward unilateral exploitation of the resources in disputed areas are stealing Chinese territory. In 2009, the Philippine Congress enacted a law that officially defines some of the Spratly Islands as Philippine territory. Vietnam and the Philippines have recently stepped up surveys in disputed areas in defiance of Chinese warnings. These actions, the Chinese would argue, violate both the DoC and the Joint Marine Seismic Undertaking that China, Vietnam, and the Philippines agreed to in 2005. From China's point of view, Vietnam and the Philippines have challenged

China's claim. The Chinese fear that without a firm Chinese response, the region would conclude the PRC has tacitly accepted a new status quo with a shrunken Chinese claim.

Nevertheless, even with these mitigating circumstances factored in, the PRC stands out as the most aggressive of the claimants because of the audacity of its claims and because of the tactics the Chinese have employed to enforce them. Beijing's policy in the South China Sea has been to declare Chinese ownership over a maritime area that the rest of the world sees as disputed or international territory, behave accordingly, and wait until the region defers to China's overwhelming relative strength. The Chinese have made selective use of international law where it supports their claims. The Chinese discard UNCLOS, however, when it conflicts with their agenda. Ultimately, China's positions are explained by the objective of achieving a Chinese sphere of influence over the near seas. China seeks to restore the region to the arrangement that preceded the encroachment of the Western powers and the emergence of Japan as a regional hegemon. As the events of 2010 demonstrated, preserving the extensive Chinese sovereignty claims in the regional oceans takes precedence over keeping up the image that the PRC is peaceful and cooperative.

Chapter Twelve

CHINA AND GLOBAL SECURITY ISSUES

In addition to regional issues, China's rise will have an effect on global security issues. Chinese and other critics of U.S. policy would argue that the rise of China contributes to world peace by challenging the U.S. superpower monopoly.

Washington says a strong U.S. presence in the Asia-Pacific and other regions upholds peace and stability. Some governments agree, but others do not. Countries that have suffered pressure, threats, or attacks from the United States are not enthusiastic about maintaining an international order that features unchecked U.S. power. From the standpoint of governments disgruntled with American preeminence, a stronger China might enhance global security in three ways. First, with a great-power PRC in the picture, the United States would be more restrained in its use of force and would be more likely to seek China's approval and cooperation in the pursuit of America's strategic agenda. Second, if China became so powerful as to replace the United States as the dominant power in the Asia-Pacific region, the current tensions stemming from U.S.-China competition would be eliminated, replaced by a Chinese hegemony. Some might see this as a favorable trade. Third, a powerful China would reshape the ideology of how to conduct international affairs away from U.S. or Western values and toward Chinese values. According to the Chinese, if they had their way, principles such as nonintervention, nonaggression, mutual benefit, and great-power benevolence would prevail. Some countries might prefer to give China a chance at global leadership.

There are, however, problems with this position. Gaining stability or peace at the expense of loss of freedom of action is not necessarily a bargain.

Hegemony might increase "security" in the sense of reducing the frequency of war, but the cost might be another kind of insecurity: governments and their peoples being forced by a dominant power to act against their own preferences.

In practice, China's commitment to a "principled" foreign policy might prove highly conditional. While the PRC government claims that morality drives China's behavior, many analysts argue the opposite: that China is "an über-realist power" or "the high church of realpolitik."[1] Realism and realpolitik refer to a policy of pursuing national self-interest without being constrained by morals, ethics, or ideology.

One could certainly argue that the United States has been self-interested and hypocritical in its foreign policy. This argument, however, does nothing to prove that a strong China would not behave in a similar way. On the contrary, it underscores the fact that great powers tend to fall into a familiar pattern.

In my view, liberal democracy (including protection of civil and political human rights), free trade, and adherence to international law are generally good for security, particularly "human security"—the protection of people from life-threatening dangers *other than* being killed by foreign soldiers. Not everyone would agree with this premise. Cases could be made that democracy leads to disorder or impedes economic development, that free trade benefits a small group of elites rather than the masses, and that international law serves the former imperialist Western powers. Nevertheless, I hold that overall, these forces improve the prospects for peace, prosperity, and quality of life. In this respect, the rise of Chinese power relative to U.S. power has a downside for the four-fifths of humanity outside China. The United States has promoted (even if inconsistently) democracy, freer trade, and adherence to international law. The PRC has been markedly less supportive.

China's dedication to global norms is selective. Beijing generally falls in line with widely held international opinion and abides by international agreements when doing so is in harmony with China's agenda. China's behavior is less consistent with global norms and rules, however, when they conflict with China's objectives. Thus, we can expect that the rise of China will have a positive effect on global security issues only where the international community's interests overlap with China's narrowly defined national interests.

China has proven itself as capable of hypocrisy as the other great powers. A few examples will make the point. Although China is a signatory of the International Covenant on Civil and Political Rights, the Chinese government regularly and blatantly violates that agreement through the imprisonment of peaceful dissidents, state-sanctioned physical abuse of detainees, and the unannounced "disappearance" of suspects for indefinite periods in unknown locations. Second example: the PRC argues that since the United States is vastly more powerful than North Korea, the Americans should be magnanimous and make concessions that would address North Korea's sense of insecurity. In the case of the South China Sea disputes, however, despite being much larger than the other claimants, China makes the most expansive claims, has been the most aggressive country in trying to enforce its claims, and insists that Chinese negotiations with the other claimant states must be one-on-one bilateral meetings. Third example: in cases where Western governments have used or threatened to use economic sanctions against countries that have friendly relations with China, Beijing has said it opposes economic sanctions in principle as an ineffective way to solve problems. In cases that involve perceived challenges to China's sovereignty, however, Beijing has frequently used economic sanctions as a way of displaying its anger. When the United States announced an arms sale to Taiwan in 2010, some Chinese elites publicly raised the threat of China boycotting the American corporations that make the weapons systems Taiwan planned to buy. After the Senkaku Islands incident later that year, China cut supplies of rare-earth minerals to Japan in violation of international trade rules and reportedly slowed down customs inspections of Japanese imports. When a Norwegian committee awarded the 2010 Nobel Prize to Chinese dissident Liu Xiaobo, Beijing cancelled planned economic talks with Norwegian officials and threatened to cut business with Norwegian firms.

Beijing's economic policies demonstrate neither good international citizenship nor a commitment to free international trade. China's approach can be described as mercantilist: the state controls important aspects of the economy, the state harnesses the economy to the goal of serving narrow national interests, and the government tries to achieve a trade surplus while protecting domestic industries. Mercantilism is the nemesis of free trade. Adam Smith's famous book *Wealth of Nations* is largely a critique of mercantilism. By the middle of the nineteenth century, the West came to accept Smith's ideology that free-market economics creates the greatest potential for prosperity both globally and within individual societies. Some Western analysts argue that China has no fundamental interest in the principles of free or fair trade but rather seeks to cultivate success for a group of preselected Chinese firms within a protected domestic market. China has violated some of the commitments it made when it joined the World Trade Organization. The PRC is widely accused of intentionally keeping its currency undervalued relative to other world currencies, giving Chinese exports an unfair advantage on the international market. China has layers of discrimination that give unfair advantages to Chinese state-owned enterprises that the government has decided to champion. For example, foreign companies engaged in the otherwise normal collection of business-related data are subject to prosecution for violating Chinese law protecting "state secrets." In a 2011 survey conducted by the European Union Chamber of Commerce in China, nearly half of respondents said they believed Chinese policies were becoming more discriminatory against foreign businesses in China despite claims to the contrary by the Chinese government. Paul Krugman, Princeton University economist and Nobel Prize winner, calls China "a rogue economic superpower, unwilling to play by the rules."[2]

Cyberwar

China's undeclared cyberwar against the United States and other countries illustrates how the PRC approach to international affairs can sometimes be cynical as well as ruthless. Part of the Chinese campaign is the looting of economically valuable information and ideas. The Internet security company McAfee revealed in 2011 that Chinese hackers had systematically sifted through the nonpublic information files of dozens of private sector and government institutions in the United States and thirteen other countries over a period of several years in the largest theft of secrets and intellectual property in history. Chinese commercial counterfeiting and piracy, part of which is carried out through computer hacking, cost U.S. companies an estimated $50 billion per year. The U.S. government's Office of the National Counterintelligence Executive concludes that "Chinese actors are the world's most active and persistent perpetrators of economic espionage."[3]

A more ominous part of the campaign of malicious cyber activity from China involves sabotage and espionage. In June 2011, for example, Google revealed details of a phishing attack targeting the e-mail accounts of "senior U.S. government officials, Chinese political activists, officials in several Asian countries (predominantly South Korea), military personnel, and journalists." Similar attacks hit Yahoo and Hotmail e-mail services. The attacks originated from Jinan, China, and demonstrated a high degree of sophistication in the wording of e-mail messages designed to gain the trust of their recipients. The attackers likely worked under the supervision of the PLA.[4] Indeed, the evidence that Chinese government agencies are complicit in at least some of these cyber attacks has become overwhelming. Yet Chinese officials flatly deny PRC government involvement in any cyber attacks against foreign countries. This is not the first time Beijing has played dirty while at the same time denying it was playing dirty. In this case, however, the misbehavior is massive, systematic, and highly damaging. It is also dangerous. Understandably, U.S. officials are raising the question of whether massive cyber attacks by a foreign government can be considered an act of war justifying a military response by the United States.[5]

Arms Sales

In the first decade of the twenty-first century, China became one of the world's top five arms sellers, along with the United States, the United Kingdom, France, and Russia. Chinese arms sales reached $3.8 billion in 2007. Nearly all Chinese weapons sales are to developing countries. Often the main purpose of the sale is political rather than strictly economic: the Chinese charge a discounted "friendship price," but the real compensation for Beijing is to strengthen the basis for future bilateral cooperation or to gain exclusive access to a partner's oil or mineral wealth. The PRC has demonstrated little concern about supplying arms to countries the international community considers pariah states. China has sold short-range ballistic missiles to Pakistan and antiship cruise missiles to Iran and reportedly to Hezbollah, the radical Lebanon-based Islamist organization dedicated to the destruction of the state of Israel. PRC arms sales exhibit a disturbing pattern of Chinese interests in particular bilateral relationships trumping the international community's concern for global stability.

In a recent case, Beijing was caught double dealing with revolution-torn Libya. Beijing simultaneously preached nonintervention, made contact with the anti-Gaddafi rebels' National Transition Council, and continued to shop arms to the dying Gaddafi regime. When forces battling Gaddafi entered the capital of Tripoli in 2011, they discovered documents indicating that as the regime was losing ground to the rebels, state-owned Chinese arms companies offered to sell $200 million worth of weaponry to Gaddafi's beleaguered government. At the time, a UN sanction prohibited sales of weapons to Gaddafi's forces. The weapons discussed included surface-to-air missiles for use against the NATO aircraft that were assisting the rebels. The Chinese companies proposed delivering the weapons through intermediary countries such as South Africa or Algeria to shield China from criticism. Confronted with the evidence, a PRC Ministry of Foreign Affairs spokeswoman said the Chinese government did not know about the meeting between the Chinese representatives and the Libyan officials. She added that "China exercises strict management over all military exports," which in this case seemed untrue at best.[6]

Nonproliferation

Nuclear nonproliferation (preventing countries that do not have nuclear weapons from getting them) is an international norm, the vast majority of the world's governments having joined the Nuclear Nonproliferation Treaty. During the Cold War, the PRC flouted this norm while claiming to honor it. Nonproliferation was another case where China's self-interests departed from and took priority over the international community's security agenda.

In the 1960s through the 1980s, Beijing criticized the nonproliferation regime as an unjust arrangement designed by the nuclear states to preserve their monopoly on nuclear weapons. Beijing still said that China would not proliferate. But despite this pledge, China helped Pakistan develop nuclear weapons and helped North Korea develop missiles. Many analysts also believe the Chinese at a minimum tacitly approved of the sharing of expertise between Pakistan and North Korea that accelerated the acquisition of advanced missiles by the Pakistanis and nuclear weapons by the North Koreans. Although denied by both the Chinese and North Koreans, it is almost certain that China knowingly assisted in the DPRK's development of nuclear weapons. China also helped Pakistan get the bomb.[7] The PRC originally proliferated for strategic reasons: (1) to nurture U.S. adversaries that could threaten the United States while China remained on the sidelines, (2) to punish the United States for policies the Chinese opposed (such as selling arms to Taiwan), and (3) to strengthen China's relationships with some of its quasi-allies.

In the post-Mao period, China was eager to win international recognition as a responsible and law-abiding country. Consequently, Beijing at first denied proliferating. Then, when the accumulation of evidence implicating China made denial untenable, Beijing began phasing out much of its nuclear cooperation and demonstrated a serious commitment to nonproliferation. During the 1990s, the types and frequency of Chinese proliferation declined and the remaining Chinese assistance to other countries became less direct. China joined the Nuclear Nonproliferation Treaty in 1992, committing itself to stop helping non-nuclear weapon states get the bomb. Beijing became a member of other nonproliferation groups, including the Zangger Committee and the Nuclear Suppliers Group (NSG). In 2003, Beijing released a White Paper on Chinese nonproliferation policy that expressed commitments and principles consistent with those of the international community. Chinese nonproliferation behavior has illustrated the principle that Beijing tends to fall in line where there is foreign pressure and a clear international consensus on an issue that the Chinese don't perceive as a challenge to PRC territoriality or CCP legitimacy. At the same time, the outlook emerged among Chinese elites that nuclear proliferation suits China's interests less in a world where the PRC needs to trade with the United States and its allies rather than destabilize them.

Although much reduced compared to the past, Chinese proliferation activity has persisted into the twenty-first century. Much of this seems to result from gaps in enforcement rather than from strategic decisions by the central government. A large number of Chinese organizations possess technical knowledge or hardware related to making missiles or nuclear weapons. Illicit sales to international customers can be lucrative, and a system that effectively detects and thwarts all Chinese violators may be beyond the capacity of the PRC government. A new problem, then, is the Chinese leadership's willingness to devote sufficient resources to upholding Beijing's nonproliferation pledges. Nonproliferation can be seen as one of many areas in which the Chinese government has difficulty enforcing its own regulations across China's massive and fast-growing economy. This larger problem is evident in the prevalence of cases of tainted food, unsafe toys, industrial accidents, substandard construction, local corruption, and so on. Even the Bush administration's Assistant Secretary of State for Verification, Compliance, and Implementation Paula A. DeSutter recently said it was unclear whether continued Chinese transfer of proscribed technology "reflects an inability or unwillingness to stop proliferation."[8]

The strategic element is not completely absent from lingering Chinese proliferation. The PRC is less cooperative if the suspected proliferation involves a Chinese client state. Beijing went ahead in 2011 with the controversial sale of nuclear reactors to Pakistan in violation of NSG guidelines, claiming there was no connection to a weapons program and that the sale was a continuation of an arrangement made before China joined the NSG. The Chinese have reportedly ignored requests from U.S. officials for information about the possibility that North Korean missile parts bound for Iran passed through China.[9]

Beijing has also declined to embrace the Proliferation Security Initiative (PSI) founded by the Bush administration in 2003 as part of the U.S. reaction to the September 11, 2001 terrorist attacks. PSI is an agreement by participating countries to coordinate efforts to stop the international trafficking of weapons of mass destruction. In particular, PSI establishes a basis for interdicting ships suspected of carrying contraband in foreign ports or on the high seas. Washington announced PSI a few months after an embarrassing and frustrating incident in which a ship was discovered transporting fifteen Scud missiles from North Korea to Yemen. The U.S. government let the ship and its cargo proceed after determining there was no legal framework that would allow for confiscating the missiles. Ninety-eight countries have endorsed PSI, but China has not (nor has India, Indonesia, or Malaysia). Beijing says the interdiction of suspicious ships under PSI might violate international law. China is sensitive about this kind of situation, having been at the receiving end of a U.S. naval interdiction. In 1993 the U.S. government said it had reason to believe a Chinese cargo ship, the *Yinhe*, was carrying chemical-weapons precursors to Iran. The U.S. Navy detained the ship at sea for three weeks before the Chinese government agreed to a joint U.S.-Saudi search of the ship in a Saudi port. A thorough search turned up no contraband chemicals in any of the containers on the ship. Beijing called the incident harassment, and Washington never officially apologized.

If Beijing persisted in supplying nuclear weapons technology, components, or material to a state or group hostile to the United States, this could transform U.S.-China relations into an openly adversarial relationship. Fortunately, this scenario is unlikely. As China becomes more powerful, its interest in nonproliferation is growing. Like the United States today, China as a great power will have interests in managing and maintaining stability in the international system. A weak, developing China that perceived its territory and political system under imminent threat from the great powers might have seen advantages in checking or constraining them through strengthened proxies. A strong and globally engaged China, however, would see little if any advantage to a terrorist nuclear attack on a country representing an important foreign market, not to mention the resulting rampage by the enraged and still-powerful United States. As it evolves from a regional to a global outlook, China is likely to gravitate toward a belief in nonproliferation for some of the same reasons that the United States has. A greater number of states deploying nuclear arsenals deflates the value of the weapons possessed by the early "nuclear club" members such as China. More importantly, proliferation increases the possibility of the use of a nuclear weapon in anger, which under any circumstances would produce massive political shock and economic disruption. These would disproportionately harm a heavily trade-reliant country such as China. Effective Chinese enforcement of its own nonproliferation laws at home will also likely improve as China continues its economic development.

Even if it moves toward stronger opposition to proliferation in principle, Beijing will continue to make exceptions according to the demands of Chinese national interests, as in the North Korea and Iran cases. If the United States, despite being one of the leading sponsors of nonproliferation, has treated various proliferators differently depending on their political relationship with Washington, we should not expect more from great-power China.

Terrorism

From the point of view of some other countries, China's antiterrorism record has been in some instances too permissive and in other cases excessive. This is because the Chinese approach to counterterrorism reflects the basic PRC self-interests of preserving the Chinese empire and encouraging global opposition to US hegemony.

Superficially, China seems to have checked all the right boxes. The PRC is a signatory to the United Nations' major international antiterrorism treaties. Beijing also joins the United States, Japan, and the European countries in supporting the United Nations' proposed Comprehensive Convention on International Terrorism, which has been deadlocked by opposition from the Organization of the Islamic Conference over the issue of whether resistance against a foreign occupying military force should be considered "terrorism." Beijing also has bilateral antiterrorism agreements with Southeast and Central Asian countries. China has opened its ports of Shenzhen and Shanghai to participation in the Container Security Initiative, a counterterrorism measure that allows U.S. officials in foreign ports to inspect cargo containers bound for the United States.

Closer inspection, however, shows that the Chinese government has its own ideas about who counts as a terrorist and about how to fight terrorism. Beijing's geopolitical interests have sometimes translated into Chinese support for groups and governments accused of using terrorist methods (a charge also leveled against the United States), including the Palestine Liberation Organization, the Khmer Rouge, and the governments of Sudan, Iran, and Syria. Beijing is enthusiastic about supporting the global effort against terrorism in the cases that matter most to the Chinese government: separatist campaigns by ethnic minorities in the PRC. Indeed, according to Uighur activists, counterterrorism is a useful excuse and an opportunity for Beijing to seek international approbation for heavy-handed crackdowns against peaceful dissenters in Xinjiang. The Chinese government has called Rebiya Kadeer, an exiled former member of the PRC National People's Congress and Uighur rights activist, a terrorist. Outside China, however, she is a heroine. Kadeer is a winner of Norway's Rafto Prize for Human Rights. President George W. Bush and other prominent figures have praised her. Beijing lobbied the U.S. government for months to get the U.S. Department of State to label the East Turkestan Islamic Movement (ETIM) a terrorist group in August 2002. Some observers saw this as a U.S. concession to keep the PRC from vetoing UN Security Council action that would authorize the U.S.-led invasion of Iraq, which eventually came in March 2003. Outside experts on the Chinese Uighur community have questioned whether the ETIM is a significant force in China. Critics charge it is a manufactured threat to justify Chinese repression of Uighur nationalism.[10]

In other cases, Chinese seem to believe that a little terrorism is a good thing. After the September 11, 2001 attacks in the United States, many Chinese in various walks of life cheered the news of the destruction of the towers of New York's World Trade Center. In their view, the mighty superpower was getting its just desserts for arrogantly and often violently intervening in the Third World in pursuit of U.S. national self-interest. This view was found among educated as well as uneducated Chinese.[11] Chinese government-controlled media organs including China Central Television, Beijing Television, and Xinhua News Agency produced DVDs for the Chinese mass market that glorified the attacks and included taunting commentary such as "This is the America the whole world has wanted to see. . . . We will never fear these people again. They have been shown to be soft-bellied paper tigers." The Chinese media commentator Mo Zhixu reported that based on his research, 90 percent of the Chinese public was pleased by the 9/11 attacks. When China's Phoenix TV conducted an online poll asking Chinese how they felt about the death of Osama bin Laden in 2011, 60 percent of the half-million respondents said they were "saddened, because an anti-American fighter has fallen."[12]

Officially, PRC President Jiang Zemin quickly expressed sympathy for and solidarity with the United States after the 2001 terrorist attacks. This was a wise business decision by Beijing. It was an opportunity for China to gain international recognition for the PRC's domestic terrorism problems stemming from ethnic Muslim nationalism in Xinjiang. And as many Americans were beginning to see China as their top potential adversary, declaring antiterrorist solidarity with the United States allowed China to yield this unwanted position to al Qaeda.

Subsequently, however, China disagreed with the United States on the prosecution of the "war on terror." Immediately after 9/11, the PRC Foreign Ministry tried to link Chinese support for the U.S. global antiterrorism campaign to U.S. support for China's fight against "separatism" (i.e., a halt to U.S. arms sales to Taiwan). The resulting media discussion embarrassed Beijing into quickly retracting this line of discussion. Beijing opposed the U.S.-led invasion of Iraq (although declining to use its UN Security Council veto power), called for an early withdrawal of U.S. troops from Afghanistan, and decried U.S. missile attacks on suspected terrorists in Pakistan.

Since much of the rest of the world also opposed at least parts of the U.S. war on terror, it could be argued that in this case China did a better job of adhering to international norms than America did. In the future, however, it may be China that is the strong power pursuing a unique counterterrorism agenda based on its self-interests over the objections of the international community.

Oil Security

China's torrid economic growth requires a lot of oil. China is currently the world's second largest oil consumer, burning about nine million barrels per day and about 10 percent of the oil produced in the world. The United States consumes the most, at over eighteen million barrels per day, but because of the rapid increase in Chinese demand the PRC may surpass America around the year 2030. China has already surpassed the United States as the world's largest buyer of automobiles.

The Chinese are heavily and increasingly dependent on imports to meet their voracious thirst for oil. Chinese territory contains substantial reserves, but much of the remaining oil is in areas that are difficult and expensive to extract from, making it more cost effective for the Chinese to increase oil imports. China became a net oil importer in 1993. Oil production within China has steadily decreased since 1996. China now imports about half of the oil it uses. That percentage will rise to 70 percent by 2035. The vast majority of China's imported oil comes from the potentially unstable regions of the Middle East and Africa. China is trying to diversify its suppliers by increasing imports from Russia, Central Asia, and South America. The Arab Spring revolts of 2011 and the fears in 2012 that tensions between Iran and the Western countries might lead to a closure of the Persian Gulf sharpened Chinese worries about depending too heavily on conflict-prone sources of oil. But for the foreseeable future, China's main oil suppliers will continue to be in the Middle East and Africa.[13]

The heavy reliance on sea lanes makes the Chinese feel insecure about their oil supplies. The PRC is trying to address this insecurity through the construction of overland pipelines. The amount of oil brought into China by pipelines will indeed grow, but not nearly as quickly as China's oil consumption. By 2015, even with three pipelines (through Kazakhstan, Russia, and Burma) in operation and delivering a total of about a million barrels per day, China is still projected to rely on ships for 85 to 90 percent of its oil imports.[14]

Some Chinese elites take an approach to energy security that could be called liberal. They argue that China should rely on buying from international energy markets. This approach is law abiding and relatively non-threatening. If China and the other major powers all took this route, the chances of a military conflict over scarce energy supplies would be minimal, except possibly in the event of a sudden shock to the global energy supply, the results of which are unpredictable but might include desperate behavior by a country with strong armed forces.

According to this Chinese liberal view, the role of governments should be limited to reducing the barriers to the production and trade of energy resources throughout the globe. A competing Chinese view is that energy supplies are a zero-sum game: the goal is to "own" them, thereby ensuring one's own self-sufficiency and denying them to one's enemies. The state should oversee foreign and domestic oil production activities as an adjunct of national security policy and should be willing to resort to military force if necessary to protect foreign-sourced supplies. The latter view is visible in some Chinese policies, leading to tensions between Beijing and other governments, especially Washington.

When Beijing sees oil as a military problem, the solution inevitably increases friction with the United States. Many Chinese analysts believe the United States is committed to controlling the outflows of Middle East oil. This, they believe, was the main reason that Washington sent U.S. forces to invade Iraq in 2003. With its powerful navy and worldwide network of bases, the United States could cut off China's seaborne oil supply line in the event of a U.S.-China conflict. The United States has predominant influence over the Persian Gulf through its ties with Saudi Arabia and other smaller Gulf states, the shorelines of which form the southern edge of the gulf. Some Chinese strategists argue, therefore, that China should counter U.S. influence in the gulf through the Chinese partnership with Iran, the coast of which runs along the northern edge of the gulf. With a Chinese ally on one shore of the gulf, the U.S. Navy could not easily cut off the flow of oil to China through the Persian Gulf. In addition to driving China closer to the United States' antagonist Iran, China's interest in ensuring the security of its energy imports along the global supply network contributes to the rationale for building a large blue-water PLA Navy, possibly with overseas bases in the future. This capability increases the chances of conflict with the navies of the United States and other maritime nations outside of eastern Asia.

A second source of international friction is the perception that Beijing is attempting to "lock up" global oil sources through exclusive agreements with oil-producing governments rather than buying oil from an open international energy market. Critics complain that this Chinese practice reduces the supply of oil to the open market, keeping prices higher and limiting supply options for everyone else. These criticisms are overstated. The

Chinese cannot really own resources under the surface of another country's territory. A foreign producer cannot get away with buying the host country's oil at below market prices. Western countries have been trying to acquire overseas oil fields for over a century. Chinese oil companies have established themselves mostly in countries that the United States and European countries have vacated or are not interested in, such as Venezuela, Iran, Sudan, and Uzbekistan. Because of transportation and other logistical costs, much of the oil produced in China's overseas concessions is sold on the international market rather than being shipped to China. In this sense, Chinese foreign investment in exploration and oil production increases the worldwide availability of oil. Disproportionate though it may be, the charge that China is trying to buy up the world's oilfields adds to international anxiety about the rise of China.

Finally, China's search for oil sometimes conflicts with efforts by the major democratic powers to promote good governance and lawful behavior in the Third World. China's urgent attempts to solidify relationships with current suppliers and to forge ties with new ones, combined with Beijing's nonjudgmental approach to bilateral economic relations, finds the Chinese conducting "oil diplomacy" in the Middle East, Africa, and South America. The Chinese have done business with unsavory regimes such as those in Iran, Venezuela, Sudan, and Uzbekistan. In some cases the Chinese provide pariah regimes with weapons as direct or indirect payment for oil.

Human Security

The destinies of people in countries such as Cambodia, North Korea, Pakistan, and Tanzania might be very different in a world dominated by Chinese values as opposed to a world in which Western values prevail. Would the Third World be better off with China as a great power? The answer depends largely on one's ideological orientation. Western liberals would argue that democratization promotes human security both by improving governance and by unleashing economic dynamism. An opposing point of view, held by many Chinese, is that the Western notion of democracy spawns social pathologies and interferes with equitable economic development because of an overemphasis on individual liberties.

From the Western liberal standpoint, China's relatively laissez-faire approach to foreign economic aid undercuts efforts to improve human security worldwide. When the major Western countries give economic aid to a poor and badly managed country, they typically make the aid conditional on the recipient country making improvements in government performance. Aid recipients must take steps toward democratization or political liberalization, better protect human rights, reduce corruption, enhance working conditions, or increase the transparency in how the rulers manage public funds. These conditions reflect what were originally called Western values, but these Western values have largely become global values.

By contrast, China's approach to giving economic aid to what are commonly called "developing" countries is completely different. Beijing does not require improvements in the fairness or efficiency of government as conditions for aid. If Beijing imposes conditions, they involve either the recipient country supporting China's position on a political issue (such as Taiwan) or China gaining preferential consideration for a future bilateral economic deal. This approach gives China a comparative advantage in establishing relationships with developing countries that are strategically important or control valuable resources. Beijing understands that Third World governments resent the intrusiveness of Western aid groups. The Chinese can present themselves as much less demanding alternative partner. In Africa, where Chinese trade and construction are sweeping the continent, local leaders are sensitive to hints of what they would see as Western neocolonialism. In contrast to Western governments, the Chinese do not try to proselytize or pressure African governments to adopt new values or ideology.

The denial of aid or commerce to regimes that treat their own people badly is one of the most important tools available to the international community to increase human security. China's willingness to carry out value-free business with these regimes undermines international efforts to pressure them to meet higher standards of governance.

China's permissive approach toward poorly governed countries obviously harms global human security by alleviating the pressure on offender regimes to provide for their people's well-being. Chinese nonjudgmental policy also indirectly contributes to the global terrorism threat. Terrorist groups are less likely to emerge from societies in which citizens are not brutalized by their rulers, can freely discuss political issues, and find opportunities to prosper. On the other hand, the opposite conditions are fertile ground for the frustration that can lead to terrorist activity, and poorly governed states often contain lawless areas in which terror groups can establish bases or havens. In this sense, China helps perpetuate the conditions that give rise to terrorism.

A second obstacle to promoting human security in the Third World is China's nonintervention principle. A consensus within the international community believes in the principle of "responsibility to protect," which means that outside countries should intervene to rescue a people whose own government is guilty of massive abuse or an egregious failure of governance. Situations that would qualify for intervention include genocide, ethnic cleansing, and widespread starvation. This directly conflicts with one of the staples of China's "principled" foreign policy: that countries should practice "nonintervention in each other's internal affairs." PRC leaders have specifically said that China "opposes the intervention of external forces in their internal affairs with the excuse of human rights."[15] In March 2011, for example, NATO aircraft began attacks on Libyan government forces to prevent a bloodbath among rebels and civilians in Benghazi and other cities by a vengeful Gaddafi regime. Beijing complained that "armed action against sovereign countries . . . is a blow to the United Nations Charter and the rules of international relations."[16] Beijing reverted to its familiar position in the case of Syria in early 2012. When the UN Security Council produced a draft resolution condemning the Syrian regime for massacring crowds protesting the despotic rule of Bashar al-Assad, China (along with Russia) voted against it, explaining that China was opposed to foreign pressure on the regime. Instead, Beijing echoed Assad's call for rebels to stop fighting against Syrian government forces. The appeal of the nonintervention principle to Chinese is not surprising in light of China's historical experience with Western intrusion and Japanese invasion plus what the Chinese see as U.S. obstruction of Chinese unification by meddling in the "domestic" issue of Taiwan. The United Nations endorsed the responsibility to protect beginning in 2005. This was a major disappointment to China, which saw a large part of the United Nations' value in its ability to impede intervention by the other great powers. China's initial response to the United Nations' action was to raise several objections: (1) the UN Charter recognizes the right to use force only in self-defense or to maintain international peace, not for humanitarian intervention; (2) legalizing the international use of force would create an incentive for groups fighting a domestic conflict to escalate the violence in the hope of drawing in outside forces rather than negotiating a peaceful solution; and (3) outsiders might exploit the principle of intervention by using moral reasons as a cover for pursuing their self-interested political agenda. Nonintervention has become a convenient position for a rising China. It provides intellectual underpinning for Beijing's cross-strait policy, for the PRC's global drive to gain access to markets and resources, and for Chinese diplomatic efforts to protect friendly pariah regimes.

As China rises, Chinese expatriate communities and investments in Third World countries grow. This has put Beijing's nonintervention principle under pressure. Some Chinese official statements suggest the principle could be relaxed under some circumstances, while some Chinese elites are calling it obsolete. The commitment to noninterference is evolving into a recognition that selective intervention serves China's interests. There are two reasons for the change in China's approach. The first is international opinion. Increasingly recognized as an influential global actor, China must use its influence constructively or risk being criticized for poor international citizenship. The second reason is that Beijing has concluded that supporting unpopular and sometimes unstable regimes is not the most effective way to protect its investments and citizens abroad.

In the latter half of the first decade of the twenty-first century, Beijing pulled back from its previously unstinting defense of disreputable authoritarian regimes. In some cases Beijing showed a greater willingness to pressure regimes to make changes that would improve their image, legitimacy, and stability. China's involvement in the Darfur conflict is an illustration. In 2003 the world learned of allegations that the ethnic Arab-dominated Sudanese government was supporting military forces and militiamen carrying out a campaign of massacre and destruction against the black African inhabitants of Sudan's Darfur region. China came under international criticism as an indirect supporter of genocide because of heavy Chinese investment in Sudan's oil production and Chinese weapons sales to the Sudan government. Beijing maintained that the Darfur massacres were a domestic issue. In early 2006 China abstained on a UN Security Council measure to sanction the Sudan government. In the summer of 2006, however, the escalating conflict threatened China's plans to invest in the oil industry in neighboring Chad and increased the likelihood of military intervention by the Western powers. Equally importantly, Darfur threatened to tarnish Beijing's hosting of the 2008 Olympic Games. China compromised its nonintervention principle, pressuring the Sudanese government to accept a twenty-thousand-strong international peacekeeping force in Darfur. The U.S. government praised Beijing for helping to bring about the agreement.

Under international pressure, Beijing has recently become more supportive of efforts to promote reform in Burma. The PRC backed Burma's ethnic Chinese Prime Minister Khin Nyunt, who appeared relatively moderate and reform minded, only to see him purged in 2004 by more conservative members of the junta. China's pressure on the junta to reform became more transparent in the latter part of the decade. In 2007 Beijing began pressuring the Burmese junta toward domestic reform and greater openness toward the international community. When the regime responded brutally to protesting Buddhist monks in September 2007, China (along with Russia) tried to restrain and weaken UN Security Council action, but at the same time China also pursued its own form of intervention. Senior Chinese diplomat Tang Jiaxuan told the Burmese prime minister that China wants to see Burma "push forward a democracy process that is appropriate for the country."[17] By this Tang almost certainly meant partial political reforms that could help make the country more prosperous (the Chinese model), not Western-style multiparty democracy will the full range of civil liberties. In recent years, Chinese diplomats have quietly expressed agreement with the U.S. position that the ruling regime in Burma should implement political reforms. Clearly, however, China's goals for Burma are different from the West's goals. In contrast to Western pressure aimed at inducing political liberalization or a changing out of the military regime, Beijing presses the Burmese government to make the regime more stable and efficient. Beijing's priority is preventing an overthrow of the regime rather than good governance. The PRC has no intrinsic interest in improving human rights in Burma and has reason to oppose democratization.

Beijing would argue that China has kept its promise to act as a force for peace and stability by standing up against the plans of the United States and other governments to violate the sovereignty of certain states. According to the Chinese, these states are unfairly singled out based on an unstated political agenda, and an intervention worsens problems rather than solving them. From the perspective of most of the major democratic governments, China's lack of interest in using its economic, political, or military power to pressure outlaw states to abide by internationally accepted norms shows a lack of responsible behavior. A partial convergence of Chinese and Western views on intervention might help alleviate this ideological dispute. But while a more powerful China will be more willing to intervene in problem-plagued Third World countries, Chinese intervention will still be in accordance with Chinese interests. China will promote stability, efficiency, and preferential Chinese access, not democracy or liberty.

Chinese Security Versus Global Security

China's rise could be a blessing to the world if Beijing saw its self-interests closely aligned with global norms that promote the security interests of the international community. Unfortunately, China's support for international norms has been inconsistent and highly conditional. While in some cases (such as nuclear nonproliferation) a stronger China might take on a more managerial outlook that could lead to greater convergence between Chinese and global values, Beijing is likely to disregard the sentiments of the international community when global norms challenge basic and sensitive PRC concerns such as national sovereignty and CCP legitimacy. In those cases where China is unsupportive of global norms, Chinese policies will do greater damage to global security as the PRC becomes stronger.

Chapter Thirteen

CONCLUSION

The previous chapters have generated findings that I will summarize below.

Several regional bilateral disputes are sharpening because of the rise of China. Chinese interests in avoiding conflict with foreign governments help form pacifying bulwarks. On balance, however, several virulent forces appear poised to break or slip through the bulwarks.

As an emerging great power, China is ambitious because it can be. Two additional factors drive China's ambition: the Chinese believe their country is historically destined to be the leader of the region, and they see heavy American influence in Asia as threatening and constraining rather than benign.

Chinese feelings of greater entitlement because of China's rise are overlapping with a residual sense of historical victimization stemming from past weakness.

Although China presently has neither the desire nor the ability to be a superpower, as China's relative capabilities increase, Beijing is aspiring to greater levels of control over the external environment. Chinese assurances that "China does not seek regional hegemony or a sphere of influence" should not be taken seriously.[1] If China's relative strength continues to grow, Beijing's calculations about the costs and risks of trying to expand Chinese influence will change. In a sense, even if China's current leaders had only the most benign intentions, they could not speak authoritatively about the PRC's future foreign policies.

As China's relative power grows, patience will likely diminish and assertiveness increase. Typical of a rising great power, China is already struggling to contain its impatience. Chinese heads understand that the PRC should avoid international confrontation while consolidating economic development and bringing domestic problems under control, but Chinese hearts demand greater accommodation and respect from other countries now that China is powerful.

As we have seen, Chinese and some non-Chinese analysts argue that the PRC will not be a serious threat to regional security even if the Chinese economy continues its present rate of growth. According to this argument, surpassing the United States as the world's largest economy will not by itself make China the world's most powerful country. Most of China will still be poor, forcing the PRC central government to concentrate funds on raising living standards across the country. Thus, the PRC will still be too poor to build a military that could dominate China's neighbors. This argument, however, is already disproved by China's rapid military buildup. Even with the objective of nationwide economic development far from accomplished, Beijing is already laying aside plenty of resources for expanding and strengthening the PRC's nuclear weapons arsenal; developing new generations of ships, missiles, and aircraft; and deploying aircraft carriers.

A safety net of pacifying international forces largely keeps China playing within the rules of accepted global interaction. In some areas, however, this net is not strong enough to prevent crises. China is less likely to compromise, less likely to be deterred, and more likely to overreact when it comes to the hearth issues: disputes regarding territory within China's perceived sphere of influence, respectful or disrespectful treatment of China by foreigners, and the legitimacy of the CCP. On these issues, nationalism trumps the Chinese wish to avoid the appearance of domineering or aggressive behavior. The PRC feels entitled to and intends to establish a Chinese sphere of influence in eastern Asia in which major foreign policy decisions and external military activity by neighboring countries would be subject to Beijing's approval. The Chinese government eventually wants to uproot U.S. military alliances and bases from the Asia-Pacific region and to circumscribe the areas in which U.S. military units can operate. China will defend its claims over disputed maritime territories with gradually increasing strength. The outlook is dim for the Southeast Asian claimants in the South China Sea disputes securing China's agreement to a roughly equal settlement. Similarly, Taiwan is in danger of losing its autonomy as a consequence of China's rise.

We can anticipate differences as well as continuity between the premodern regional hegemon China and the twenty-first-century great-power

PRC. In contrast to the premodern era, the China of our time will have a global outlook and interests that will push Beijing toward an internationalist foreign policy that seeks to shape world events to produce outcomes favorable to China. This will include taking leadership roles in multilateral organizations and, most likely, establishing military bases (or base-like arrangements) outside of China. What carries over from premodern to modern times is the sphere of influence mentality. Like ancient China, the resurgent PRC will expect deference from neighboring countries and will view itself as a moral exemplar within the international community. With this somewhat dissonant combination, Beijing will prefer to dominate the region not through warfare and conquest but through what could be described as self-righteous bullying: political and economic pressure (backed by superior military force) carried out with pompous moralism. A PRC that attains preeminence will routinely lean on regional governments to accept Chinese preferences in economic, political, and strategic matters.

East Asia has already been a showcase of security dilemmas. The problem is intensified by a rising China's hypersensitivity to the security policies of states in the U.S. camp, combined with Chinese undersensitivity to the security fears of its neighbors. Beijing is aware of the challenge of rising without alarming neighbors into forming a defensive coalition. Nevertheless, the PRC is struggling, and perhaps failing, to avoid policies and postures that will make the region fear a strong China. The states that can are balancing against China, mostly in subtle ways that allow them to maintain constructive economic relationships with the PRC. The Asia-Pacific countries want to trade with China, but they also generally want the United States to remain a strategic player, if not a strategic partner. They are interested not in intimidating or containing China but in maintaining an insurance policy against possible Chinese aggression. The growth of China makes the United States more rather than less welcome.

U.S.-China relations are conflicted and rife with mutual suspicions. Washington and Beijing cooperate extensively in some areas, especially in trade and investment, but are also hedging against each other. Serious conflict is not inevitable, but neither is it impossible. China and the United States have a common interest in managing global affairs to maintain peace and stability. U.S. willingness to accede to the rise of China if the Chinese generally play by the widely accepted rules of international affairs offers hope of a peaceful ascendance by the PRC into a region of heavy U.S. influence. The two countries are divided, however, by strategic competition and clashing values. These divisions will continue to bedevil Sino-U.S. cooperation on difficult but important international issues. Chinese and Americans fundamentally disagree on the need for a strong U.S. strategic role in the western Pacific region. The Chinese see this as a strictly self-serving policy to enable the United States to dominate and exploit Asia. Americans see their role as crucial to maintaining the stability that allows regional states to prosper. China's modernizing military forces make it more difficult for U.S. forces to protect allies and friends in the region in the event of belligerent Chinese behavior.

The effect of the rise of China on the current international system of rules, norms, and institutions has been mixed. As a stronger player, China can be a more influential supporter of the system, a more damaging violator, and a more compelling proponent of changes in the rules. Beijing has done some of each. In the future, China's support for international norms will be inconsistent and often reluctant except in cases where these norms coincide with narrow PRC self-interests.

Some form of democratization is likely in the PRC during the next two decades, but a shift to a democratic political system would not by itself sweep away China's strategic disputes with the United States, Japan, India, or Taiwan.

My analysis up to now about the PRC's effects on international security is based on the assumption that China will maintain its rapid economic growth and domestic political stability. We must recognize, however, that for both the United States and China, the continuation of the economic capacity to field large and technologically advanced military forces is uncertain. In 2012, the U.S. government announced adjustments that would gradually downsize its military forces because of America's weakened financial foundation. China's economy, as well, could falter, forcing a reconsideration of the current expectation that China will challenge America for regional hegemony. The strategies that produced rapid growth in the PRC during the last three decades probably cannot sustain high growth rates into the future. Up to now China has relied heavily on exports, but it is increasingly difficult for the outside world to absorb all of what China produces for export. Much of China's recent growth is based on state-guided investment in infrastructure and real estate. The returns on this investment are shrinking from overinvestment, increased competition, and in some cases government policy. China's economy requires rebalancing toward more modest growth rates, greater domestic consumption, and intensive rather than extensive growth (with emphasis on such areas as research and development and technologies that save energy and resources). Chinese leaders must make policy adjustments that will be politically difficult. They might hesitate to make these adjustments or fail to make them successfully.[2]

But if China continues to churn forward as it has for the past three decades, the other Asia-Pacific countries face a formidable challenge. They have three general choices. The first is continuing to hedge, with the understanding that if an overly assertive China intrudes on certain critically important interests, states in the region will increase their defense cooperation and signal a determination to defend those interests even at the risk of a conflict with the PRC. A second possible strategy is to accommodate China early, even though resistance is still feasible. This strategy would accept the premise that China will eventually win by building an overwhelming advantage in capabilities that the United States and other regional states cannot match. Giving the game away might buy goodwill in Beijing that would pay off in a smoother relationship once China attains dominance as anticipated. But this would require submitting to China's preferences on strategic disputes: Taiwan and the near seas today, U.S. alliances tomorrow. A third possibility is for Washington and Beijing to agree to divide or share the responsibility for maintaining stability in the region, with each recognizing and not interfering in the other's key interests by mutual agreement. To obtain China's assent would probably require the Americans to demonstrate "sincerity" by accepting the sphere of influence the Chinese want, meaning the United States would have to end policies such as arms sales to Taiwan and surveillance from within China's EEZ. In sum, if China's relative power continues to grow, the other Asia-Pacific states must either accept compromises in their freedom of action or be prepared to pay a higher price to maintain it.

The rise of China from a poor, weak country to a prosperous and secure country that contributes to global economic vitality is almost universally accepted as a positive development. The desire of the Chinese people for their country to be developed, powerful, and safe from foreign molestation is understandable and legitimate. Unfortunately, their gain will probably be someone else's loss. China's continued growth into a great power or a regional hegemon will likely lead to a net reduction in security for most of the world.

NOTES

1. Introduction

1. Kathy Chu, "Most Americans Think China Is No. 1 Economy; It Isn't," *USA Today* (February 15, 2011), http://www.usatoday.com/money/economy/2011-02-14-chinapoll14_ST_N.htm.

2. Tom Curry, "China Foes in House Deploy Nazi Analogy," *MSNBC* (October 24, 2007), http://www.msnbc.msn.com/id/21449421/ns/politics/; Constantine Christopher Menges, *China: The Gathering Threat* (Nashville, Tenn.: Nelson Current, 2005), xvi; Jed Babbin and Edward Timperlake, *Showdown: Why China Wants War with the United States* (Washington, D.C.: Regnery, 2006), 2; Zbigniew Brzezinski, "Make Money, Not War," *Foreign Policy* 146 (January–February 2005): 46.

3. Robert Jervis, *Perception and Misperception in International Politics* (Princeton, N.J.: Princeton University Press, 1978), 58–113.

4. See Gideon Rose, "Neoclassical Realism and Theories of Foreign Policy," *World Politics* 51, no. 1 (October 1998): 144–172.

5. M. Taylor Fravel, "International Relations Theory and China's Rise: Assessing China's Potential for Territorial Expansion," *International Studies Review* 12, no. 4 (December 2010): 506.

6. Robert G. Sutter, *U.S.-Chinese Relations: Perilous Past, Pragmatic Present* (Lanham, Md.: Rowman & Littlefield, 2010); Avery Goldstein, *Rising to the Challenge* (Stanford, Calif.: Stanford University Press, 2005); Robert S. Ross and Zhu Feng, *China's Ascent: Power, Security, and the Future of International Relations* (Ithaca, N.Y.: Cornell University Press, 2008); Aaron L. Friedberg, *A Contest for Supremacy: China, America, and the Struggle for Mastery in Asia* (New York: Norton, 2011); Susan Shirk, *China: Fragile Superpower* (New York: Oxford University Press, 2007); David Kang, *China Rising: Peace, Power, and Order in East Asia* (New York: Columbia University Press, 2007); Andrew Nathan and Andrew Scobell, *China's Search for Security* (New York: Columbia University Press, 2012).

2. A Chinese View of the World

1. Brian Spegele, "China Says Foreigners Fuel Unrest in Mongolia," *Wall Street Journal* (May 31, 2011), http://online.wsj.com/article/SB10001424052702304563104576357273803568478.html?mod=WSJ_hpp_sections_world.

2. "China's Xi Vows to Speed Up Tibet's Development While Fighting Separatism," *Xinhua News Service* (July 19, 2011), http://news.xinhuanet.com/english2010/china/2011-07/19/c_13994659.htm.

3. Brian L. Job, "The Insecurity Dilemma: Nation, Regime, and State Securities in the Third World," in *The Insecurity Dilemma*, ed. Brian L. Job (London: Lynne Rienner, 1992).

4. "China: Is It a Threat, or an Opportunity?" *People's Daily* (August 23, 2005), http://english.peopledaily.com.cn/200508/23/eng20050823_204164.html.

5. Wang Gungwu, "Early Ming Relations with Southeast Asia: A Background Essay," in *The Chinese World Order: Traditional China's Foreign Relations*, ed. John King Fairbank (Cambridge, Mass.: Harvard University Press, 1968), 61.

6. PRC Premier Wen Jiabao, speech at the University of Cambridge (February 2, 2009), http://www.china.org.cn/international/2009-02/03/content_17214156.htm.

7. "Peace, Harmony, Good-Neighborliness—Goal of China's Diplomacy," *Xinhua News Service* (November 15, 2010), http://english.people.com.cn/90001/90776/90883/7198913.html.

8. Geoffrey Wade, "The Ming *Shi-lu* as a Source for the Study of Southeast Asian History," Asian Research Institute, National University of Singapore (2005), 28, http://epress.nus.edu.sg/msl/MSL.pdf; Charles Horner, *Rising China and Its Postmodern Fate* (Athens: University of Georgia Press, 2009), 51–52.

9. See, for example, Alastair Iain Johnston, *Cultural Realism: Strategic Culture and Grand Strategy in Chinese History* (Princeton, N.J.: Princeton University Press, 1995).

10. Christopher J. Pehrson, "String of Pearls: Meeting the Challenge of China's Rising Power Across the Asian Littoral," Strategic Studies Institute, U.S. Army War College, Carlisle, Penn., July 2006, http://www.strategicstudiesinstitute.army.mil/pdffiles/PUB721.pdf; James R. Holmes and Toshi Yoshihara, "Is China a 'Soft' Naval Power?" *China Brief* 9, no. 17 (August 20, 2009): 4–7; Geoffrey Wade, "The Zheng He Voyages: A Reassessment," Asia Research Institute Working Paper 31, National University of Singapore (October 2004), 1, 11–16.

11. Wang Jisi, "Meiguo Baquan de Luoji," *Meiguo Yanjiu* 17, no. 3 (2003): 28; Kuo Shuyong, "Lun Zhongguo Jueqi yu Shijie Zhixu de Guanxi," *Taipingyang Xuebao* 6 (2005): 3–11; Liu Yantang and Liu Xinyu, "Guoji biange: Shijie yu Zhongguo de zhanlue hudong," *Liaowang Xinwen Zhoukan* 9 (February 28, 2005): 28; Qian Wenrong, "Duojihua shi Dangjin Shijie Geju Fazhen de Keguan Qushi," *Heping yu Fazhan* 3 (2004): 16; "Leguan kandai Zhongmei guanxi: zhuangfang Beijing Daxue Guoji Guanxi Xueyuan yuanzhang Wang Jisi," *Nanfengchuan* (October 2008), http://www.nfcmag.com/articles/1129.

12. Song Xiaojun et. al, *Zhonguo bu gaoxing* (China unhappy) (Nanjing: Jiangsu Renmin Chubanshe, 2009), 204.; Li Hongmei, "The U.S. Hegemony Ends, the Era of Global Multipolarity Enters," *People's Daily* online (February 24, 2009), http://english.people.com.cn/90002/96417/6599374.html.

3. U.S.-China Relations Under Hegemonic Transition

1. "China Takes Its Place on the International Stage," *China Daily* (December 30, 2006), http://english.peopledaily.com.cn/200612/30/eng20061230_337133.html. Pang Zhongying, "China, My China," *The National Interest* 83 (Spring 2006): 9–10.

2. Jing Di Wang Tian, *Daguo youxi: kan Zhongguo ruhe keying shijie* (Beijing: Shijie zhishi chubanshe, 2009); Song Xiaojun et al., *Zhonguo bu gaoxing* (China unhappy) (Nanjing: Jiangsu Renmin Chubanshe, 2009), 204; Francesco Sisci, "Vague Sea Borders Let Hawks Pick Their Fight," *Asia Times* (September 23, 2010), http://www.atimes.com/atimes/China/LI23Ad01.html.

3. Liu Mingfu, *Zhongguo Meng: Hou Meiguo Shidai de DaGuo Siwei yu Zhanlue Dingwei* (Beijing: Zhouguo Youyi Chubangongsi, 2010).

4. Luo Yuan, *People's Daily* (August 13, 2010), http://english.peopledaily.com.cn/90001/90780/91343/7103900.html.

5. Zhu Shida, "The Rise of China and the Sino-U.S. Relations," *International Review* 45 (Spring 2006), http://www.siis.org.cn/Sh_Yj_Cms/Mgz/200601/20087242258287E3K.PDF.

6. Chen Zewei, "The Development of China's National Defense Capability Is Appropriate," *Liaowang* 30 (July 25, 2005): 37–38, translated by Open Source Center.

7. U.S. Department of Defense, *Quadrennial Defense Review* (2006), http://www.defenselink.mil/qdr/report/Report20060203.pdf; U.S. Department of Defense, *Quadrennial Defense Review* (February 2010), http://www.defense.gov/qdr/images/QDR_as_of_12Feb10_1000.pdf.

8. Wang Jisi, "From Paper Tiger to Real Leviathan: China's Images of the United States Since 1949," in *Chinese Images of the United States*, ed. Carola McGiffert (Washington, D.C.: Center for Strategic and International Studies Press, 2006), 13.

9. Yang Jiemian, "China and U.S. Strategies and Measures in Response to the Transition of International System," *International Review* 45 (Winter 2006): 44, http://www.siis.org.cn/en/luntan_view_En.aspx?id=200604.

10. Yan Xuetong, "The Rise of China in Chinese Eyes," *Journal of Contemporary China* 10, no. 25 (February 2001): 36.

11. John J. Mearsheimer, *The Tragedy of Great Power Politics* (New York: Norton, 2001), 402.

12. Condoleezza Rice, "Condoleezza Rice Delivers Remarks at Sophia University" (March 19, 2005), http://findarticles.com/p/news-articles/political-transcript-wire/mi_8167/is_20050319/condoleezza-rice-delivers-remarks-sophia/ai_n50513683/pg_12/?tag=content;col1.

13. Mei Zhaorong, "EU's Historic Enlargement and Its Implications," Chinese Institute of International Studies (September 27, 2004), http://www.ciis.org.cn/item/2004-09-27/50596.html.

14. Rory Medcalf, "Shangri-La Dialogue: Sounds of Silence," Lowy Institute for International Policy (June 7, 2010), http://www.lowyinterpreter.org/post/2010/06/07/Shangri-La-Dialogue-Sounds-of-silence.aspx.

15. "Four Barriers on Japan's Way to 'Permanent Seat,'" *People's Daily* online (September 26, 2004), http://english.people.com.cn/200409/26/eng20040926_158376.html.

16. Robert B. Zoellick, "Whither China: From Membership to Responsibility?" speech to the National Committee on U.S.-China Relations, New York (September 21, 2005), http://www.asiaing.com/whither-china-from-membership-to-responsibility.html.

17. Jianwei Wang, "Building a New Conceptual Framework for U.S.-China Relations," in *Challenges to Chinese Foreign Policy: Diplomacy, Globalization, and the Next World Power*, ed. Yufan Hao, C. X. George Wei, and Lowell Dittmer (Lexington: University of Kentucky Press, 2009), 45.

4. China's Military Rise

1. Website of U.S. Pacific Command, http://www.pacom.mil/web/Site_Pages/USPACOM/Facts.shtml.

2. David Finkelstein, "Commentary on China's External Grand Strategy," Center for Naval Analyses (January 2011), 6–7.

3. Jane Perlez, "Continuing Buildup, China Boosts Military Spending More Than 11 Percent," *New York Times* (March 4, 2012), http://www.nytimes.com/2012/03/05/world/asia/china-boosts-military-spending-more-than-11-percent.html?_r=2.

4. Stockholm International Peace Research Institute, SIPRI Military Expenditure Database, http://milexdata.sipri.org/; U.S. Department of Defense, "Military and Security Developments Involving the People's Republic of China 2010," Annual Report to Congress, http://www.defense.gov/pubs/pdfs/2010_CMPR_Final.pdf; "China's Defense Budget," *Globalsecurity.org* (April 3, 2011), http://www.globalsecurity.org/military/world/china/budget.htm.

5. Testimony of Admiral Robert F. Willard to the House of Representatives' Armed Services Committee (March 23, 2010), 12, http://www.pacom.mil/web/pacom_resources/pdf/Willard_Statement_HASC_032510.pdf.

6. International Security Advisory Board report to the U.S. Department of State, "China's Strategic Modernization" (September 2008), http://www.fas.org/nuke/guide/china/ISAB2008.pdf.

7. Ross Babbage, "Australia's Strategic Edge in 2030," Kokoda Papers 15, Kokoda Foundation (February 2011), v.

8. U.S. Department of Defense, "Military and Security Developments Involving the People's Republic of China 2010," Annual Report to Congress, http://www.defense.gov/pubs/pdfs/2010_CMPR_Final.pdf, p. 1.

9. Fan Gaoyue, "China's National Defence: Challenges and Responses," in *Rising China: Power and Reassurance*, ed. Ron Huisken (Canberra: Australian National University Press, 2009), http://epress.anu.edu.au/sdsc/rc/mobile_devices/ch10.html.

10. James R. Holmes and Toshi Yoshihara, "A Chinese Turn to Mahan?" *China Brief* 9, no. 13 (June 24, 2009): 8–11.

11. Ian Storey, "China's 'Malacca Dilemma,'" *China Brief* 6, no. 8 (April 12, 2006).

12. U.S. Department of Defense, "China 2010," 1.

13. Robert S. Ross, "China's Naval Nationalism: Sources, Prospects, and the U.S. Response," *International Security* 34, no. 2 (Fall 2009): 46–81.

14. U.S. Department of Defense, "China 2010," 1–2.

15. PLA Senior Colonel Yao Yunzhu, "China's Perspective on Nuclear Deterrence," *Air and Space Power Journal* (March 1, 2010 [Spring 2010]), http://www.airpower.au.af.mil/airchronicles/apj/apj10/spr10/yao.html.

16. Robert S. Norris and Hans M. Kristensen, "Chinese Nuclear Forces, 2010," *Bulletin of the Atomic Scientists* 66, no. 6 (November–December 2010): 134.

17. Hans M. Kristensen, "State Department Arms Control Board Declares Cold War on China" (October 7, 2008), Federation of American Scientists Strategic Security Blog, http://www.fas.org/blog/ssp/2008/10/isab.php; Baohui Zhang, "American Nuclear Primacy or Mutually Assured Destruction," in *Challenges to Chinese Foreign Policy: Diplomacy, Globalization, and the Next World Power*, ed. Yufan Hao, C. X. George Wei, and Lowell Dittmer (Lexington: University of Kentucky Press, 2009), 79.

18. Russell Hsiao, "China's 'Underground Great Wall' and Nuclear Deterrence," *China Brief* 9, no. 25 (December 16, 2009): 1–2.

19. Baohui Zhang, "American Nuclear Primacy or Mutually Assured Destruction," in *Challenges to Chinese Foreign Policy: Diplomacy, Globalization, and the Next World Power*, ed. Yufan Hao, C. X. George Wei, and Lowell Dittmer (Lexington: University of Kentucky Press, 2009), 78, 80.

20. Wu Chunsi, "Zhong-Mei he guanxi de zouxiang," in *Weishe yu wending: Zhong-Mei he guanxi*, ed. Zhu Mingquan, Wu Chunsi, and Su Changhe (Beijing: Shishi Chubanshe, 2005), 306; Hou Xiaohe and Zhang Hui, *Meiguo dandao daodan fangyu jihua toushi* (Beijing: Zhongguo Minhang Chubanshe, 2001), 248–252.

21. Mark A. Stokes, *China's Strategic Modernization: Implications for the United States* (Carlisle, Penn.: Strategic Studies Institute, U.S. Army War College, 1999), 89–91.

5. Japan and China: A Long Struggle with Bitter Resolve

1. Okazaki Hisahiko, "Politics of Business in China," *Japan Times* (June 21, 2004), http://www.okazaki-inst.jp/06212004japan-E.html.

2. Yoichiro Sato, "Tango Without Trust and Respect? Japan's Awkward Co-Prosperity with China in the Twenty-First Century," in *The Rise of China and International Security*, by Kevin J. Cooney and Yoichiro Sato (London: Routledge, 2009), 95.

3. James Brooke, "Drawing the Line on Energy," *New York Times* (March 29, 2005), http://www.nytimes.com/2005/03/29/business/worldbusiness/29joust.html.

4. "Ex-Japan PM says China Eyeing Nazi-Type *Lebensraum*," *Indianexpress.com* (October 19, 2010), http://www.indianexpress.com/news/china-is-the-most-aggressive-country-in-the-world/699541/.

5. A copy of the Guidelines is posted at http://www.nti.org/db/china/engdocs/usjguide.htm.

6. Joint Statement of the U.S.-Japan Security Consultative Committee (February 19, 2005), http://www.cfr.org/publication/15104/joint_statement_of_the_usjapan_security_consultative_committee.html.

7. Japan Ministry of Foreign Affairs website, "Japan-U.S. Security Consultative Committee," http://www.mofa.go.jp/region/n-america/us/security/scc/.

8. National Institute for Defense Studies, "East Asian Strategic Review 2011," http://www.nids.go.jp/english/publication/east-asian/pdf/2011/east-asian_e2011_overview.pdf; "White Paper Calls China 'Overbearing,'" *Daily Yomiuri* (August 2, 2011), http://www.yomiuri.co.jp/dy/national/T110802005930.htm.

9. "Chinese Minister Enraged by Okada's Calls for Nuclear Arsenal Cut," *Kyodo News Service* (May 24, 2010), http://www.japantoday.com/category/politics/view/chinese-minister-enraged-by-okadas-calls-for-nuke-arsenal-cut; John Pomfret, "U.S.-China Talks

End Without Accords on Key Issues," *Washington Post* (May 26, 2010), http://www.washingtonpost.com/wp-dyn/content/article/2010/05/25/AR2010052503244.html.

10. "Japan Finds China's Defense Buildup Worrying," *Agence France-Presse* (April 3, 2011), http://globalnation.inquirer.net/news/breakingnews/view/20110304–323474/Japan-finds-Chinas-defense-build-up-worrying; "Japan Voices Grave Concern About China's 2011 Defense Budget Plan," *Kyodo News Service* (March 5, 2011), http://www.mcot.net/cfcustom/cache_page/177435.html.

11. National Institute for Defense Studies, "East Asian Strategic Review 2011," http://www.nids.go.jp/english/publication/east-asian/pdf/2011/east-asian_e2011_04.pdf.

12. Christopher W. Hughes, "Japan's Response to China's Rise: Regional Engagement, Global Containment, Dangers of Collision," *International Affairs* 85, no. 4 (2009): 837–856.

13. Elena Atanassova-Cornelis, "Political and Security Dynamics of Japan-China Relations: Strategic Mistrust, Fragile Stability, and the U.S. Factor," Political Science Association conference paper (March 2010), 6.

14. Lin Zhaowei, "China 'Driving Japan Closer to U.S.,'" *Straits Times* (March 10, 2011), http://www.asianewsnet.net/home/news.php?id=17834.

15. Yoichi Funabashi, "Japan-China Relations Stand at Ground Zero," *Asahi.com* (October 9, 2010), http://www.asahi.com/english/TKY201010080462.html.

6. Pressure on China's Neighbors

1. Indian Prime Minister Jawaharlal Nehru, *India's Foreign Policy* (New Delhi: Publications Division, Ministry of Information and Broadcasting, 1961), 36.

2. Mohan Malik, "War Talk: Perceptual Gaps in 'Chindia' Relations," *China Brief* 9, no. 20 (October 7, 2009), 6–9.

3. J. Mohan Malik, "South Asia in China's Foreign Relations," *Pacifica Review* 13, no. 1 (February 2001): 89; Iskander Rehman, "Keeping the Dragon at Bay: India's Counter-Containment of China in Asia," *Asian Security* 5, no. 2 (2009): 114.

4. Sudha Ramachandran, "India Frets as China and Pakistan Embrace," *Asia Times* (November 8, 2003), http://www.atimes.com/atimes/South_Asia/EK08Df06.html.

5. Lee Addams, Giulio Boccaletti, Mike Kerlin, and Martin Stuchtey, *Charting Our Water Future: Economic Frameworks to Inform Decision Making*, McKinsey and Company, 2009, http://www.mckinsey.com/App_Media/Reports/Water/Charting_Our_Water_Future_Full_Report_001.pdf.

6. "Drying Up," *The Economist* (May 19, 2005), http://www.economist.com/research/articlesBySubject/PrinterFriendly.cfm?Story_ID=4000643&subjectID=348924.

7. Sudha Ramachandran, "India Quakes Over China's Water Plan," *Asia Times* (December 9, 2008), http://www.atimes.com/atimes/China/JL09Ad01.html.

8. Brantly Womack, *China Among Unequals: Asymmetric Foreign Relationships in Asia* (Singapore: World Scientific Publishing Co., 2010), 513; Ian Storey, *Southeast Asia and the Rise of China: The Search for Security* (New York: Routledge, 2011), 102-106.

9. Professor Carl Thayer, correspondence to author, June 23, 2011.

10. "China Must React to Vietnam's Provocation," *Global Times* (June 21, 2011), http://www.globaltimes.cn/NEWS/tabid/99/articleType/ArticleView/articleId/662453/China-must-react-to-Vietnams-provocation.aspx.

11. Brock A. Taylor, "USS *John S. McCain* Arrives in Vietnam to Commemorate 15th Anniversary of Diplomatic Relations," US Navy website (August 8, 2010), http://www.navy.mil/search/display.asp?story_id=55216.

12. Peter Symonds, "U.S. Forges Closer Military Ties with Vietnam," World Socialist website (August 26, 2010), http://www.wsws.org/articles/2010/aug2010/viet-a26.shtml.

13. Tessa Jamandre, "China Fired at Filipino Fishermen in Jackson Atoll," *VERA Files* (March 6, 2011), *ABS-CBN News* (Philippines), http://www.abs-cbnnews.com/-depth/06/02/11/china-fired-filipino-fishermen-jackson-atoll.

14. "China Communist Party Newspaper Cautions Vietnam," *Associated Press* (June 11, 2011), http://www.google.com/hostednews/ap/article/ALeqM5hvKWMcZN3XRwXHcoo7R4HQ1d-uiA.

15. "Foreign Ministry Spokesperson Hong Lei's Remarks on Vietnamese Ships Chasing Away Chinese Fishing Boats in the Waters off the Nansha Islands," PRC Foreign Ministry website (June 9, 2011), http://www.mfa.gov.cn/eng/xwfw/s2510/t829427.htm.

16. Margie Mason, "Vietnam, China Hold Joint Naval Patrol Amid Spat," *Associated Press* (June 21, 2011), http://old.news.yahoo.com/s/ap/20110621/ap_on_re_as/as_vietnam_china_patrol.

17. Su Qiang and Li Xiaokun, "China, Russia Quit Dollar," *China Daily* (November 24, 2010), http://www.chinadaily.com.cn/china/2010-11/24/content_11599087.htm.

18. Alexander Lukin, *The Bear Watches the Dragon: Russia's Perceptions of China and the Evolution of Russian-Chinese Relations Since the Eighteenth Century* (Armonk, N.Y.: M. E. Sharpe, 2003), 305.

19. Author discussions with track-two dialogue participants, 2010–2011.

20. Yong Deng, "Remolding Great Power Politics: China's Strategic Partnerships with Russia, the European Union, and India," *Journal of Strategic Studies* 30, no. 4–5 (August–October 2007): 869–870; Lowell Dittmer, "The Sino-Russian Strategic Relationship," in *Challenges to Chinese Foreign Policy: Diplomacy, Globalization, and the Next World Power*, ed. Yufan Hao, C. X. George Wei, and Lowell Dittmer (Lexington: University of Kentucky Press, 2009), 100.

21. Mickhail Alexseen, "Chinese Migration in the Russian Far East: Security Threat and Incentives for Cooperation in Primorskii Krai," in *Russia's Far East: A Region at Risk*, ed. Judith Thornton and Charles E. Ziegler (Seattle: National Bureau of Asian Research and University of Washington Press, 2002), 319.

22. Woo-Jun Kim, "Cooperation and Conflict Among Provinces: The Three Northeastern Provinces of China, the Russian Far East, and Sinuiju, North Korea," *Issues & Studies* 44, no. 3 (September 2008): 219.

23. Stephen Blank, "Toward a New Chinese Order in Asia: Russia's Failure," National Bureau of Asian Research, NBR Special Report 26 (March 2011); Stephen Blank, "China's Russian Far East," *China Brief* 9, no. 16 (August 5, 2009): 8–10.

24. Kim Hyun-Wook, "U.S. Fiscal Crisis and Its Impact on Korea-U.S. Relations," Jeju Peace Institute (October 20, 2011).

25. John F. Fei, "Beyond Rivalry and Camaraderie: Explaining Varying Asian Responses to China," RAND Corporation, RGSD-279 (February 2011), 184.

26. Bertil Lintner, "China Embrace Too Strong for Naypyidaw," *Asia Times* online (November 29, 2011), http://www.atimes.com/atimes/Southeast_Asia/MK29Ae01.html.

27. Andrew Selth, "Irrawaddy: Chinese Whispers: The Great Coco Island Mystery," *BurmaNet News* (January 9, 2007), http://www.burmanet.org/news/2007/01/09/irrawaddy-chinese-whispers-the-great-coco-island-mystery-andrew-selth/.

7. Mitigating Factors

1. Robert Sutter, *U.S.-China Relations: Perilous Past, Pragmatic Present* (Lanham, Md.: Rowman & Littlefield, 2010), 276.

2. Tao Xie and Benjamin I. Page, "Americans and the Rise of China as a World Power," *Journal of Contemporary China* 19, no. 65 (June 2010): 479–501.

3. Jianwei Wang, "Building a New Conceptual Framework for U.S.-China Relations," in *Challenges to Chinese Foreign Policy: Diplomacy, Globalization, and the Next World Power*, ed. Yufan Hao, C. X. George Wei, and Lowell Dittmer (Lexington: University of Kentucky Press, 2009), 40.

4. Qian Qichen, "Heping Fazhan Shi Zhongguo de Zhanlue Jueze," *Renmin Ribao* (November 21, 2005): 1.

5. Jia Qingguo, "China's New Leadership and Strategic Relations with the United States," in *Challenges to Chinese Foreign Policy: Diplomacy, Globalization, and the Next World Power*, ed. Yufan Hao, C. X. George Wei, and Lowell Dittmer (Lexington: University of Kentucky Press, 2009), 59; "China Eager to Establish New International Order," *Xinhua News Service* (February 28, 1991); "Multilateralism a Preferred Path for Diplomatic Work," *China Daily* (October 22, 2007), http://www.china.org.cn/english/congress/229189.htm; Michael A. Glosny, "China and the BRICs: A Real (but Limited) Partnership in a Unipolar World," *Polity* 42, no. 1 (January 2010): 116–117.

6. Dong Fangxiao, "Zhibian qiubian," *Xiandai Guoji Guanxi* 4 (April 20, 2003): 26–28.

7. Xinning Song, "The European Union and China," in *Challenges to Chinese Foreign Policy: Diplomacy, Globalization, and the Next World Power*, ed. Yufan Hao, C. X. George Wei, and Lowell Dittmer (Lexington: University of Kentucky Press, 2009), 118; Xia Liping, "How China Thinks About National Security," in *Rising China: Power and Reassurance*, ed. Ron Huisken (Canberra: Australian National University Press, 2009), http://epress.anu.edu.au/sdsc/rc/mobile_devices/ch09.html.

8. Shen Dingli, "The 2010 U.S. QDR and Its Impact on China," *Asia Pacific Bulletin* (East-West Center–Washington) 61 (May 13, 2010).

9. "Foreign Ministry Spokesperson Jiang Yu's Remarks on the Death of Gaddafi's Son and Others in NATO's Air Strikes," PRC Ministry of Foreign Affairs website (May 2, 2011), http://www.mfa.gov.cn/eng/xwfw/s2510/2535/t819910.htm.

10. Global public goods are benefits shared in by states that do not pay for them. An example is the U.S. Navy providing security in international waters, which aids non-U.S. as well as U.S. shipping.

11. Robert G. Sutter, *Chinese Foreign Relations: Power and Policy Since the Cold War* (Lanham, Md.: Rowman & Littlefield, 2008), 403.

12. G. John Ikenberry, "The Rise of China and the Future of the West: Can the Liberal System Survive?" *Foreign Affairs* 87, no. 1 (January–February 2008): 23–37; G. John Ikenberry, "The Rise of China: Power, Institutions, and the Western Order," in *China's Ascent: Power, Security, and the Future of International Politics*, ed. Robert S. Ross and Zhu Feng (Ithaca, N.Y.: Cornell University Press, 2008), 89–114.

13. Robert Pape, "Soft Balancing Against the United States," *International Security* 30, no. 1 (Summer 2005): 7–45.

14. Singapore's former prime minister is credited with this phrase. "In the Balance," *The Economist* (December 2, 2010), http://www.economist.com/node/17601463.

15. Agence France Presse, "Japan Calls on India to Join Asian 'Arc of Freedom,'"

Channel News Asia (August 22, 2007), http://www.channelnewsasia.com/stories/afp_asia pacific_business/view/295416/1/.html.

16. "Summary of National Defense Program Guidelines, FY 2011," Japan Ministry of Defense (December 17, 2010), http://www.mod.go.jp/e/d_act/d_policy/pdf/summaryFY 2011-.pdf.

17. Benigno S. Aquino III, "State of the Nation Address," Quezon City (July 25, 2011), http://www.bakitwhy.com/PNoy-SONA-2011-English-Translation.

18. Shi Yinhong, "Guoji Zhengzhi de Shijixing Guilu jiqi dui Zhongguo de Qishi," *Zhanlue yu Guanli* 5 (1995): 1–3; Tang Yongsheng, "Guoji Zhengzhi Changzhouqi Guilu zai Dangdai de Yanbian," *Zhanlue yu Guanli* 1 (1996): 46–51.

19. Zheng Bijian, *Collection of Zheng Bijian's Essays*, vol. 3 (Shanghai: Shanghai People's Press, 2005); Zheng Bijian, "China's 'Peaceful Rise' to Great Power Status," *Foreign Affairs* 84, no. 5 (September–October 2005): 18–24.

8. Persistent Risk of Conflict

1. PRC Information Office of the State Council, "China's Peaceful Development," Beijing (September 2011), http://www.chinadaily.com.cn/china/2011-09/06/content_13630926_2.htm.

2. "Premier Wen Meets the Press," PRC Embassy in Pakistan (March 14, 2005), http://pk.china-embassy.org/eng/zgxw/t189022.htm.

3. Claude Arpi, "Which Direction for China in 2011?" *Indian Defence Review* (January 14, 2011), http://www.indiandefencereview.com/geopolitics/Which-direction-for-China-in-2011.html.

4. Jian Junbo, "China Takes New Tack in Maritime Diplomacy," *Asia Times* (July 14, 2010), http://www.atimes.com/atimes/China/LG14Ad01.html.

5. Willy Lam, "Beijing's Great Leap Outward: Power Projection with Chinese Characteristics," *China Brief* 7, no. 3 (May 9, 2007).

6. Ian Johnson and Jackie Calmes, "As U.S. Looks to Asia, It Sees China Everywhere," *New York Times* (November 15, 2011).

7. Andrew Scobell, *China's Use of Military Force: Beyond the Great Wall and the Long March* (New York: Cambridge University Press, 2003).

8. Mohan Malik, "The Strategies and Objectives of China's Foreign Affairs and Asian Reactions to China's Rise," testimony to U.S.-China Economic and Security Review Commission (March 18, 2008), Washington, D.C., http://www.uscc.gov/hearings/2008hearings/written_testimonies/08_03_18_wrts/08_03_18_malik_statement.pdf; Amir Mir, "China Seeks Military Bases in Pakistan," *Asia Times* online (October 26, 2011), http://www.atimes.com/atimes/South_Asia/MJ26Df03.html; "China Needs Overseas Bases for Global Role," *Global Times* (May 25, 2011), http://opinion.globaltimes.cn/chinese-press/2011-05/658995.html.

9. John Mearsheimer, "The Gathering Storm: China's Challenge to U.S. Power in Asia," fourth annual Michael Hintze Lecture in International Security, Sydney University (August 4, 2010), http://sydney.edu.au/business/_data/assets/pdf_file/0003/75450/Transcript_4th_Hintze_Lecture_John_Mearsheimer_100804.pdf.

10. Robert S. Ross and Zhu Feng, "The Rise of China: Theoretical and Policy Perspectives," *China's Ascent: Power, Security, and the Future of International Politics*, ed. Robert S. Ross and Zhu Feng (Ithaca, N.Y.: Cornell University Press, 2008).

11. Donald K. Emmerson, "China's 'Frown Diplomacy' in Southeast Asia," *Asia Times* online (October 5, 2010), http://www.atimes.com/atimes/China/LJ05Ad02.html.

12. "China Hearts Putin; Beijing Projects Its National Neuroses on Butcher of Chechnya," *Wall Street Journal* (November 18, 2011): 16.

13. "Three Tibetans Self-Immolate in Western China: Report," *Reuters* (February 5, 2012), http://www.reuters.com/article/2012/02/05/us-china-tibet-idUSTRE8120BQ20120205.

14. Fei-Ling Wang, "Beijing's Incentive Structure: The Pursuit of Preservation, Prosperity, and Power," in *China Rising: Power and Motivation in Chinese Foreign Policy*, ed. Yong Deng and Fei-Ling Wang (Lanham, Md.: Rowman & Littlefield, 2005), 22, 28.

15. Ambrose Evans-Pritchard, "China's Young Officers and the 1930s Syndrome," *The Telegraph* (September 7, 2010), http://blogs.telegraph.co.uk/finance/ambroseevans-pritchard/100007519/china%E2%80%99s-young-officers-and-the-1930s-syndrome/.

16. Shaun Tandon, "Study Shows Sharp Gaps in China Views of U.S.," *Agence France-Presse* (April 19, 2012), http://news.yahoo.com/study-shows-sharp-gaps-china-views-us-155347462.html.

17. Rowan Callick, "China Learns to Deploy Its Soft Power," *The Australian* (November 27, 2010), http://www.theaustralian.com.au/news/opinion/china-learns-to-deploy-its-soft-power/story-e6frg6zo-1225961313024.

18. Patrice Hill, "China Mocks U.S. Political Model," *Washington Times* (November 9, 2011), http://www.washingtontimes.com/news/2011/nov/9/beijing-blueprint/.

19. Edward D. Mansfield and Jack Snyder, *Electing to Fight: Why Emerging. Democracies Go to War* (Cambridge, Mass.: MIT Press, 2005).

20. Najmeh Bozorgmehr and Geoff Dyer, "China Overtakes EU as Iran's Top Trade Partner," *Financial Times* (February 8, 2010), http://www.ft.com/cms/s/0/f220dfac-14d4-11df-8f1d-00144feab49a.html.

21. Michael Swaine, "Beijing's Tightrope Walk on Iran," *China Leadership Monitor* (Hoover Institute) 33 (2010): 8.

9. North Korea: Bothersome Client State

1. David E. Sanger, "Leaked Cables Depict a World Guessing About North Korea," *New York Times* (November 29, 2010), http://www.nytimes.com/2010/11/30/world/asia/30korea.html?pagewanted=1&hp.

2. Stephanie Kleine-Ahlbrandt and Andrew Small, "China's New Dictatorship Diplomacy," *New York Times* (January 28, 2008), http://www.nytimes.com/cfr/world/20080101faessay_v87n1_kleine.html.

3. Cai Jian, "How Should China Respond to the Resurgence of the North Korean Nuclear Issue," *Shijie Zhishi* (May 1, 2009), Open Source Center (OSC), CPP20090514671009; Ren Weidong, "The DPRK-U.S. Relationship is the Crucial Point in the Peninsula Issue," *Liaowang* 26 (June 29, 2009): 58, OSC, CPP20090707710015.

4. Chris Buckley, "China Fends off Obama Pressure Over North Korea," *Reuters* (June 29, 2010), http://www.reuters.com/article/idUSTRE65S1PI20100629.

5. Xinhua News Service, "Chinese FM Calls for Restraint, Dialogue After DPRK's Satellite Launch," *Sina.com* (April 13, 2012), http://english.sina.com/china/p/2012/0413/457903.html.

6. David Barboza, "Senior Chinese Official Meets North Korean Leader," *New York Times* (December 9, 2010), http://www.nytimes.com/2010/12/10/world/asia/10north.html?_r=1&ref=global-home.

7. Confidential leaked cable from the U.S. Embassy in Beijing, reprinted in "A Selection From the Cache of Diplomatic Dispatches," *New York Times* (November 29, 2010), http://www.nytimes.com/interactive/2010/11/28/world/20101128-cables-viewer.html#report/korea-09BEIJING1634.

8. International Crisis Group, *China and North Korea: Comrades Forever?* Asia Report 112 (Brussels, 2005), 9.

9. Shen Dingli, "North Korea's Strategic Significance to China," *China Security* (Autumn 2006): 20–21; Shen Dingli, "Cooperative Denuclearization Toward North Korea," *Washington Quarterly* 32, no. 4 (October 2009): 180–187.

10. Taiwan in the PRC's Lengthening Shadow

1. Patrick Tyler, *A Great Wall* (New York: Public Affairs, 1999), 172; Xinhua News Service, "Full Text: Deng Xiaoping's Remarks on 'One Country, Two Systems,'" *Xinhuanet* (February 19, 2004), http://news.xinhuanet.com/english/2004-02/19/content_1322422.htm.

2. Jiang Zemin, "Continue to Promote the Reunification of the Motherland," PRC Ministry of Foreign Affairs website (January 30, 1995), http://www.fmprc.gov.cn/eng/ljzg/3568/t17784.htm; Dai Bingguo, "Stick to the Path of Peaceful Development," *U.S.-China Focus* (March 2, 2011), http://www.chinausfocus.com/foreign-policy/stick-to-the-path-of-peaceful-development/.

3. "Changes in the Taiwanese/Chinese Identity of Taiwanese," Election Studies Center, National Chengchi University (July 2011), http://esc.nccu.edu.tw/english/modules/tinyd2/content/pic/trend/People201106.jpg.

4. Peng Guangqian and Yao Youzhi, *Zhanlue Xue* (Beijing: Zhunxue Chubanshe, 2005), 443.

5. Chicago Council on Global Affairs, "Aware of China's Rise, Worried Americans Still Prefer to Engage" (2008), 2, http://www.thechicagocouncil.org/UserFiles/File/POS_Topline%20Reports/POS%202008/2008%20POS_Chinas%20rise.pdf.

6. David Alexander, "Gates Says U.S.-China Military Ties at 'Pretty Good Place,'" *Reuters* (June 1, 2011), http://www.reuters.com/article/2011/06/02/us-usa-military-gates-idUSTRE75109V20110602; Rich Chang, "Taiwan Renews Drive for Advanced Fighter Aircraft," *Taipei Times* (March 16, 2009), http://www.taipeitimes.com/News/front/archives/2009/03/16/2003438588/1.

7. "Transcript: Adm. Willard Delivers Asian Pacific Military Overview Briefing," Washington Foreign Press Center, Washington, D.C. (September 27, 2011), http://www.pacom.mil/web/Site_Pages/Media/News_2011/09/27-Willard-Delivers-Overview.shtml.

8. Foster Klug, "U.S. Official Warns of China, Taiwan Conflict," *Associated Press* (February 14, 2009), http://www.chinapost.com.tw/china/national-news/2009/02/14/195982/U.S.-official.htm.

9. Robert Burns, "Panetta Praises China for Arms Sale Reaction," *Associated Press* (October 23, 2011), http://www.airforcetimes.com/news/2011/10/ap-military-leon-panetta-praises-china-taiwan-arms-sale-reaction-102311/.

10. "President Chen Shui-bian's Speech," *BBC News* (August 5, 2002), http://news.bbc.co.uk/2/hi/asia-pacific/2172970.stm.

11. Jens Kastner, "Taiwan Lowers Its Military Sights," *Asia Times* (August 2, 2011), http://www.atimes.com/atimes/China/MH02Ad02.html.

12. William Murray, "Revisiting Taiwan's Defense Strategy," *Naval War College Review* 61, no. 3 (Summer 2008): 13–38.

11. The South China Sea Dispute

1. The statement is from the PRC Ministry of Foreign Affairs spokesman Hong Lei. "Foreign Ministry Spokesperson Hong Lei's Remarks on Philippine Foreign Ministry's Comments on the South China Sea," PRC Ministry of Foreign Affairs website (June 7, 2011), http://www.mfa.gov.cn/eng/xwfw/s2510/t829425.htm.

2. "China to Strengthen Maritime Forces Amid Disputes," *People Daily* online (June 17, 2011), http://english.people.com.cn/90001/90776/90883/7412388.html.

3. Kazuto Tsukamoto, Fusako Go, and Takeshi Fujitani, "S.E. Asia Grapples with a Rising Power," *Asahi.com* (January 1, 2011), http://www.asahi.com/english/TKY201012310142.html.

4. Testimony of ADM Robert F. Willard to a House of Representatives subcommittee (April 14, 2011), 10, http://www.pacom.mil/web/PACOM_Resources/pdf/TestimonyofAdmRobertWillardUSNavy-14April2011.pdf.

5. Jian Junbo, "China-U.S. Spat a Drop in the Ocean," *Asia Times* online (March 14, 2009), http://www.atimes.com/atimes/China/KC14Ad01.html.

6. Hillary Rodham Clinton, "Remarks at Press Availability," Hanoi (July 23, 2010), U.S. Department of State website, http://www.state.gov/secretary/rm/2010/07/145095.htm.

7. "Foreign Minister Yang Jiechi Refutes Fallacies on the South China Sea Issue," PRC Foreign Ministry website (July 26, 2010), http://www.fmprc.gov.cn/eng/zxxx/t719460.htm; Geoff Dyer, "Beijing's Elevated Aspirations," *Financial Times* (November 10, 2010), http://www.ft.com/intl/cms/s/0/1cfa57c4-ed03-11df-9912-00144feab49a.html#axzz1hsuZM8I8.

8. Michael Sainsbury, "Our Hard Line Turns out to Be Prescient," *The Australian* (January 8, 2011), http://www.theaustralian.com.au/news/features/our-hard-line-turns-out-to-be-prescient/story-e6frg6z6–1225983871740.

9. Ian Storey, "China's Missteps in Southeast Asia: Less Charm, More Offensive," *China Brief* (Jamestown Foundation) 10, no. 25 (December 17, 2010): 4–7.

10. "NIDS China Security Report," National Institute of Defense Studies, Tokyo (2011), 16, http://www.nids.go.jp/english/publication/chinareport/pdf/china_report_EN_4C_A01.pdf.

11. Qin Jize, Li Xiaokun, and Cheng Guangjin, "Japan Atoll Expansion 'Hurts Neighbors,'" *China Daily* (February 11, 2010), http://www.chinadaily.com.cn/world/2010-02/11/content_9461259.htm.

12. "China's Submarine No Threat to Japan," *People's Daily* (November 19, 2003), http://www.chinadaily.com.cn/en/doc/2003–11/19/content_282937.htm.

13. "Foreign Ministry Spokesperson Qin Gang's Regular Press Conference on July 8, 2010," PRC Ministry of Foreign Affairs website, http://www.fmprc.gov.cn/eng/xwfw/s2510/2511/t715219.htm; Liang Jun, *People's Daily* online (June 12, 2010), http://english

.peopledaily.com.cn/90001/90780/91343/7024204.html; Shen Dingli, "U.S.-S. Korean maritime war games needlessly provocative," *Global Times* (July 14, 2010), http://www.globaltimes.cn/opinion/commentary/2010–07/551234.html.

14. Taylor Fravel, "Explaining Stability in the Senkaku (Diaoyu) Dispute," in *Getting the Triangle Straight: Managing China-Japan-U.S. Relations*, ed. Gerald Curtis, Ryosei Kokubun, and Wang Jisi (Washington, D.C.: Brookings Institution Press, 2010), 147.

12. China and Global Security Issues

1. Robert D. Kaplan, "The Geography of Chinese Power," *Foreign Affairs* 89, no. 3 (May/June 2010): 24; Thomas J. Christensen, "Chinese Realpolitik," *Foreign Affairs* 75, no. 5 (September/October 1996): 37.

2. "China's Frustrated 'Old Friends': Beijing's Domestic Protectionism Is Alienating Allies," *Wall Street Journal* online (July 8, 2010), http://online.wsj.com/article/SB10001424052748704111704575354241858131862.html; Laurie Burkitt, "China Climate Faulted in Poll," *Wall Street Journal* online (May 26, 2011), http://online.wsj.com/article/SB10001424052702304066504576344222233947258.html; Paul Krugman, "Rare and Foolish," *New York Times* (October 17, 2010), http://www.nytimes.com/2010/10/18/opinion/18krugman.html?_r=1&src=me&ref=general.

3. Jamie Metzl, "China's Threat to World Order," *Wall Street Journal* online (August 17, 2011), http://online.wsj.com/article/SB10001424053111904006104576500690087766626.html; Office of the National Counterintelligence Executive, "Foreign Spies Stealing U.S. Economic Secrets in Cyberspace" (October 2011), Washington, D.C.

4. L. Gordon Crovitz, "China Goes Phishing," *Wall Street Journal* online, http://online.wsj.com/article/SB10001424052702303657404576363374283504838.html; "China Directed Google Hacking: Leaked U.S. Documents," *Agence France Presse* (November 28, 2010), http://news.yahoo.com/s/afp/20101128/pl_afp/usdiplomacymilitaryinternetwikileakschinagoogle.

5. Ellen Nakashima, "U.S. Cyber Approach 'Too Predictable' for One Top General," *Washington Post* (July 14, 2011), http://www.washingtonpost.com/national/national-security/us-cyber-approach-too-predictable-for-one-top-general/2011/07/14/gIQAYJC6EI_story.html.

6. Anne Barnard, "China Sought to Sell Arms to Qaddafi, Documents Suggest," *New York Times* (September 5, 2011): 9; Michael Wines, "China Says State-Run Arms Makers Talked to Libyans," *New York Times* (September 6, 2011): 12.

7. Thomas C. Reed and Danny B. Stillman, *The Nuclear Express: A Political History of the Bomb and Its Proliferation* (Minneapolis, Minn.: Zenith, 2009).

8. Testimony of Paula A. DeSutter to U.S.-China Economic and Security Review Commission, Washington, D.C. (September 14, 2006), http://www.uscc.gov/hearings/2006hearings/transcripts/sept_14/06_09_14_trans.pdf.

9. "China Reluctant to Talk Much to U.S. About North," *Joong Ang Daily* (November 30, 2010), http://joongangdaily.joins.com/article/view.asp?aid=2929027.

10. Rebiya Kadeer, "China's Double Game on Terrorism," *Wall Street Journal* online (September 23, 2011), http://online.wsj.com/article/SB10001424053111903703604576584550167314960.html; Chris Buckley, "Analysis: Far West Attacks Expose Violence's Homegrown Roots," *Reuters News Service* (August 4, 2011), http://www.reuters.com/article/2011/08/04/us-china-xinjiang-pakistan-idUSTRE7731P720110804.

11. See Chen Shengluo, "Chinese College Students' Views of America After September 11, 2001," in *Chinese Images of the United States*, ed. Carola McGiffert (Washington, D.C.: Center for Strategic and International Studies, 2005), 106–109.

12. Damien McElroy, "Beijing Produces Videos Glorifying Terrorist Attacks on 'Arrogant' U.S.," *The Telegraph* (November 4, 2001), http://www.telegraph.co.uk/news/worldnews/asia/china/1361461/Beijing-produces-videos-glorifying-terrorist-attacks-on-arrogant-US.html; Miles Yu, "China on Bin Laden," *Washington Times* (May 4, 2011), http://www.washingtontimes.com/news/2011/may/4/inside-china-567382461/?page=all.

13. David Scott, *The Chinese Century? The Challenges to Global Order* (Hampshire: Palgrave Macmillan, 2008), 67; U.S. Energy Information Administration webpage on China, http://www.eia.doe.gov/countries/cab.cfm?fips=CH; U.S. Department of Defense, "Military and Security Developments Involving the People's Republic of China 2010," Annual Report to Congress, http://www.defense.gov/pubs/pdfs/2010_CMPR_Final.pdf.

14. I thank my colleague Kang Wu for these figures.

15. Yan Liang, "Hu Meets Guests of Party of European Socialists," *Xinhua News Service* (July 5, 2007), http://english.gov.cn/2007-07/05/content_674553.htm; "Russian President Putin Met with Chinese Premier Wen Jiabao in Kremlin, Moscow," Chinese Ministry of Foreign Affairs website (November 7, 2007), http://www.fmprc.gov.cn/eng/wjb/wjbz/2467/t379410.htm.

16. "Chinese Paper Condemns Libya Air Strikes," *China Daily* (March 21, 2011), http://usa.chinadaily.com.cn/china/2011-03/21/content_12205091.htm.

17. Michael Bristow, "Chinese Dilemma Over Burma Protests," *BBC News* (September 25, 2007), http://news.bbc.co.uk/2/hi/asia-pacific/7011746.stm.

13. Conclusion

1. The quote comes from the PRC State Council's white paper on "China's Peaceful Development" published in September 2011.

2. Damien Ma, "Is Chinese Growth Sustainable?" *Atlantic Monthly* (August 18, 2011), http://www.theatlantic.com/international/archive/2011/08/is-chinese-growth-sustainable/243795/.

INDEX